S0-BAZ-253

A. W.

TOZER

THREE SPIRITUAL CLASSICS
IN ONE VOLUME

MOODY PUBLISHERS

CHICAGO

The Knowledge of the Holy

The Pursuit of God

God's Pursuit of Man

The Knowledge of the Holy
Copyright © 1961 by Aiden Wilson Tozer
Published by arrangement with HarperOne, an imprint of HarperCollins Publishers.
All Rights Reserved.

The Pursuit of God
Copyright © 1948, 1982, 1993, 2006 by
The Moody Bible Institute of Chicago

God's Pursuit of Man was previously published
under the titles *The Divine Conquest* and *The Pursuit of Man*
and is a sequel to *The Pursuit of God.*
Copyright © 1950, renewed 1978 by Lowell Tozer

All rights reserved. No part of this book may be reproduced in any form without permission in
writing from the publisher, except in the case of brief quotations embodied in critical articles or
reviews.

Unless otherwise indicated, all Scripture quotations are taken from the King James Version.
Scripture quotations marked ASV are taken from the American Standard Version.

Interior and cover design: Erik M. Peterson

Library of Congress Cataloging-in-Publication Data

Names: Tozer, A. W. (Aiden Wilson), 1897-1963, author.
Title: Three spiritual classics in one volume / A.W. Tozer.
Description: Chicago : Moody Publishers, 2018. | Includes bibliographical
   references.
Identifiers: LCCN 2018008744 | ISBN 9780802418616
Subjects: LCSH: Christian life. | Spiritual life--Christianity. | God
   (Christianity)--Attributes. | God (Christianity)--Worship and love.
Classification: LCC BV4501.3 .T723 2018 | DDC 248.4--dc23 LC record available at
   https://lccn.loc.gov/2018008744

ISBN: 978-0-8024-1861-6

We hope you enjoy this book from Moody Publishers. Our goal is to provide high-quality,
thought-provoking books and products that connect truth to your real needs and challenges.
For more information on other books and products written and produced from a biblical perspective, go to www.moodypublishers.com or write to:

Moody Publishers
820 N. LaSalle Boulevard
Chicago, IL 60610

5 7 9 10 8 6

Printed in the United States of America

CONTENTS

The Knowledge of the Holy

The Pursuit of God

God's Pursuit of Man

The Knowledge
of the Holy

PREFACE

True religion confronts earth with heaven and brings eternity to bear upon time. The messenger of Christ, though he speaks from God, must also, as the Quakers used to say, "speak to the condition" of his hearers; otherwise he will speak a language known only to himself. His message must be not only timeless but timely. He must speak to his own generation.

The message of this book does not grow out of these times but it is appropriate to them. It is called forth by a condition which has existed in the Church for some years and is steadily growing worse. I refer to the loss of the concept of majesty from the popular religious mind. The Church has surrendered her once lofty concept of God and has substituted for it one so low, so ignoble, as to be utterly unworthy of thinking, worshiping men. This she has done not deliberately, but little by little and without her knowledge; and her very unawareness only makes her situation all the more tragic.

The low view of God entertained almost universally among Christians is the cause of a hundred lesser evils everywhere among us. A whole new philosophy of the Christian life has resulted from this one basic error in our religious thinking.

With our loss of the sense of majesty has come the further loss of religious awe and consciousness of the divine Presence. We have lost our spirit of worship and our ability to withdraw inwardly to meet God in adoring silence. Modern Christianity is simply not producing the kind of Christian who can appreciate or experience the life in the Spirit. The words, "Be still, and know that I am God," mean next to nothing to the self-confident, bustling worshiper in this middle period of the twentieth century.

This loss of the concept of majesty has come just when the forces of religion are making dramatic gains and the churches are more prosperous than at any time within the past several hundred years. But the alarming thing is that our gains are mostly external and our losses wholly internal; and since it is the quality of our religion that is affected by internal conditions, it may be that our supposed gains are but losses spread over a wider field.

The only way to recoup our spiritual losses is to go back to the cause of them and make such corrections as the truth warrants. The decline of the knowledge of the holy has brought on our troubles. A rediscovery of the majesty of God will go a long way toward curing them. It is impossible to keep our moral practices sound and our inward attitudes right while our idea of God is erroneous or inadequate. If we would bring back spiritual power to our lives, we must begin to think of God more nearly as He is.

As my humble contribution to a better understanding of the Majesty in the heavens I offer this reverent study of the attributes of God. Were Christians today reading such works as those of Augustine or Anselm a book like this would have no reason for being. But such illuminated masters are known to modern Christians only by name. Publishers dutifully reprint their books and in due time these appear on the shelves of our studies. But the whole trouble lies right there: they remain on the shelves. The current religious mood makes the reading of them virtually impossible even for educated Christians.

Apparently not many Christians will wade through hundreds of pages of heavy religious matter requiring sustained concentration. Such books remind too many persons of the secular classics they were forced to read while they were in school and they turn away from them with a feeling of discouragement.

For that reason an effort such as this may be not without some beneficial effect. Since this book is neither esoteric nor technical, and since it is written in the language of worship with no pretension to elegant literary style, perhaps some persons may be drawn to read it. While I believe that nothing will be found here contrary to sound Christian theology, I yet write not for professional theologians but for plain persons whose hearts stir them up to seek after God Himself.

It is my hope that this small book may contribute somewhat to the promotion of personal heart religion among us; and should a few persons by reading it be encouraged to begin the practice of reverent meditation on the being of God, that will more than repay the labor required to produce it.

A.W.T.

———————•———————

CHAPTER 1

Why We Must Think Rightly About God

O Lord God Almighty, not the God of the philosophers and the wise but the God of the prophets and apostles; and better than all, the God and Father of our Lord Jesus Christ, may I express Thee unblamed?

They that know Thee not may call upon Thee as other than Thou art, and so worship not Thee but a creature of their own fancy; therefore enlighten our minds that we may know Thee as Thou art, so that we may perfectly love Thee and worthily praise Thee.

In the name of Jesus Christ our Lord. *Amen.*

What comes into our minds when we think about God is the most important thing about us.

The history of mankind will probably show that no people has ever risen above its religion, and man's spiritual history will positively demonstrate that no religion has ever been greater than its idea of God. Worship is pure or base as the worshiper entertains high or low thoughts of God.

For this reason the gravest question before the Church is always God Himself, and the most portentous fact about any man is not what he at a given time may say or do, but what he in his deep heart conceives God to be like. We tend by a secret law of the soul to move toward our mental image of God. This is true not only of the individual Christian, but of the company of Christians that composes the Church. Always the most revealing thing about the Church is her idea of God, just as her most significant message is what she says about Him or leaves unsaid, for her silence is often more eloquent than her speech. She can never escape the self-disclosure of her witness concerning God.

Were we able to extract from any man a complete answer to the question, "What comes into your mind when you think about God?" we might predict with certainty the spiritual future of that man. Were we able to know exactly what our most influential religious leaders think of God today, we might be able with some precision to foretell where the Church will stand tomorrow.

Without doubt, the mightiest thought the mind can entertain is the thought of God, and the weightiest word in any language is its word for God. Thought and speech are God's gifts to creatures made in His image; these are intimately associated with Him and impossible apart from Him. It is highly significant that the first word was the Word: "And the Word was with God, and the Word was God." We may speak because God spoke.

In Him word and idea are indivisible.

That our idea of God correspond as nearly as possible to the true being of God is of immense importance to us. Compared with our actual thoughts about Him, our creedal statements are of little consequence. Our real idea of God may lie buried under the rubbish of conventional religious notions and may require an intelligent and vigorous search before it is finally unearthed and exposed for what it is. Only after an ordeal of painful self-probing are we likely to discover what we actually believe about God.

A right conception of God is basic not only to systematic theology but to practical Christian living as well. It is to worship what the foundation is to the temple; where it is inadequate or out of plumb the whole structure must sooner or later collapse. I believe there is scarcely an error in doctrine or a failure in applying Christian ethics that cannot be traced finally to imperfect and ignoble thoughts about God.

It is my opinion that the Christian conception of God current in these middle years of the twentieth century is so decadent as to be utterly beneath the dignity of the Most High God and actually to constitute for professed believers something amounting to a moral calamity.

All the problems of heaven and earth, though they were to confront us together and at once, would be nothing compared with the overwhelming problem of God: That He is; what He is *like*; and what we as moral beings must do about Him.

The man who comes to a right belief about God is relieved of ten thousand temporal problems, for he sees at once that these have to do with matters which at the most cannot concern him for very long; but even if the multiple burdens of time may be lifted from him, the one mighty single burden of eternity begins to press down upon him with a weight more crushing than all the woes of the world piled one upon another. That mighty burden is his obligation to God. It includes an instant and lifelong duty to love God with every power of mind and soul, to obey Him perfectly, and to worship Him acceptably. And when the man's laboring conscience tells him that he has done none of these things, but has from childhood been guilty of foul revolt against the Majesty in the heavens, the inner pressure of self-accusation may become too heavy to bear.

The gospel can lift this destroying burden from the mind, give beauty for ashes, and the garment of praise for the spirit of heaviness. But unless the weight of the burden is felt the gospel can mean nothing to the man; and until he sees a vision of God high and lifted up, there will be no woe and no burden. Low views of God destroy the gospel for all who hold them.

Among the sins to which the human heart is prone, hardly any other is more hateful to God than idolatry, for idolatry is at bottom a libel on His character. The idolatrous heart assumes that God is other than He is—in itself a monstrous sin—and substitutes for the true God one made after its own likeness. Always this God will conform to the image of the one who created it and will be base or pure, cruel or kind, according to the moral state of the mind from which it emerges.

A god begotten in the shadows of a fallen heart will quite naturally be no true likeness of the true God. "Thou thoughtest," said the Lord to the wicked man in the psalm, "that I was altogether such a one as thyself." Surely this must be a serious affront to the Most High God before whom cherubim and seraphim continually do cry, "Holy, holy, holy, Lord God of Sabaoth."

Let us beware lest we in our pride accept the erroneous notion that idolatry consists only in kneeling before visible objects of adoration, and that civilized peoples are therefore free from it. The essence of idolatry is the entertainment of thoughts about God that are unworthy of Him. It begins in the mind and may be present where no overt act of worship has taken place. "When they knew God," wrote Paul, "they glorified him not as God, neither were thankful; but became vain in their imaginations, and their foolish heart was darkened."

Then followed the worship of idols fashioned after the likeness of men and birds and beasts and creeping things. But this series of degrading acts began in the mind. Wrong ideas about God are not only the fountain from which the polluted waters of idolatry flow; they are themselves idolatrous. The idolater simply imagines things about God and acts as if they were true.

Perverted notions about God soon rot the religion in which they appear. The long career of Israel demonstrates this clearly enough, and the history of the Church confirms it. So necessary to the Church is a lofty concept of God that when that concept in any measure declines, the Church with her worship and her moral standards declines along with it. The first step down for any church is taken when it surrenders its high opinion of God.

Before the Christian Church goes into eclipse anywhere there must first be a corrupting of her simple basic theology. She simply gets a wrong answer to the question, "What is God like?" and goes on from there. Though she may continue to cling to a sound nominal creed, her practical working creed has become false. The masses of her adherents come to believe that God is different from what He actually is; and that is heresy of the most insidious and deadly kind.

The heaviest obligation lying upon the Christian Church today is to purify and elevate her concept of God until it is once more worthy of Him—and of her. In all her prayers and labors this should have first place. We do the greatest service to the next generation of Christians by passing on to them undimmed and undiminished that noble concept of God which we received from our Hebrew and Christian fathers of generations past. This will prove of greater value to them than anything that art or science can devise.

O God of Bethel, by whose hand
   Thy people still are fed;
Who through this weary pilgrimage
   Hast all our fathers led!

Our vows, our prayers we now present
   Before Thy throne of grace:
God of our fathers! be the God
   Of their succeeding race.

                    Philip Doddridge

———————•———————

CHAPTER 2

God Incomprehensible

Lord, how great is our dilemma! In Thy Presence silence best becomes us, but love inflames our hearts and constrains us to speak.

Were we to hold our peace the stones would cry out; yet if we speak, what shall we say? Teach us to know that we cannot know, for the things of God knoweth no man, but the Spirit of God. Let faith support us where reason fails, and we shall think because we believe, not in order that we may believe.

In Jesus' name. *Amen.*

The child, the philosopher, and the religionist have all one question: "What is God like?

But sin has introduced complications and has made those very gifts of God a potential source of ruin to the soul.

This book is an attempt to answer that question. Yet at the outset I must acknowledge that it cannot be answered except to say that God is not like anything; that is, He is not *exactly* like anything or anybody.

We learn by using what we already know as a bridge over which we pass to the unknown. It is not possible for the mind to crash suddenly past the familiar into the totally unfamiliar. Even the most vigorous and daring mind is unable to create something out of nothing by a spontaneous act of imagination. Those strange beings that populate the world of mythology and superstition are not pure creations of fancy. The imagination created them by taking the ordinary inhabitants of earth and air and sea and extending their familiar forms beyond their normal boundaries, or by mixing the forms of two or more so as to produce something new. However beautiful or grotesque these may be, their prototypes can always be identified. They are like something we already know.

The effort of inspired men to express the ineffable has placed a great strain upon both thought and language in the Holy Scriptures. These being often a revelation of a world *above* nature, and the minds for which they were written being a *part* of nature, the writers are compelled to use a great many "like" words to make themselves understood.

When the Spirit would acquaint us with something that lies beyond the field of our knowledge, He tells us that this thing is like something we already know, but He is always careful to phrase His description so as to save us from slavish literalism. For example, when the prophet Ezekiel saw heaven opened and beheld visions of God, he found himself looking at that which he had no language to describe. What he was seeing was wholly different from anything he had ever known before, so he fell back upon the language of resemblance. "As for the likeness of the living creatures, their appearance was like burning coals of fire." The nearer he approaches to the burning throne the less sure his words become: "And above the firmament that was over their heads was the likeness of a throne, as the appearance of a sapphire stone: and upon the likeness of the throne was the likeness as the appearance of a man above upon it. And I saw as the colour of amber, as the appearance of fire round about within it. . . . This was the appearance of the likeness of the glory of the Lord."

Strange as this language is, it still does not create the impression of unreality. One gathers that the whole scene is very real but entirely alien to anything men know on earth. So, in order to convey an idea of what he sees, the prophet must employ such words as "likeness," "appearance," "as it were," and "the likeness of the appearance." Even the throne becomes "the appearance of a throne" and He that sits upon it, though like a man, is so unlike one that He can be described only as "the likeness of the appearance of a man."

When the Scripture states that man was made in the image of God, we dare not add to that statement an idea from our own head and make it mean "in the exact image." To do so is to make man a replica of God, and that is to lose the unicity of God and end with no God at all.

It is to break down the wall, infinitely high, that separates That-which-is-God from that-which-is-not-God. To think of creature and Creator as alike in essential being is to rob God of most of His attributes and reduce Him to the status of a creature. It is, for instance, to rob Him of His infinitude: there cannot be two unlimited substances in the universe. It is to take away His sovereignty: there cannot be two absolutely free beings in the universe, for sooner or later two completely free wills must collide. These attributes, to mention no more, require that there be but one to whom they belong.

When we try to imagine what God is like we must of necessity use that-which-is-not-God as the raw material for our minds to work on; hence whatever we visualize God to be, He is not, for we have constructed our image out of that which He has made and what He has made is not God. If we insist upon trying to imagine Him, we end with an idol, made not with hands but with thoughts; and an idol of the mind is as offensive to God as an idol of the hand.

"The intellect knoweth that it is ignorant of Thee," said Nicholas of Cusa, "because it knoweth Thou canst not be known, unless the unknowable could be known, and the invisible beheld, and the inaccessible attained."[1]

"If anyone should set forth any concept by which Thou canst be conceived," says Nicholas again, "I know that that concept is not a concept of Thee, for every concept is ended in the wall of Paradise. . . . So too, if any were to tell of the understanding of Thee, wishing to supply a means whereby Thou mightest be understood, this man is yet far from Thee . . . forasmuch as Thou art absolute above all the concepts which any man can frame."[2]

Left to ourselves we tend immediately to reduce God to manageable terms. We want to get Him where we can use Him, or at least know where He is when we need Him. We want a God we can in some measure control. We need the feeling of security that comes from knowing what God is like, and what He is like is of course a composite of all the religious pictures we have seen, all the best people we have known or heard about, and all the sublime ideas we have entertained.

If all this sounds strange to modern ears, it is only because we have for a full half century taken God for granted. The glory of God has not been revealed to this generation of men. The God of contemporary Christianity is only slightly superior to the gods of Greece and Rome, if indeed He is not actually inferior to them in that He is weak and helpless while they at least had power.

If what we conceive God to be He is not, how then shall we think of Him? If He is indeed incomprehensible, as the Creed declares Him to be, and unapproachable, as Paul says He is, how can we Christians satisfy our longing after Him? The hopeful words, "Acquaint now thyself with him, and be at peace," still stand after the passing of the centuries; but how shall we acquaint ourselves with One who eludes all the straining efforts of mind and heart? And how shall we be held accountable to know what cannot be known?

"Canst thou by searching find out God?" asks Zophar the Naamathite; "canst thou find out the Almighty unto perfection? It is as high as heaven; what canst thou do? deeper than hell; what canst thou know?" "Neither knoweth any man the Father, save the Son," said our Lord, "and he to whomsoever the Son will reveal him." The Gospel according to John reveals the helplessness of the human mind before the great Mystery which is God, and Paul in First Corinthians teaches that God can be known only as the Holy Spirit performs in the seeking heart an act of self-disclosure.

The yearning to know What cannot be known, to comprehend the Incomprehensible, to touch and taste the Unapproachable, arises from the image of God in the nature of man. Deep calleth unto deep, and though polluted and landlocked by the mighty disaster theologians call the Fall, the soul senses its origin and longs to return to its Source. How can this be realized?

The answer of the Bible is simply "through Jesus Christ our Lord." In Christ and by Christ, God effects complete self-disclosure, although He shows Himself not to reason but to faith and love. Faith is an organ of knowledge, and love an organ of experience. God came to us in the incarnation; in atonement He reconciled us to Himself, and by faith and love we enter and lay hold on Him.

"Verily God is of infinite greatness," says Christ's enraptured troubadour, Richard Rolle; "more than we can think; . . . unknowable by created things; and can never be comprehended by us as He is in Himself. But even here and now, whenever the heart begins to burn with a desire for God, she is made able to receive the uncreated light and, inspired and fulfilled by the gifts of the Holy Ghost, she tastes the joys of heaven. She transcends all visible things and is raised to the sweetness of eternal life. . . . Herein truly is perfect love; when all the intent of the mind, all the secret working of the heart, is lifted up into the love of God."[3]

That God can be known by the soul in tender personal experience while remaining infinitely aloof from the curious eyes of reason constitutes a paradox best described as

> *Darkness to the intellect*
> *But sunshine to the heart.*
> > Frederick W. Faber

The author of the celebrated little work *The Cloud of Unknowing* develops this thesis throughout his book. In approaching God, he says, the seeker discovers that the divine Being dwells in obscurity, hidden behind a cloud of unknowing; nevertheless he should not be discouraged but set his will with a naked intent unto God. This cloud is between the seeker and God so that he may never see God clearly by the light of understanding nor feel Him in the emotions. But by the mercy of God faith can break through into His Presence if the seeker but believe the Word and press on.[4]

Michael de Molinos, the Spanish saint, taught the same thing. In his *Spiritual Guide* he says that God will take the soul by the hand and lead her through the way of pure faith, "and causing the understanding to leave behind all considerations and reasonings He draws her forward. . . . Thus He causes her by means of a simple and obscure knowledge of faith to aspire only to her Bridegroom upon the wings of love."[5]

For these and similar teachings Molinos was condemned as a heretic by the Inquisition and sentenced to life imprisonment. He soon died in prison, but the truth he taught can never die. Speaking of the Christian soul he says: "Let her suppose that all the whole world and the most refined conceptions of the wisest intellects can tell her nothing, and that the goodness and beauty of her Beloved infinitely surpass all their knowledge, being persuaded that all creatures are too rude to inform her and to conduct her to the true knowledge of God. . . . She ought then to go forward with her love, leaving all her understanding behind. Let her love God as He is in Himself, and not as her imagination says He is, and pictures Him."[6]

"What is God like?" If by that question we mean "What is God like *in Himself*?" there is no answer. If we mean "What has God disclosed *about Himself* that the reverent reason can comprehend?" there is, I believe, an answer both full and satisfying. For while the name of God is secret and His essential nature incomprehensible, He in condescending love has by revelation declared certain things to be true of Himself. These we call His attributes.

> *Sovereign Father, heavenly King,*
> *Thee we now presume to sing;*
> *Glad thine attributes confess,*
> *Glorious all, and numberless.*
>
> Charles Wesley

CHAPTER 3

A Divine Attribute: Something True About God

O Majesty unspeakable, my soul desires to behold Thee. I cry to Thee from the dust.

Yet when I inquire after Thy name it is secret. Thou art hidden in the light which no man can approach unto. What Thou art cannot be thought or uttered, for Thy glory is ineffable.

Still, prophet and psalmist, apostle and saint have encouraged me to believe that I may in some measure know Thee. Therefore, I pray, whatever of Thyself Thou hast been pleased to disclose, help me to search out as treasure more precious than rubies or the merchandise of fine gold: for with Thee shall I live when the stars of the twilight are no more and the heavens have vanished away and only Thou remainest. *Amen.*

The study of the attributes of God, far from being dull and heavy, may for the enlightened Christian be a sweet and absorbing spiritual exercise. To the soul that is athirst for God, nothing could be more delightful.

> *Only to sit and think of God,*
> *Oh what a joy it is!*
> *To think the thought, to breathe the Name*
> *Earth has no higher bliss.*
>
> Frederick W. Faber

It would seem to be necessary before proceeding further to define the word *attribute* as it is used in this volume. It is not used in its philosophical sense nor confined to its strictest theological meaning. By it is meant simply whatever may be correctly ascribed to God. For the purpose of this book an *attribute of God is whatever God has in any way revealed as being true of Himself.*

And this brings us to the question of the number of the divine attributes. Religious thinkers have differed about this. Some have insisted that there are seven, but Faber sang of the "God of a *thousand* attributes," and Charles Wesley exclaimed,

> *Glory thine attributes confess,*
> *Glorious all and numberless.*

True, these men were worshiping, not counting; but we might be wise to follow the insight of the enraptured heart rather than the more cautious reasonings of the theological mind. If an attribute is something that is true of God, we may as well not try to enumerate them. Furthermore, to this meditation on the being of God the number of the attributes is not important, for only a limited few will be mentioned here.

If an attribute is something true of God, it is also something that we can *conceive* as being true of Him. God, being infinite, must possess attributes about which we can know nothing. An attribute, as we can know it, is a mental concept, an intellectual response to God's self-revelation. It is an answer to a question, the reply God makes to our interrogation concerning Himself.

What is God like? What kind of God is He? How may we expect Him to act toward us and toward all created things? Such questions are not merely academic. They touch the far-in reaches of the human spirit, and their answers affect life and character and destiny. When asked in reverence and their answers sought in humility, these are questions that cannot but be pleasing to our Father which art in heaven. "For He willeth that we be occupied in knowing and loving," wrote Julian of Norwich, "till the time that we shall be fulfilled in heaven. . . . For of all things the beholding and the loving of the Maker maketh the soul to seem less in his own sight, and most filleth him with reverent dread and true meekness; with plenty of charity for his fellow Christians." [7]

To our questions God has provided answers; not all the answers, certainly, but enough to satisfy our intellects and ravish our hearts. These answers He has provided in nature, in the Scriptures, and in the person of His Son.

The idea that God reveals Himself in the creation is not held with much vigor by modern Christians; but it is, nevertheless, set forth in the inspired Word, especially in the writings of David and Isaiah in the Old Testament and in Paul's Epistle to the Romans in the New. In the Holy Scriptures the revelation is clearer:

> *The heavens declare Thy glory, Lord,*
> *In every star Thy wisdom shines;*
> *But when our eyes behold Thy Word,*
> *We read Thy name in fairer lines.*
> Isaac Watts

And it is a sacred and indispensable part of the Christian message that the full sun-blaze of revelation came at the incarnation when the Eternal Word became flesh to dwell among us.

Though God in this threefold revelation has provided answers to our questions concerning Him, the answers by no means lie on the surface. They must be sought by prayer, by long meditation on the written Word, and by earnest and well-disciplined labor. However brightly the light may shine, it can be seen only by those who are spiritually prepared to receive it. "Blessed are the pure in heart, for they shall see God."

If we would think accurately about the attributes of God, we must learn to reject certain words that are sure to come crowding into our minds—such words as *trait*, *characteristic*, *quality*, words which are proper and necessary when we are considering created beings but altogether inappropriate when we are thinking about God. We must break ourselves of the habit of thinking of the Creator as we think of His creatures. It is probably impossible to think without words, but if we permit ourselves to think with the wrong words, we shall soon be entertaining erroneous thoughts; for words, which are given us for the expression of thought, have a habit of going beyond their proper bounds and determining the content of thought. "As nothing is more easy than to think," says Thomas Traherne, "so nothing is more difficult than to think well."[8] If we ever think well it should be when we think of God.

A man is the sum of his parts and his character the sum of the traits that compose it. These traits vary from man to man and may from time to time vary from themselves within the same man. Human character is not constant because the traits or qualities that constitute it are unstable. These come and go, burn low or glow with great intensity throughout our lives. Thus a man who is kind and considerate at thirty may be cruel and churlish at fifty. Such a change is possible because man is *made*; he is in a very real sense a composition; he is the sum of the traits that make up his character.

We naturally and correctly think of man as a work wrought by the divine Intelligence. He is both created and made. How he was created lies undisclosed among the secrets of God; how he was brought from not-being to being, from no-thing to something is not known and may never be known to any but the One who brought him forth. How God *made* him, however, is less of a secret, and while we know only a small portion of the whole truth, we do know that man possesses a body, a soul, and a spirit; we know that he has memory, reason, will, intelligence, sensation, and we know that to give these meaning he has the wondrous gift of consciousness. We know, too, that these, together with various qualities of temperament, compose his total human self. These are gifts from God arranged by infinite wisdom, notes that make up the score of creation's loftiest symphony, threads that compose the master tapestry of the universe.

But in all this we are thinking creature-thoughts and using creature-words to express them. Neither such thoughts nor such words are appropriate to the Deity. "The Father is made of none," says the Athanasian Creed, "neither created nor begotten. The Son is of the Father alone, not made, nor created, but begotten. The Holy Spirit is of the Father and the Son: not made nor created, nor begotten, but proceeding."[9] God exists in Himself and of Himself. His being He owes to no one. His substance is indivisible. He has no parts but is single in His unitary being.

The doctrine of the divine unity means not only that there is but one God; it means also that God is simple,

uncomplex, one with Himself. The harmony of His being is the result not of a perfect balance of parts but of the
absence of parts. Between His attributes no contradiction
can exist. He need not suspend one to exercise another,
for in Him all His attributes are one. All of God does all
that God does; He does not divide Himself to perform a
work, but works in the total unity of His being.

An attribute, then, is not a part of God. It is how God
is, and as far as the reasoning mind can go, we may say
that it is what God is, though, as I have tried to explain,
exactly what He is He cannot tell us. Of what God is conscious when He is conscious of self, only He knows. "The
things of God knoweth no man, but the Spirit of God."
Only to an equal could God communicate the mystery
of His Godhead; and to think of God as having an equal
is to fall into an intellectual absurdity.

The divine attributes are what we know to be true of
God. He does not possess them as qualities; they are how
God is as He reveals Himself to His creatures. Love, for
instance, is not something God has and which may grow
or diminish or cease to be. His love is the way God is, and
when He loves He is simply being Himself. And so with
the other attributes.

> *One God! one Majesty!*
> *There is no God but Thee!*
> *Unbounded, unextended Unity!*

Unfathomable Sea!
All life is out of Thee,
And Thy life is Thy blissful Unity.
Frederick W. Faber

CHAPTER 4

The Holy Trinity

God of our fathers, enthroned in light, how rich, how musical is the tongue of England! Yet when we attempt to speak forth Thy wonders, our words how poor they seem and our speech how unmelodious. When we consider the fearful mystery of Thy Triune Godhead we lay our hand upon our mouth. Before that burning bush we ask not to understand, but only that we may fitly adore Thee, One God in Persons Three. *Amen.*

To meditate on the three Persons of the Godhead is to walk in thought through the garden eastward in Eden and to tread on holy ground. Our sincerest effort to grasp the incomprehensible mystery of the Trinity must remain forever futile, and only by deepest reverence can it be saved from actual presumption.

Some persons who reject all they cannot explain have denied that God is a Trinity. Subjecting the Most High to their cold, level-eyed scrutiny, they conclude that it is impossible that He could be both One and Three. These forget that their whole life is enshrouded in mystery. They fail to consider that any real explanation of even the simplest phenomenon in nature lies hidden in obscurity and can no more be explained than can the mystery of the Godhead.

Every man lives by faith, the nonbeliever as well as the saint; the one by faith in natural laws and the other by faith in God. Every man throughout his entire life constantly accepts without understanding. The most learned sage can be reduced to silence with one simple question, "*What?*" The answer to that question lies forever in the abyss of unknowing beyond any man's ability to discover. "God understandeth the way thereof, and he knoweth the place thereof," but mortal man never.

Thomas Carlyle, following Plato, pictures a man, a deep pagan thinker, who had grown to maturity in some hidden cave and is brought out suddenly to see the sun rise. "What would his wonder be," exclaims Carlyle, "his rapt astonishment at the sight we daily witness with indifference! With the free, open sense of a child, yet with the ripe faculty of a man, his whole heart would be kindled by that sight. . . . This green flowery rock-built earth, the trees, the mountains, rivers, many-sounding seas; that great deep sea of azure that swims overhead; the winds sweeping through it; the black cloud fashioning itself together, now pouring out fire, now hail and rain; what is it? Ay, what? At bottom we do not yet know; we can never know at all."[10]

How different are we who have grown used to it, who have become jaded with a satiety of wonder. "It is not by our superior insight that we escape the difficulty," says Carlyle, "it is by our superior levity, our inattention, our *want* of insight. It is by not thinking that we cease to wonder at it. . . . We call that fire of the black thundercloud 'electricity,' and lecture learnedly about it, and grind the like of it out of glass and silk: but what is it? Whence comes it? Whither goes it? Science has done much for us; but it is a poor science that would hide from us the great deep sacred infinitude of Nescience, whither we can never penetrate, on which all science swims as a mere superficial film. This world, after all our science and sciences, is still a miracle; wonderful, inscrutable, magical and more, to whosoever will think of it."

These penetrating, almost prophetic, words were written more than a century ago, but not all the breath-taking advances of science and technology since that time have invalidated one word or rendered obsolete as much as one period or comma. Still we do not know. We save face by repeating frivolously the popular jargon of science. We harness the mighty energy that rushes through our world; we subject it to fingertip control in our cars and our kitchens; we make it work for us like Aladdin's jinn, but still we do not know what it is. Secularism, materialism, and the intrusive presence of *things* have put out the light in our souls and turned us into a generation of zombies. We cover our deep ignorance with words, but we are ashamed to wonder, we are afraid to whisper "mystery."

The Church has not hesitated to teach the doctrine of the Trinity. Without pretending to understand, she has given her witness, she has repeated what the Holy Scriptures teach. Some deny that the Scriptures teach the Trinity of the Godhead on the ground that the whole idea of trinity in unity is a contradiction in terms; but since we cannot understand the fall of a leaf by the roadside or the hatching of a robin's egg in the nest yonder, why should the Trinity be a problem to us? "We think more loftily of God," says Michael de Molinos, "by knowing that He is incomprehensible, and above our understanding, than by conceiving Him under any image, and creature beauty, according to our rude understanding."[11]

Not all who called themselves Christians through the centuries were Trinitarians, but as the presence of God in the fiery pillar glowed above the camp of Israel throughout the wilderness journey, saying to all the world, "These are My people," so belief in the Trinity has since the days of the apostles shone above the Church of the Firstborn as she journeyed down the years. Purity and power have followed this faith. Under this banner have gone forth apostles, fathers, martyrs, mystics, hymnists, reformers, revivalists, and the seal of divine approval has rested on their lives and their labors. However they may have differed on minor matters, the doctrine of the Trinity bound them together.

What God declares the believing heart confesses without the need of further proof. Indeed, to seek proof is to admit doubt, and to obtain proof is to render faith superfluous. Everyone who possesses the gift of faith will recognize the wisdom of those daring words of one of the early Church fathers: "I believe that Christ died for me because it is incredible; I believe that He rose from the dead because it is impossible."

That was the attitude of Abraham, who against all evidence waxed strong in faith, giving glory to God. It was the attitude of Anselm, "the second Augustine," one of the greatest thinkers of the Christian era, who held that faith must precede all effort to understand. Reflection upon revealed truth naturally follows the advent of faith, but faith comes first to the hearing ear, not to the cogitating mind. The believing man does not ponder the Word and arrive at faith by a process of reasoning, nor does he seek confirmation of faith from philosophy or science. His cry is, "O earth, earth, earth, hear the word of the LORD. Yea, let God be true, but every man a liar."

Is this to dismiss scholarship as valueless in the sphere of revealed religion? By no means. The scholar has a vitally important task to perform within a carefully prescribed precinct. His task is to guarantee the purity of the text, to get as close as possible to the Word as originally given. He may compare Scripture with Scripture until he has discovered the true meaning of the text. But right there his authority ends. *He must never sit in judgment upon what is written.* He dare not bring the meaning of the Word before the bar of his reason. He dare not commend or condemn the Word as reasonable or unreasonable, scientific or unscientific. After the meaning is discovered, that meaning judges him; never does he judge it.

The doctrine of the Trinity is truth for the heart. The spirit of man alone can enter through the veil and penetrate into that Holy of Holies. "Let me seek Thee in longing," pleaded Anselm, "let me long for Thee in seeking; let me find Thee in love, and love Thee in finding."[12] Love and faith are at home in the mystery of the Godhead. Let reason kneel in reverence outside.

Christ did not hesitate to use the plural form when speaking of Himself along with the Father and the Spirit. "We will come unto him, and make our abode with him." Yet again He said, "I and my Father are one." It is most important that we think of God as Trinity in Unity, neither confounding the Persons nor dividing the Substance. Only so may we think rightly of God and in a manner worthy of Him and of our own souls.

It was our Lord's claim to equality with the Father that outraged the religionists of His day and led at last to His crucifixion. The attack on the doctrine of the Trinity two centuries later by Arius and others was also aimed at Christ's claim to deity. During the Arian controversy 318 Church fathers (many of them maimed and scarred by the physical violence suffered in earlier persecutions) met at Nicaea and adopted a statement of faith, one section of which runs:

I believe in one Lord Jesus Christ,
The Only-begotten Son of God,
Begotten of Him before all ages,
God of God, Light of Light,
Very God of Very God,
Begotten, not made,
Being of one substance with the Father,
By whom all things were made.

For more than sixteen hundred years this has stood as the final test of orthodoxy, as well it should, for it condenses in theological language the teaching of the New Testament concerning the position of the Son in the Godhead.

The Nicene Creed also pays tribute to the Holy Spirit as being Himself God and equal to the Father and the Son:

I believe in the Holy Spirit
The Lord and giver of life,
Which proceedeth from the Father and the Son,
Who with the Father and Son together
Is worshipped and glorified.

Apart from the question of whether the Spirit proceeds from the Father alone or from the Father and the Son, this tenet of the ancient creed has been held by the Eastern and Western branches of the Church and by all but a tiny minority of Christians.

The authors of the Athanasian Creed spelled out with

great care the relation of the three Persons to each other, filling in the gaps in human thought as far as they were able while staying within the bounds of the inspired Word. "In this Trinity," runs the Creed, "nothing is before or after, nothing is greater or less: but all three Persons coeternal, together and equal."

How do these words harmonize with the saying of Jesus, "My Father is greater than I"? Those old theologians knew, and wrote into the Creed, "Equal to His Father, as touching His Godhead; less than the Father, as touching His manhood," and this interpretation commends itself to every serious-minded seeker after truth in a region where the light is all but blinding.

To redeem mankind the Eternal Son did not leave the bosom of the Father; while walking among men He referred to Himself as "the only begotten Son, which is in the bosom of the Father," and spoke of Himself again as "the Son of man which is in heaven." We grant mystery here, but not confusion. In His incarnation the Son veiled His deity, but He did not void it. The unity of the Godhead made it impossible that He should surrender anything of His deity. When He took upon Him the nature of man, He did not degrade Himself or become even for a time less than He had been before. God can never become less than Himself. For God to become anything that He has not been is unthinkable.

The Persons of the Godhead, being one, have one will. They work always together, and never one smallest act is done by one without the instant acquiescence of the other two. Every act of God is accomplished by the Trinity in Unity. Here, of course, we are being driven by necessity to conceive of God in human terms. We are thinking of God by analogy with man, and the result must fall short of ultimate truth; yet if we are to think of God at all, we must do it by adapting creature-thoughts and creature-words to the Creator. It is a real if understandable error to conceive of the Persons of the Godhead as conferring with one another and reaching agreement by interchange of thought as humans do. It has always seemed to me that Milton introduces an element of weakness into his celebrated Paradise Lost when he presents the Persons of the Godhead conversing with each other about the redemption of the human race.

When the Son of God walked the earth as the Son of Man, He spoke often to the Father and the Father answered Him again; as the Son of Man, He now intercedes with God for His people. The dialogue involving the Father and the Son recorded in the Scriptures is always to be understood as being between the Eternal Father and the Man Christ Jesus. That instant, immediate communion between the Persons of the Godhead which has been from all eternity knows not sound nor effort nor motion.

> *Amid the eternal silences*
> *God's endless Word was spoken;*
> *None heard but He who always spake,*
> *And the silence was unbroken.*

O marvellous! O worshipful!
No song or sound is heard
But everywhere and every hour
In love, in wisdom, and in power,
The Father speaks His dear Eternal Word.

Frederick W. Faber

A popular belief among Christians divides the work of God between the three Persons, giving a specific part to each, as, for instance, creation to the Father, redemption to the Son, and regeneration to the Holy Spirit. This is partly true but not wholly so, for God cannot so divide Himself that one Person works while another is inactive. In the Scriptures the three Persons are shown to act in harmonious unity in all the mighty works that are wrought throughout the universe.

In the Holy Scriptures the work of *creation* is attributed to the Father (Gen. 1:1), to the Son (Col. 1:16), and to the Holy Spirit (Job 26:13 and Ps. 104:30). The *incarnation* is shown to have been accomplished by the three Persons in full accord (Luke 1:35), though only the Son became flesh to dwell among us. At Christ's *baptism* the Son came up out of the water, the Spirit descended upon Him, and the Father's voice spoke from heaven (Matt. 3:16, 17). Probably the most beautiful description of the work of *atonement* is found in Hebrews 9:14, where it is stated that Christ, through the Eternal Spirit, offered Himself without spot to God; and there we behold the three Persons operating together.

The *resurrection* of Christ is likewise attributed variously to the Father (Acts 2:32), to the Son (John 10:17, 18), and to the Holy Spirit (Rom. 1:4). The *salvation* of the individual man is shown by the apostle Peter to be the work of all three Persons of the Godhead (I Pet. 1:2), and the *indwelling* of the Christian man's soul is said to be by the Father, the Son, and the Holy Spirit (John 14:15–23).

The doctrine of the Trinity, as I have said before, is truth for the heart. The fact that it cannot be satisfactorily explained, instead of being against it, is in its favor. Such a truth had to be revealed; no one could have imagined it.

> *O Blessed Trinity!*
> *O simplest Majesty! O Three in One!*
> *Thou art for ever God alone.*
> *Holy Trinity!*
> *Blessed equal Three.*
> *One God, we praise Thee.*
>
> Frederick W. Faber

CHAPTER 5

The Self-existence of God

Lord of all being! Thou alone canst affirm I AM THAT I AM; yet we who are made in Thine image may each one repeat "I am," so confessing that we derive from Thee and that our words are but an echo of Thine own. We acknowledge Thee to be the great Original of which we through Thy goodness are grateful if imperfect copies. We worship Thee, O Father Everlasting. *Amen.*

"God has no origin," said Novatian,[13] and it is precisely this concept of no-origin which distinguishes That-which-is-God from whatever is not God.

Origin is a word that can apply only to things created. When we think of anything that has origin we are not thinking of God. God is self-existent, while all created things necessarily originated somewhere at some time. Aside from God, nothing is self-caused.

By our effort to discover the origin of things we confess our belief that everything was made by Someone who was made of none. By familiar experience we are taught that everything "came from" something else. Whatever exists must have had a cause that antedates it and was at least equal to it, since the lesser cannot produce the greater. Any person or thing may be at once both caused and the cause of someone or something else; and so, back to the One who is the cause of all but is Himself caused by none.

The child by his question, "Where did God come from?" is unwittingly acknowledging his creaturehood. Already the concept of cause and source and origin is firmly fixed in his mind. He knows that everything around him came from something other than itself, and he simply extends that concept upward to God. The little philosopher is thinking in true creature-idiom and, allowing for his lack of basic information, he is reasoning correctly. He must be told that God has no origin, and he will find this hard to grasp since it introduces a category with which he is wholly unfamiliar and contradicts the bent toward origin-seeking so deeply ingrained in all intelligent beings, a bent that impels them to probe ever back and back toward undiscovered beginnings.

To think steadily of that to which the idea of origin cannot apply is not easy, if indeed it is possible at all. Just as under certain conditions a tiny point of light can be seen, not by looking directly at it but by focusing the eyes slightly to one side, so it is with the idea of the Uncreated. When we try to focus our thought upon One who is pure uncreated being we may see nothing at all, for He dwelleth in light that no man can approach unto. Only by faith and love are we able to glimpse Him as He passes by our shelter in the cleft of the rock. "And although this knowledge is very cloudy, vague and general," says Michael de Molinos, "yet, being supernatural, it produces a far more clear and perfect cognition of God than any sensible or particular apprehension that can be formed in this life; since all corporeal and sensible images are immeasurably remote from God."[14]

The human mind, being created, has an understandable uneasiness about the Uncreated. We do not find it comfortable to allow for the presence of One who is wholly outside of the circle of our familiar knowledge. We tend to be disquieted by the thought of One who does not account to us for His being, who is responsible to no one, who is self-existent, self-dependent, and self-sufficient.

Philosophy and science have not always been friendly toward the idea of God, the reason being that they are dedicated to the task of accounting for things and are impatient with anything that refuses to give an account of itself. The philosopher and the scientist will admit that there is much that they do not know; but that is quite another thing from admitting that there is something which they can never know, which indeed they have no technique for discovering. To admit that there is One who lies beyond us, who exists outside of all our categories, who will not be dismissed with a name, who will not appear before the bar of our reason, nor submit to our curious inquiries: this requires a great deal of humility, more than most of us possess, so we save face by thinking God down to our level, or at least down to where we can manage Him. Yet how He eludes us! For He is everywhere while He is nowhere, for "where" has to do with matter and space, and God is independent of both. He is unaffected by time or motion, is wholly self-dependent and owes nothing to the worlds His hands have made.

> *Timeless, spaceless, single, lonely,*
> *Yet sublimely Three,*
> *Thou art grandly, always, only*
> *God in Unity!*
> *Lone in grandeur, lone in glory,*
> *Who shall tell Thy wondrous story?*
> *Awful Trinity!*
>
> Frederick W. Faber

It is not a cheerful thought that millions of us who live in a land of Bibles, who belong to churches and labor to promote the Christian religion, may yet pass our whole life on this earth without once having thought or tried to think seriously about the being of God. Few of us have let our hearts gaze in wonder at the I AM, the self-existent

Self back of which no creature can think. Such thoughts are too painful for us. We prefer to think where it will do more good—about how to build a better mousetrap, for instance, or how to make two blades of grass grow where one grew before. And for this we are now paying a too heavy price in the secularization of our religion and the decay of our inner lives.

Perhaps some sincere but puzzled Christian may at this juncture wish to inquire about the practicality of such concepts as I am trying to set forth here. "What bearing does this have on my life?" he may ask. "What possible meaning can the self-existence of God have for me and others like me in a world such as this and in times such as these?"

To this I reply that, because we are the handiwork of God, it follows that *all our problems and their solutions are theological.* Some knowledge of what kind of God it is that operates the universe is indispensable to a sound philosophy of life and a sane outlook on the world scene. The much-quoted advice of Alexander Pope

> *Know then thyself, presume not God to scan:*
> *The proper study of mankind is man,*

if followed literally would destroy any possibility of man's ever knowing himself in any but the most superficial way. We can never know who or what we are till we know at least something of what God is. For this reason the self-existence of God is not a wisp of dry doctrine, academic and remote; it is in fact as near as our breath and as practical as the latest surgical technique.

For reasons known only to Himself, God honored man above all other beings by creating him in His own image. And let it be understood that the divine image in man is not a poetic fancy, not an idea born of religious longing. It is a solid theological fact, taught plainly throughout the Sacred Scriptures and recognized by the Church as a truth necessary to a right understanding of the Christian faith.

Man is a created being, a derived and contingent self, who of himself possesses nothing but is dependent each moment for his existence upon the One who created him after His own likeness. The fact of God is necessary to the fact of man. Think God away and man has no ground of existence.

That God is everything and man nothing is a basic tenet of Christian faith and devotion; and here the teachings of Christianity coincide with those of the more advanced and philosophical religions of the East. Man for all his genius is but an echo of the original Voice, a reflection of the uncreated Light. As a sunbeam perishes when cut off from the sun, so man apart from God would pass back into the void of nothingness from which he first leaped at the creative call. Not man only, but everything that exists came out of and is dependent upon the continuing creative impulse. "In the beginning was the Word, and the Word was with God, and the Word was God. . . . All things were made by him; and without him was not any thing made that was made." That is how John explains it, and with him agrees the apostle Paul: "For by him were all things created, that are in heaven, and that are in earth, visible and invisible, whether they be thrones, or dominions, or principalities, or powers: all things were created by him, and for him: and he is before all things, and by him all things consist." To this witness the writer to the Hebrews adds his voice, testifying of Christ that He is the brightness of God's glory and the express image of His Person, and that He upholds all things by the word of His power.

In this utter dependence of all things upon the creative will of God lies the possibility for both holiness and sin. One of the marks of God's image in man is his ability to exercise moral choice. The teaching of Christianity is that man chose to be independent of God and confirmed his choice by deliberately disobeying a divine command. This act violated the relationship that normally existed between God and His creature; it rejected God as the ground of existence and threw man back upon himself. Thereafter he became not a planet revolving around the central Sun, but a sun in his own right, around which everything else must revolve.

A more positive assertion of selfhood could not be imagined than those words of God to Moses: "I AM THAT I AM." Everything God is, everything that is

God, is set forth in that unqualified declaration of independent being. Yet in God, self is not sin but the quintessence of all possible goodness, holiness, and truth.

The natural man is a sinner because and only because he challenges God's selfhood in relation to his own. In all else he may willingly accept the sovereignty of God; in his own life he rejects it. For him, God's dominion ends where his begins. For him, self becomes Self, and in this he unconsciously imitates Lucifer, that fallen son of the morning who said in his heart, "I will ascend into heaven, I will exalt my throne above the stars of God. . . . I will be like the most High."

Yet so subtle is self that scarcely anyone is conscious of its presence. Because man is born a rebel, he is unaware that he is one. His constant assertion of self, as far as he thinks of it at all, appears to him a perfectly normal thing. He is willing to share himself, sometimes even to sacrifice himself for a desired end, but never to dethrone himself. No matter how far down the scale of social acceptance he may slide, he is still in his own eyes a king on a throne, and no one, not even God, can take that throne from him.

Sin has many manifestations but its essence is one. A moral being, created to worship before the throne of God, sits on the throne of his own selfhood and from that elevated position declares, "I AM." That is sin in its concentrated essence; yet because it is natural it appears to be good. It is only when in the gospel the soul is brought before the face of the Most Holy One without the protective shield of ignorance that the frightful moral incongruity is brought home to the conscience. In the language of evangelism the man who is thus confronted by the fiery presence of Almighty God is said to be under conviction. Christ referred to this when He said of the Spirit whom He would send to the world, "And when he is come, he will reprove the world of sin, and of righteousness, and of judgment."

The earliest fulfillment of these words of Christ was at Pentecost after Peter had preached the first great Christian sermon."Now when they heard this, they were pricked in their heart, and said unto Peter and to the rest of the apostles, Men and brethren, what shall we do?" This "What shall we do?" is the deep heart cry of every man who suddenly realizes that he is a usurper and sits on a stolen throne. However painful, it is precisely this acute moral consternation that produces true repentance and makes a robust Christian after the penitent has been dethroned and has found forgiveness and peace through the gospel.

"Purity of heart is to will one thing," said Kierkegaard, and we may with equal truth turn this about and declare, "The essence of sin is to will one thing," for to set our will against the will of God is to dethrone God and make ourselves supreme in the little kingdom of Mansoul. This is sin at its evil root. Sins may multiply like the sands by the seashore, but they are yet one. Sins are because sin is. This is the rationale behind the much maligned doctrine of natural depravity which holds that the impenitent man can do nothing but sin and that his good deeds are really not good at all. His best religious works God rejects as He rejected the offering of Cain. Only when he has restored his stolen throne to God are his works acceptable. The struggle of the Christian man to be good while the bent toward self-assertion still lives within him as a kind of unconscious moral reflex is vividly described by the apostle Paul in the seventh chapter of his Roman Epistle; and his testimony is in full accord with the teaching of the prophets. Eight hundred years before the advent of Christ the prophet Isaiah identified sin as rebellion against the will of God and the assertion of the right of each man to choose for himself the way he shall go. "All we like sheep have gone astray," he said, "we have turned every one to his own way," and I believe that no more accurate description of sin has ever been given.

The witness of the saints has been in full harmony with prophet and apostle, that an inward principle of self lies at the source of human conduct, turning everything men do into evil. To save us completely Christ must reverse the bent of our nature; He must plant a new principle within us so that our subsequent conduct will spring out of a desire to promote the honor of God and the good of our fellow men. The old self-sins must die, and the only instrument by which they can be slain is the cross. "If any man will come after me, let him deny himself, and take up his cross, and follow me," said our Lord, and years later the victorious Paul could say, "I am crucified with Christ: nevertheless I live; yet not I, but Christ liveth in me."

> *My God, shall sin its power maintain*
> *And in my soul defiant live!*
> *'Tis not enough that Thou forgive,*
> *The cross must rise and self be slain.*
>
> *O God of love, Thy power disclose:*
> *'Tis not enough that Christ should rise,*
> *I, too, must seek the brightening skies,*
> *And rise from death, as Christ arose.*
>
> Greek Hymn

———————•———————

CHAPTER 6

The Self-sufficiency
of God

Teach us, O God, that nothing is necessary to Thee.
Were anything necessary to Thee that thing would be the
measure of Thine imperfection: and how could we worship
one who is imperfect? If nothing is necessary to Thee, then
no one is necessary, and if no one, then not we. Thou dost
seek us though Thou does not need us. We seek Thee
because we need Thee, for in Thee we live and move and
have our being. *Amen.*

"T he Father hath life in himself," said our Lord, and
it is characteristic of His teaching that He thus in
a brief sentence sets forth truth so lofty as to transcend
the highest reaches of human thought. God, He said, is
self-sufficient; He is what He is in *Himself*, in the final
meaning of those words.

Whatever God is, and all that God is, He is in Himself. All life is in and from God, whether it be the lowest

form of unconscious life or the highly self-conscious, intelligent life of a seraph. No creature has life in itself; all life is a gift from God.

The life of God, conversely, is not a gift from another. Were there another from whom God could receive the gift of life, or indeed any gift whatever, that other would be God in fact. An elementary but correct way to think of God is as the One who contains all, who gives all that is given, but who Himself can receive nothing that He has not first given.

To admit the existence of a need in God is to admit incompleteness in the divine Being. Need is a creature-word and cannot be spoken of the Creator. God has a voluntary relation to everything He has made, but He has no *necessary* relation to anything outside of Himself. His interest in His creatures arises from His sovereign good pleasure, not from any need those creatures can supply nor from any completeness they can bring to Him who is complete in Himself.

Again we must reverse the familiar flow of our thoughts and try to understand that which is unique, that which stands alone as being true in this situation and nowhere else. Our common habits of thought allow for the existence of need among created things. Nothing is complete in itself but requires something outside itself in order to exist. All breathing things need air; every organism needs food and water. Take air and water from the earth and all life would perish instantly. It may be stated as an axiom that to stay alive every created thing needs some other created thing and all things need God. To God alone nothing is necessary.

The river grows larger by its tributaries, but where is the tributary that can enlarge the One out of whom came everything and to whose infinite fullness all creation owes its being?

> *Unfathomable Sea: all life is out of Thee,*
> *And Thy life is Thy blissful Unity.*
>   Frederick W. Faber

The problem of why God created the universe still troubles thinking men; but if we cannot know why, we can at least know that He did not bring His worlds into being to meet some unfulfilled need in Himself, as a man might build a house to shelter him against the winter cold or plant a field of corn to provide him with necessary food. The word necessary is wholly foreign to God.

Since He is the Being supreme over all, it follows that God cannot be elevated. Nothing is above Him, nothing beyond Him. Any motion in His direction is elevation for the creature; away from Him, descent. He holds His position out of Himself and by leave of none. As no one can promote Him, so no one can degrade Him. It is written that He upholds all things by the word of His power. How can He be raised or supported by the things He upholds?

Were all human beings suddenly to become blind, still the sun would shine by day and the stars by night, for these owe nothing to the millions who benefit from their light. So, were every man on earth to become atheist, it could not affect God in any way. He is what He is in Himself without regard to any other. To believe in Him adds nothing to His perfections; to doubt Him takes nothing away.

Almighty God, just because He is almighty, needs no support. The picture of a nervous, ingratiating God fawning over men to win their favor is not a pleasant one; yet if we look at the popular conception of God that is precisely what we see. Twentieth-century Christianity has put God on charity. So lofty is our opinion of ourselves that we find it quite easy, not to say enjoyable, to believe that we are necessary to God. But the truth is that God is not greater for our being, nor would He be less if we did not exist. That we do exist is altogether of God's free determination, not by our desert nor by divine necessity.

Probably the hardest thought of all for our natural egotism to entertain is that God does not need our help. We commonly represent Him as a busy, eager, somewhat frustrated Father hurrying about seeking help to carry out His benevolent plan to bring peace and salvation to the world, but, as said the Lady Julian, "I saw truly that God doeth all-thing, be it never so little."[15] The God who worketh all things surely needs no help and no helpers.

Too many missionary appeals are based upon this fancied frustration of Almighty God. An effective speaker can easily excite pity in his hearers, not only for the heathen but for the God who has tried so hard and so long to save them and has failed for want of support. I fear that thousands of younger persons enter Christian service from no higher motive than to help deliver God from the embarrassing situation His love has gotten Him into and His limited abilities seem unable to get Him out of. Add to this a certain degree of commendable idealism and a fair amount of compassion for the underprivileged and you have the true drive behind much Christian activity today.

Again, God needs no defenders. He is the eternal Undefended. To communicate with us in an idiom we can understand, God in the Scriptures makes full use of military terms; but surely it was never intended that we should think of the throne of the Majesty on high as being under siege, with Michael and his hosts or some other heavenly beings defending it from stormy overthrow. So to think is to misunderstand everything the Bible would tell us about God. Neither Judaism nor Christianity could approve such puerile notions. A God who must be defended is one who can help us only while someone is helping Him. We may count upon Him only if He wins in the cosmic seesaw battle between right and wrong. Such a God could not command the respect of intelligent men; He could only excite their pity.

To be right we must think worthily of God. It is morally imperative that we purge from our minds all ignoble concepts of the Deity and let Him be the God in our minds that He is in His universe. The Christian religion has to do with God and man, but its focal point is God, not man. Man's only claim to importance is that he was created in the divine image; in himself he is nothing. The psalmists and prophets of the Scriptures refer in sad scorn to weak man whose breath is in his nostrils, who grows up like the grass in the morning only to be cut down and wither before the setting of the sun. That God exists for Himself and man for the glory of God is the emphatic teaching of the Bible. The high honor of God is first in heaven as it must yet be in earth.

From all this we may begin to understand why the Holy Scriptures have so much to say about the vital place of faith and why they brand unbelief as a deadly sin. Among all created beings, not one dare trust in itself. God alone trusts in Himself; all other beings must trust in Him. Unbelief is actually perverted faith, for it puts its trust not in the living God but in dying men. The unbeliever denies the self-sufficiency of God and usurps attributes that are not his. This dual sin dishonors God and ultimately destroys the soul of the man.

In His love and pity God came to us as Christ. This has been the consistent position of the Church from the days of the apostles. It is fixed for Christian belief in the doctrine of the incarnation of the Eternal Son. In recent times, however, this has come to mean something different from, and less than, what it meant to the early church. The Man Jesus as He appeared in the flesh has been equated with the Godhead and all His human weaknesses and limitations attributed to the Deity. The truth is that the Man who walked among us was a demonstration, not of unveiled deity but of perfect humanity. The awful majesty of the Godhead was mercifully sheathed in the soft envelope of human nature to protect mankind. "Go down," God told Moses on the mountain, "charge the people, less they break through unto the Lord to gaze, and many of them perish"; and later, "Thou canst not see my face: for there shall no man see me, and live."

Christians today appear to know Christ only after the flesh. They try to achieve communion with Him by divesting Him of His burning holiness and unapproachable majesty, the very attributes He veiled while on earth but assumed in fullness of glory upon His ascension to the Father's right hand. The Christ of popular Christianity has a weak smile and a halo. He has become Someone-up-There who likes people, at least some people, and these are grateful but not too impressed. If they need Him, He also needs them.

Let us not imagine that the truth of the divine self-sufficiency will paralyze Christian activity. Rather it will stimulate all holy endeavor. This truth, while a needed rebuke to human self-confidence, will when viewed in its Biblical perspective lift from our minds the exhausting load of mortality and encourage us to take the easy yoke of Christ and spend ourselves in Spirit-inspired toil for the honor of God and the good of mankind. For the blessed news is that the God who needs no one has in sovereign condescension stooped to work by and in and through His obedient children.

If all this appears self-contradictory—*Amen*, be it so. The various elements of truth stand in perpetual antithesis, sometimes requiring us to believe apparent opposites while we wait for the moment when we shall know as we are known. Then truth which now appears to be in conflict with itself will arise in shining unity and it will be seen that the conflict has not been in the truth but in our sin-damaged minds.

In the meanwhile our inner fulfillment lies in loving obedience to the commandments of Christ and the inspired admonitions of His apostles. "It is God which worketh in you." *He needs no one*, but when faith is present *He works through anyone*. Two statements are in this sentence, and a healthy spiritual life requires that we accept both. For a full generation the first has been in almost total eclipse, and that to our deep spiritual injury.

> *Fountain of good, all blessing flows*
> *From Thee; no want Thy fulness knows;*
> *What but Thyself canst Thou desire?*
> *Yet, self-sufficient as Thou art,*
> *Thou dost desire my worthless heart;*
> *This, only this, dost Thou require.*
>   Johann Scheffler

CHAPTER 7

---•---

The Eternity of God

This day our hearts approve with gladness what our reason can never fully comprehend, even Thine eternity, O Ancient of Days. Art Thou not from everlasting, O Lord, my God, mine Holy One?

We worship Thee, the Father Everlasting, whose years shall have no end; and Thee, the love-begotten Son whose goings forth have been ever of old; we also acknowledge and adore Thee, Eternal Spirit, who before the foundation of the world didst live and love in coequal glory with the Father and the Son.

Enlarge and purify the mansions of our souls that they may be fit habitations for Thy Spirit, who dost prefer before all temples the upright heart and pure. *Amen.*

The concept of everlastingness runs like a lofty mountain range throughout the entire Bible and looms large in orthodox Hebrew and Christian thought. Were we to reject the concept, it would be altogether impossible for us to think again the thoughts of prophets and apostles, so full were they of the long dreams of eternity.

Because the word *everlasting* is sometimes used by the sacred writers to mean no more than long-lasting (as "the everlasting hills"), some persons have argued that the concept of unending existence was not in the minds of the writers when they used the word but was supplied later by the theologians. This is of course a serious error, and, as far as I can see, has no ground in serious scholarship. It has been used by certain teachers as an escape from the doctrine of eternal punishment. These reject the eternity of moral retribution, and to be consistent they are forced to weaken the whole idea of endlessness. This is not the only instance where an attempt was made to slay a truth to keep it quiet lest it appear as a material witness against an error. The truth is that if the Bible did not teach that God possessed endless being in the ultimate meaning of that term, we would be compelled to infer it from His other attributes, and if the Holy Scriptures had no word for absolute everlastingness, it would be necessary for us to coin one to express the concept, for it is assumed, implied, and generally taken for granted everywhere throughout the inspired Scriptures. The idea of endlessness is to the kingdom of God what carbon is to the kingdom of nature. As carbon is present almost everywhere, as it is an essential element in all living matter and supplies all life with energy, so the concept of everlastingness is necessary to give meaning to any Christian doctrine. Indeed I know of no tenet of the Christian creed that could retain its significance if the idea of eternity were extracted from it.

"From everlasting to everlasting, thou art God," said Moses in the Spirit. "From the vanishing point to the vanishing point" would be another way to say it quite in keeping with the words as Moses used them. The mind looks backward in time till the dim past vanishes, then turns and looks into the future till thought and imagination collapse from exhaustion; and God is at both points, unaffected by either.

Time marks the beginning of created existence, and because God never began to exist it can have no application to Him. "Began" is a time-word, and can have no personal meaning for the high and lofty One that inhabiteth eternity.

> *No age can heap its outward years on Thee;*
> *Dear God! Thou art, Thyself, Thine own eternity.*
> Frederick W. Faber

Because God lives in an everlasting now, He has no past and no future. When time-words occur in the Scriptures they refer to our time, not to His. When the four living creatures before the throne cry day and night, "Holy, holy, holy, LORD God Almighty, which was, and is, and is to come," they are identifying God with the flow of creature-life with its familiar three tenses; and this is right and good, for God has sovereignly willed so to identify Himself. But since God is uncreated, He is not Himself affected by that succession of consecutive changes we call time.

God dwells in eternity but time dwells in God. He has already lived all our tomorrows as He has lived all our yesterdays. An illustration offered by C. S. Lewis may help us here. He suggests that we think of a sheet of paper infinitely extended. That would be eternity. Then on that paper draw a short line to represent time. As the line begins and ends on that infinite expanse, so time began in God and will end in Him.

That God appears at time's beginning is not too difficult to comprehend, but that He appears at the beginning and end of time *simultaneously* is not so easy to grasp; yet it is true. Time is known to us by a succession of events. It is the way we account for consecutive changes in the universe. Changes take place not all at once but in succession, one after the other, and it is the relation of "after" to "before" that gives us our idea of time. We wait for the sun to move from east to west or for the hour hand to move around the face of the clock, but God is not compelled so to wait. For Him everything that will happen has already happened.

This is why God can say, "I am God, . . . and there is none like me, declaring the end from the beginning." He sees the end and the beginning in one view. "For infinite duration, which is eternity's self, includeth all succession," says Nicholas of Cusa, "and all which seemeth to us to be in succession existeth not posterior to Thy concept, which is eternity. . . . Thus, because Thou art God almighty, Thou dwellest within the wall of Paradise, and this wall is that coincidence where later is one with earlier, where the end is one with the beginning, where Alpha and Omega are the same. . . . For NOW and THEN coincide in the circle of the wall of Paradise. But, O my God, the Absolute and Eternal, it is beyond the present and the past that Thou dost exist and utter speech."[16]

When he was a very old man, Moses wrote the psalm from which I have quoted earlier in this chapter. In it he celebrates the eternity of God. To him this truth is a solid theological fact as firm and hard as that Mount Sinai with which he was so familiar, and for him it had two practical meanings: since God is eternal, He can be and continue forever to be the one safe home for His time-driven children. "Lord, thou hast been our dwelling place in all generations." The second thought is less comforting: God's eternity is so long and our years on earth are so few, how shall we establish the work of our hands? How shall we escape the abrasive action of events that would wear us out and destroy us? God fills and dominates the psalm, so it is to Him that Moses makes his plaintive appeal, "So teach us to number our days, that we may apply our hearts unto wisdom." May the knowledge of Thy eternity not be wasted on me!

We who live in this nervous age would be wise to meditate on our lives and our days long and often before the face of God and on the edge of eternity. For we are made for eternity as certainly as we are made for time, and as responsible moral beings we must deal with both.

"He hath set eternity in their heart," said the Preacher, and I think he here sets forth both the glory and the misery of men. To be made for eternity and forced to dwell in time is for mankind a tragedy of huge proportions. All within us cries for life and permanence, and everything around us reminds us of mortality and change. Yet that God has made us of the stuff of eternity is both a glory yet to be realized and a prophecy yet to be fulfilled.

I hope it will not be found unduly repetitious if I return again to that important pillar of Christian theology, the image of God in man. The marks of the divine image have been so obscured by sin that they are not easy to identify, but is it not reasonable to believe that one mark may be man's insatiable craving for immortality?

> Thou wilt not leave us in the dust:
> Thou madest man, he knows not why;
> He thinks he was not made to die
> And Thou hast made him: Thou art just.[17]

So reasons Tennyson, and the deepest instincts of the normal human heart agree with him. The ancient image of God whispers within every man of everlasting hope; somewhere he will continue to exist. Still he cannot rejoice, for the light that lighteth every man that cometh into the world troubles his conscience, frightening him with proofs of guilt and evidences of coming death. So is he ground between the upper millstone of hope and the nether stone of fear.

Just here the sweet relevancy of the Christian message appears. "Jesus Christ . . . hath abolished death, and hath brought life and immortality to light through the gospel." So wrote the greatest Christian of them all just before he went out to meet his executioner. God's eternity and man's mortality join to persuade us that faith in Jesus Christ is not optional. For every man it must be Christ or eternal tragedy. Out of eternity our Lord came into time to rescue His human brethren whose moral folly had made them not only fools of the passing world but slaves of sin and death as well.

> *Brief life is here our portion,*
> *Brief sorrow, short-lived care;*
> *The life that knows no ending,*
> *The tearless life is there.*
>
> *There God, our King and Portion,*
> *In fullness of His grace,*
> *We then shall see forever,*
> *And worship face to face.*
>
> Bernard of Cluny

———————•———————

CHAPTER 8

God's Infinitude

Our Heavenly Father: Let us see Thy glory, if it must be from the shelter of the cleft rock and from beneath the protection of Thy covering hand. Whatever the cost to us in loss of friends or goods or length of days let us know Thee as Thou art, that we may adore Thee as we should. Through Jesus Christ our Lord. *Amen.*

The world is evil, the times are waxing late, and the glory of God has departed from the church as the fiery cloud once lifted from the door of the Temple in the sight of Ezekiel the prophet.

The God of Abraham has withdrawn His conscious Presence from us, and another God whom our fathers knew not is making himself at home among us. This God we have made and because we have made him we can understand him; because we have created him he can never surprise us, never overwhelm us, nor astonish us, nor transcend us.

The God of glory sometimes revealed Himself like a sun to warm and bless, indeed, but often to astonish, overwhelm, and blind before He healed and bestowed permanent sight. This God of our fathers wills to be the God of their succeeding race. We have only to prepare Him a habitation in love and faith and humility. We have but to want Him badly enough, and He will come and manifest Himself to us.

Shall we allow a saintly and thoughtful man to exhort us? Hear Anselm; or better still, heed his words:

> Up now, slight man! Flee for a little while thy occupations; hide thyself for a time from thy disturbing thoughts. Cast aside now thy burdensome cares, and put away thy toilsome business. Yield room for some little time to God, and rest for a little time in Him. Enter the inner chamber of thy mind; shut out all thoughts save that of God and such as can aid thee in seeking Him. Speak now, my whole heart! Speak now to God, saying, I seek Thy face; Thy face, Lord, will I seek.[18]

Of all that can be thought or said about God, His infinitude is the most difficult to grasp. Even to try to conceive of it would appear to be self-contradictory, for such conceptualization requires us to undertake something which we know at the outset we can never accomplish. Yet we must try, for the Holy Scriptures teach that God is infinite and, if we accept His other attributes, we must of necessity accept this one too.

From the effort to understand, we must not turn back because the way is difficult and there are no mechanical aids for the ascent. The view is better farther up and the journey is not one for the feet but for the heart. Let us seek, therefore, such "trances of thought and mountings of the mind" as God may be pleased to grant us, knowing that the Lord often pours eyesight on the blind and whispers to babes and sucklings truths never dreamed of by the wise and prudent. Now the blind must see and the deaf hear. Now we must expect to receive the treasures of darkness and the hidden riches of secret places.

Infinitude, of course, means limitlessness, and it is obviously impossible for a limited mind to grasp the Unlimited. In this chapter I am compelled to think one step short of that about which I am writing, and the reader must of necessity think a degree under that about which he is trying to think. O, the depths of the riches both of the wisdom and knowledge of God! How unsearchable are His judgments, and His ways past finding out!

The reason for our dilemma has been suggested before. We are trying to envision a mode of being altogether foreign to us, and wholly unlike anything we have known in our familiar world of matter, space, and time.

"Here, and in all our meditations upon the qualities and content of God," writes Novalian, "we pass beyond our power of fit conception, nor can human eloquence put forth a power commensurate with His greatness. At the contemplation and utterance of His majesty all eloquence is rightly dumb, all mental effort is feeble. For God is greater than mind itself. His greatness cannot be conceived. Nay, could we conceive of His greatness He would be less than the human mind which could form the conception. He is greater than all language, and no statement can express Him. Indeed, if any statement could express Him, He would be less than human speech which could by such statement comprehend and gather up all that He is. All our thoughts about Him will be less than He, and our loftiest utterances will be trivialities in comparison with Him."[19]

Unfortunately the word *infinite* has not always been held to its precise meaning, but has been used carelessly to mean simply *much* or a *great deal*, as when we say that an artist takes infinite pains with his picture or a teacher shows infinite patience with her class. Properly, the word can be used of no created thing, and of no one but God. Hence, to argue about whether or not space is infinite is to play with words. Infinitude can belong to but One. There can be no second.

When we say that God is infinite we mean that He knows *no bounds*. Whatever God is and all that God is, He is without limit. And here again we must break away from the popular meaning of words. "Unlimited wealth" and "boundless energy" are further examples of the misuse of words. Of course no wealth is unlimited and no energy boundless unless we are speaking of the wealth and energy of God.

Again, to say that God is infinite is to say that He is measureless. Measurement is the way created things have of accounting for themselves. It describes limitations, imperfections, and cannot apply to God. Weight describes the gravitational pull of the earth upon material bodies; distance describes intervals between bodies in space; length means extension in space, and there are other familiar measurements such as those for liquid, energy, sound, light, and numbers for pluralities. We also try to measure abstract qualities, and speak of great or little faith, high or low intelligence, large or meager talents.

Is it not plain that all this does not and cannot apply to God? It is the way we see the works of His hands, but not the way we see Him. He is above all this, outside of it, beyond it. Our concepts of measurement embrace mountains and men, atoms and stars, gravity, energy, numbers, speed, but never God. We cannot speak of measure or amount or size or weight and at the same time be speaking of God, for these tell of degrees and there are no degrees in God. All that He is He is without growth or addition or development. Nothing in God is less or more, or large or small. He is what He is in Himself, without qualifying thought or word. He is simply God.

In the awful abyss of the divine Being may lie attributes of which we know nothing and which can have no meaning for us, just as the attributes of mercy and grace can have no personal meaning for seraphim or cherubim. These holy beings may know of these qualities in

God but be unable to feel them sympathetically for the reason that they have not sinned and so do not call forth God's mercy and grace. So there may be, and I believe there surely are, other aspects of God's essential being which He has not revealed even to His ransomed and Spirit-illuminated children. These hidden facets of God's nature concern His relation to none but Himself. They are like the far side of the moon, which we know is there but which has never been explored and has no immediate meaning for men on earth. There is no reason for us to try to discover what has not been revealed. It is enough to know that God is God.

> *Thine own Self forever filling*
> *With self-kindled flame,*
> *In Thyself Thou art distilling*
> *Unctions without name!*
> *Without worshipping of creatures,*
> *Without veiling of Thy features,*
> *God always the same!*
>
> Frederick W. Faber

But God's infinitude belongs to us and is made known to us for our everlasting profit. Yet, just what does it mean to us beyond the mere wonder of thinking about it? Much every way, and more as we come to know ourselves and God better.

Because God's nature is infinite, everything that flows

out of it is infinite also. We poor human creatures are constantly being frustrated by limitations imposed upon us from without and within. The days of the years of our lives are few, and swifter than a weaver's shuttle. Life is a short and fevered rehearsal for a concert we cannot stay to give. Just when we appear to have attained some proficiency we are forced to lay our instruments down. There is simply not time enough to think, to become, to perform what the constitution of our natures indicates we are capable of.

How completely satisfying to turn from our limitations to a God who has none. Eternal years lie in His heart. For Him time does not pass, it remains; and those who are in Christ share with Him all the riches of limitless time and endless years. God never hurries. There are no deadlines against which He must work. Only to know this is to quiet our spirits and relax our nerves. For those out of Christ, time is a devouring beast; before the sons of the new creation time crouches and purrs and licks their hands. The foe of the old human race becomes the friend of the new, and the stars in their courses fight for the man God delights to honor. This we may learn from the divine infinitude.

But there is more. God's gifts in nature have their limitations. They are finite because they have been created, but the gift of eternal life in Christ Jesus is as limitless as God. The Christian man possesses God's own life and shares His infinitude with Him. In God there is life enough for all and time enough to enjoy it. Whatever is possessed of natural life runs through its cycle from birth to death and ceases to be, but the life of God returns upon itself and ceases never. And this is life eternal: to know the only true God, and Jesus Christ whom He has sent.

The mercy of God is infinite too, and the man who has felt the grinding pain of inward guilt knows that this is more than academic. "Where sin abounded, grace did much more abound." Abounding sin is the terror of the world, but abounding grace is the hope of mankind. However sin may abound it still has its limits, for it is the product of finite minds and hearts; but God's "much more" introduces us to infinitude. Against our deep crea-ture-sickness stands God's infinite ability to cure.

The Christian witness through the centuries has been that "God so loved the world . . ."; it remains for us to see that love in the light of God's infinitude. His love is measureless. It is more: it is boundless. It has no bounds because it is not a thing but a facet of the essential nature of God. His love is something He is, and because He is infinite that love can enfold the whole created world in itself and have room for ten thousand times ten thousand worlds beside.

> *This, this is the God we adore,*
> *Our faithful, unchangeable Friend,*
> *Whose love is as great as His power,*
> *And neither knows measure nor end.*

'Tis Jesus, the first and the last,
  Whose Spirit shall guide us safe home;
We'll praise Him for all that is past,
  And trust Him for all that's to come.
                                    Joseph Hart

CHAPTER 9

The Immutability of God

O Christ our Lord, Thou hast been our dwelling place in all generations. As conies to their rock, so have we run to Thee for safety; as birds from their wanderings, so have we flown to Thee for peace. Chance and change are busy in our little world of nature and men, but in Thee we find no variableness nor shadow of turning. We rest in Thee without fear or doubt and face our tomorrows without anxiety. *Amen.*

The immutability of God is among those attributes less difficult to understand, but to grasp it we must discipline ourselves to sort out the usual thoughts with which we think of created things from the rarer ones that arise when we try to lay hold of whatever may be comprehended of God.

To say that God is immutable is to say that He never differs from Himself. The concept of a growing or developing God is not found in the Scriptures. It seems to me impossible to think of God as varying from Himself in any way. Here is why:

For a moral being to change it would be necessary that the change be in one of three directions. He must go from better to worse or from worse to better; or, granted that the moral quality remain stable, he must change within himself, as from immature to mature or from one order of being to another. It should be clear that God can move in none of these directions. His perfections forever rule out any such possibility.

God cannot change for the better. Since He is perfectly holy, He has never been less holy than He is now and can never be holier than He is and has always been. Neither can God change for the worse. Any deterioration within the unspeakably holy nature of God is impossible. Indeed I believe it impossible even to think of such a thing, for the moment we attempt to do so, the object about which we are thinking is no longer God but something else and someone less than He. The one of whom we are thinking may be a great and awesome creature, but because he is a creature he cannot be the self-existent Creator.

As there can be no mutation in the moral character of God, so there can be none within the divine essence. The being of God is unique in the only proper meaning of that word; that is, His being is other than and different from all other beings. We have seen how God differs from His creatures in being self-existent, self-sufficient, and eternal. By virtue of these attributes God is God and not some other being. One who can suffer any slightest degree of change is neither self-existent, self-sufficient, nor eternal, and so is not God.

Only a being composed of parts may change, for change is basically a shift in the relation of the parts of a whole or the admission of some foreign element into the original composition. Since God is self-existent, He is not composed. There are in Him no parts to be altered. And since He is self-sufficient, nothing can enter His being from without.

"Whatever is composed of parts," says Anselm, "is not altogether one, but is in some sort plural, and diverse from itself; and either in fact or in concept is capable of dissolution. But these things are alien to Thee, than whom nothing better can be conceived of. Hence, there are no parts in Thee Lord, nor art Thou more than one. But Thou art so truly a unitary being, and so identical with Thyself, that in no respect art Thou unlike Thyself; rather Thou art unity itself, indivisible by any conception."[20]

"All that God is He has always been, and all that He has been and is He will ever be." Nothing that God has ever said about Himself will be modified; nothing the inspired prophets and apostles have said about Him will be rescinded. His immutability guarantees this.

The immutability of God appears in its most perfect beauty when viewed against the mutability of men. In God no change is possible; in men change is impossible to escape. Neither the man is fixed nor his world, but he and it are in constant flux. Each man appears for a little while to laugh and weep, to work and play, and then to go to make room for those who shall follow him in the never-ending cycle.

Certain poets have found a morbid pleasure in the law of impermanence and have sung in a minor key the song of perpetual change. Omar the tentmaker was one who sang with pathos and humor of mutation and mortality, the twin diseases that afflict mankind. "Don't slap that clay around so roughly," he exhorts the potter, "that may be your grandfather's dust you make so free with." "When you lift the cup to drink red wine," he reminds the reveler, "you may be kissing the lips of some beauty dead long ago."

This note of sweet sorrow expressed with gentle humor gives a radiant beauty to his quatrains but, however beautiful, the whole long poem is sick, sick unto death. Like the bird charmed by the serpent that would devour it, the poet is fascinated by the enemy that is destroying him and all men and every generation of men.

The sacred writers, too, face up to man's mutability, but they are healthy men and there is a wholesome strength in their words. They have found the cure for the great sickness. God, they say, changes not. The law of mutation belongs to a fallen world, but God is immutable, and in Him men of faith find at last eternal permanence. In the meanwhile change works for the children of the kingdom, not against them. The changes that occur in them are wrought by the hand of the in-living Spirit.

"But we all," says the apostle, "with open face beholding as in a glass the glory of the Lord, are changed into the same image from glory to glory, even as by the Spirit of the Lord."

In a world of change and decay not even the man of faith can be completely happy. Instinctively he seeks the unchanging and is bereaved at the passing of dear familiar things.

> *O Lord! my heart is sick,*
> *Sick of this everlasting change;*
> *And life runs tediously quick*
> *Through its unresting race and varied range:*
> *Change finds no likeness to itself in Thee,*
> *And wakes no echo in Thy mute Eternity.*
>   Frederick W. Faber

These words of Faber find sympathetic response in every heart; yet much as we may deplore the lack of stability in all earthly things, in a fallen world such as this the very *ability* to change is a golden treasure, a gift from God of such fabulous worth as to call for constant thanksgiving. For human beings the whole possibility of redemption lies in their ability to change. To move across from one sort of person to another is the essence of repentance: the liar becomes truthful, the thief honest, the lewd pure, the proud humble. The whole moral texture of the life is altered. The thoughts, the desires, the affections are transformed, and the man is no longer what he had been before. So radical is this change that the apostle calls the man that used to be "the old man" and the man that now is "the new man, which is renewed in knowledge after the image of him that created him."

Yet the change is deeper and more basic than any external acts can reveal, for it includes also the reception of life of another and higher quality. The old man, even at his best, possesses only the life of Adam: the new man has the life of God. And this is more than a mere manner of speaking; it is quite literally true. When God infuses eternal life into the spirit of a man, the man becomes a member of a new and higher order of being.

In the working out of His redemptive processes the unchanging God makes full use of change and through a succession of changes arrives at permanence at last. In the Book of Hebrews this is shown most clearly. "He taketh away the first, that he may establish the second," is a kind of summation of the teaching of that remarkable book. The old covenant, as something provisional, was abolished, and the new and everlasting covenant took its place. The blood of goats and bulls lost its significance when the blood of the Paschal Lamb was shed. The law, the altar, the priesthood—all were temporary and subject to change; now the eternal law of God is engraven forever on the living, sensitive stuff of which the human soul is composed. The ancient sanctuary is no more, but the new sanctuary is eternal in the heavens and there the Son of God has His eternal priesthood.

Here we see that God uses change as a lowly servant to bless His redeemed household, but He Himself is outside of the law of mutation and is unaffected by any changes that occur in the universe.

> *And all things as they change proclaim*
> *The Lord eternally the same.*
> Charles Wesley

Again the question of use arises. "Of what use to me is the knowledge that God is immutable?" someone asks. "Is not the whole thing mere metaphysical speculation? Something that might bring a certain satisfaction to persons of a particular type of mind but can have no real significance for practical men?"

If by "practical men" we mean unbelieving men engrossed in secular affairs and indifferent to the claims of Christ, the welfare of their own souls, or the interests of the world to come, then for them such a book as this can have no meaning at all; nor, unfortunately, can any other book that takes religion seriously. But while such men may be in the majority, they do not by any means compose the whole of the population. There are still the seven thousand who have not bowed their knees to Baal. These believe they were created to worship God and to enjoy His presence forever, and they are eager to learn all they can about the God with whom they expect to spend eternity.

In this world where men forget us, change their attitude toward us as their private interests dictate, and revise their opinion of us for the slightest cause, is it not a source of wondrous strength to know that the God with whom we have to do changes not? That His attitude toward us now is the same as it was in eternity past and will be in eternity to come?

What peace it brings to the Christian's heart to realize that our Heavenly Father never differs from Himself. In coming to Him at any time we need not wonder whether we shall find Him in a receptive mood. He is always receptive to misery and need, as well as to love and faith. He does not keep office hours nor set aside periods when He will see no one. Neither does He change His mind about anything. Today, this moment, He feels toward His creatures, toward babies, toward the sick, the fallen, the sinful, exactly as He did when He sent His only-begotten Son into the world to die for mankind.

God never changes moods or cools off in His affections or loses enthusiasm. His attitude toward sin is now the same as it was when He drove out the sinful man from the eastward garden, and His attitude toward the sinner the same as when He stretched forth His hands and cried, "Come unto me, all ye that labour and are heavy laden, and I will give you rest."

God will not compromise and He need not be coaxed. He cannot be persuaded to alter His Word nor talked into answering selfish prayer. In all our efforts to find

God, to please Him, to commune with Him, we should remember that all change must be on our part. "I am the LORD, I change not." We have but to meet His clearly stated terms, bring our lives into accord with His revealed will, and His infinite power will become instantly operative toward us in the manner set forth through the gospel in the Scriptures of truth.

> *Fountain of being! Source of Good!*
> *Immutable Thou dost remain!*
> *Nor can the shadow of a change*
> *Obscure the glories of Thy reign.*
> *Earth may with all her powers dissolve,*
> *If such the great Creator will;*
> *But Thou for ever art the same,*
> *I AM is Thy memorial still.*

From Walker's Collection

———————•———————

CHAPTER 10

The Divine Omniscience

Lord, Thou knowest all things; Thou knowest my downsitting and mine uprising and art acquainted with all my ways. I can inform Thee of nothing and it is vain to try to hide anything from Thee. In the light of Thy perfect knowledge I would be as artless as a little child. Help me to put away all care, for Thou knowest the way that I take and when Thou hast tried me I shall come forth as gold. *Amen.*

To say that God is omniscient is to say that He possesses perfect knowledge and therefore has no need to learn. But it is more: it is to say that God has never learned and cannot learn.

The Scriptures teach that God has never learned from anyone. "Who hath directed the Spirit of the LORD, or being his counsellor hath taught him? With whom took he counsel, and who instructed him, and taught him in the path of judgment, and taught him knowledge, and shewed to him the way of understanding?" "For who hath known

the mind of the Lord? or who hath been his counsellor?"
These rhetorical questions put by the prophet Isaiah and
the apostle Paul declare that God has never learned.

From there it is only a step to the conclusion that God
cannot learn. Could God at any time or in any manner
receive into His mind knowledge that He did not possess
and had not possessed from eternity, He would be imperfect and less than Himself. To think of a God who must
sit at the feet of a teacher, even though that teacher be an
archangel or a seraph, is to think of someone other than
the Most High God, maker of heaven and earth.

This negative approach to the divine omniscience is,
I believe, quite justified in the circumstances. Since our
intellectual knowledge of God is so small and obscure,
we can sometimes gain considerable advantage in our
struggle to understand what God is like by the simple ex-
pedient of thinking what He is *not* like. So far in this examination of the attributes of God we have been driven
to the free use of negatives. We have seen that God had
no origin, that He had no beginning, that He requires
no helpers, that He suffers no change, and that in His
essential being there are no limitations.

This method of trying to make men see what God is
like by showing them what He is not like is used also by
the inspired writers in the Holy Scriptures. "Hast thou not
known? hast thou not heard," cries Isaiah, "that the everlasting God, the LORD, the Creator of the ends of the earth,
fainteth not, neither is weary?" And that abrupt statement

by God Himself, "I am the LORD, I change not," tells us more about the divine omniscience than could be told in a ten-thousand word treatise, were all negatives arbitrarily ruled out. God's eternal truthfulness is stated negatively by the apostle Paul, "God . . . cannot lie"; and when the angel asserted that "with God nothing shall be impossible," the two negatives add up to a ringing positive.

That God is omniscient is not only taught in the Scriptures, it must be inferred also from all else that is taught concerning Him. God perfectly knows Himself and, being the source and author of all things, it follows that He knows all that can be known. And this He knows instantly and with a fullness of perfection that includes every possible item of knowledge concerning everything that exists or could have existed anywhere in the universe at any time in the past or that may exist in the centuries or ages yet unborn.

God knows instantly and effortlessly all matter and all matters, all mind and every mind, all spirit and all spirits, all being and every being, all creaturehood and all creatures, every plurality and all pluralities, all law and every law, all relations, all causes, all thoughts, all mysteries, all enigmas, all feeling, all desires, every unuttered secret, all thrones and dominions, all personalities, all things visible and invisible in heaven and in earth, motion, space, time, life, death, good, evil, heaven, and hell.

Because God knows all things perfectly, He knows no thing better than any other thing, but all things equally well. He never discovers anything. He is never surprised, never amazed. He never wonders about anything nor (except when drawing men out for their own good) does He seek information or ask questions.

God is self-existent and self-contained and knows what no creature can ever know—Himself, perfectly. "The things of God knoweth no man, but the Spirit of God." Only the Infinite can know the infinite.

In the divine omniscience we see set forth against each other the terror and fascination of the Godhead. That God knows each person through and through can be a cause of shaking fear to the man that has something to hide—some unforsaken sin, some secret crime committed against man or God. The unblessed soul may well tremble that God knows the flimsiness of every pretext and never accepts the poor excuses given for sinful conduct, since He knows perfectly the real reason for it. "Thou hast set our iniquities before thee, our secret sins in the light of thy countenance." How frightful a thing to see the sons of Adam seeking to hide among the trees of another garden. But where shall they hide? "Whither shall I go from thy spirit? or whither shall I flee from thy presence? . . . If I say, Surely the darkness shall cover me; even the night shall be light about me. Yea, the darkness hideth not from thee; but the night shineth as the day."

And to us who have fled for refuge to lay hold upon the hope that is set before us in the gospel, how unutterably sweet is the knowledge that our Heavenly Father knows us completely. No talebearer can inform on us, no enemy can make an accusation stick; no forgotten skeleton can come tumbling out of some hidden closet to abash us and expose our past; no unsuspected weakness in our characters can come to light to turn God away from us, since He knew us utterly before we knew Him and called us to Himself in the full knowledge of everything that was against us. "For the mountains shall depart, and the hills be removed; but my kindness shall not depart from thee, neither shall the covenant of my peace be removed, saith the Lord that hath mercy on thee."

Our Father in heaven knows our frame and remembers that we are dust. He knew our inborn treachery, and for His own sake engaged to save us (Isa. 48:8–11). His only begotten Son, when He walked among us, felt our pains in their naked intensity of anguish. His knowledge of our afflictions and adversities is more than theoretic; it is personal, warm, and compassionate. Whatever may befall us, God knows and cares as no one else can.

> *He doth give His joy to all;*
> *He becomes an infant small;*
> *He becomes a man of woe;*
> *He doth feel the sorrow too.*
>
> *Think not thou canst sigh a sigh*
> *And thy Maker is not by;*
> *Think not thou canst weep a tear*
> *And thy Maker is not near.*

O! He gives to us His joy
That our griefs He may destroy;
Till our grief is fled and gone
He doth sit by us and moan.

William Blake

CHAPTER 11

The Wisdom of God

Thou, O Christ, who wert tempted in all points like as we are, yet without sin, make us strong to overcome the desire to be wise and to be reputed wise by others as ignorant as ourselves. We turn from our wisdom as well as from our folly and flee to Thee, the wisdom of God and the power of God. *Amen.*

In this brief study of the divine wisdom we begin with faith in God. Following our usual pattern, we shall not seek to understand in order that we may believe, but to believe in order that we may understand. Hence, we shall not seek for proof that God is wise. The unbelieving mind would not be convinced by any proof, and the worshiping heart needs none.

"Blessed be the name of God for ever and ever," cried Daniel the prophet, "for wisdom and might are his: . . . he giveth wisdom unto the wise, and knowledge to them that know understanding: he revealeth the deep and secret things: he knoweth what is in the darkness, and the light dwelleth with him." The believing man responds to this, and to the angelic chant, "Blessing, and glory, and wisdom, and thanksgiving, and honour, and power, and might, be unto our God for ever and ever." It never occurs to such a man that God should furnish proof of His wisdom or His power. Is it not enough that He is God?

When Christian theology declares that God is wise, it means vastly more than it says or can say, for it tries to make a comparatively weak word bear an incomprehensible plenitude of meaning that threatens to tear it apart and crush it under the sheer weight of the idea. "His understanding is infinite," says the psalmist. It is nothing less than infinitude that theology is here laboring to express.

Since the word *infinite* describes what is unique, it can have no modifiers. We do not say "more unique" or "very infinite." Before infinitude we stand silent.

There is indeed a secondary, created wisdom which God has given in measure to His creatures as their highest good may require; but the wisdom of any creature or of all creatures, when set against the boundless wisdom of God, is pathetically small. For this reason the apostle is accurate when he refers to God as "only wise." That is, God is wise in Himself, and all the shining wisdom of men or angels is but a reflection of that uncreated effulgence which streams from the throne of the Majesty in the heavens.

The idea of God as infinitely wise is at the root of all truth. It is a datum of belief necessary to the soundness of all other beliefs about God. Being what He is without regard to creatures, God is of course unaffected by our opinions of Him, but our moral sanity requires that we attribute to the maker and sustainer of the universe a wisdom entirely perfect. To refuse to do this is to betray the very thing in us that distinguishes us from the beasts.

In the Holy Scriptures wisdom, when used of God and good men, always carries a strong moral connotation. It is conceived as being pure, loving, and good. Wisdom that is mere shrewdness is often attributed to evil men, but such wisdom is treacherous and false. These two kinds of wisdom are in perpetual conflict. Indeed, when seen from the lofty peak of Sinai or Calvary, the whole history of the world is discovered to be but a contest between the wisdom of God and the cunning of Satan and fallen men. The outcome of the contest is not in doubt. The imperfect must fall before the perfect at last. God has warned that He will take the wise in their own craftiness and bring to nothing the understanding of the prudent.

Wisdom, among other things, is the ability to devise perfect ends and to achieve those ends by the most perfect means. It sees the end from the beginning, so there can be no need to guess or conjecture. Wisdom sees everything in focus, each in proper relation to all, and is thus able to work toward predestined goals with flawless precision.

All God's acts are done in perfect wisdom, first for His own glory, and then for the highest good of the greatest number for the longest time. And all His acts are as pure as they are wise, and as good as they are wise and pure. Not only could His acts not be better done: a better way to do them could not be imagined. An infinitely wise God must work in a manner not to be improved upon by finite creatures. O Lord, how manifold are Thy works! In wisdom hast Thou made them all. The earth is full of Thy riches!

Without the creation, the wisdom of God would have remained forever locked in the boundless abyss of the divine nature. God brought His creatures into being that He might enjoy them and they rejoice in Him. "And God saw every thing that he had made, and, behold, it was very good."

Many through the centuries have declared themselves unable to believe in the basic wisdom of a world wherein so much appears to be so wrong. Voltaire in his *Candide* introduces a determined optimist, whom he calls Dr. Pangloss, and into his mouth puts all the arguments for the "best-of-all-possible-worlds" philosophy. Of course the French cynic took keen delight in placing the old professor in situations that made his philosophy look ridiculous.

But the Christian view of life is altogether more realistic than that of Dr. Pangloss with his "sufficient reason." It is that this is not at the moment the best of all possible worlds, but one lying under the shadow of a huge calamity, the Fall of man. The inspired writers insist that the whole creation now groans and travails under the mighty shock of the Fall. They do not attempt to supply "sufficient reasons"; they assert that the "creature was made subject to vanity, not willingly, but by reason of him who hath subjected the same in hope." No effort here to justify the ways of God with men; just a simple declaration of fact. The being of God is its own defense.

But there is hope in all our tears. When the hour of Christ's triumph arrives, the suffering world will be brought out into the glorious liberty of the sons of God. For men of the new creation the golden age is not past but future, and when it is ushered in, a wondering universe will see that God has indeed abounded toward us in all wisdom and prudence. In the meantime we rest our hope in the only wise God, our Saviour, and wait with patience the slow development of His benign purposes.

In spite of tears and pain and death we believe that the God who made us all is infinitely wise and good. As Abraham staggered not at the promises of God through unbelief, but was strong in faith, giving the glory to God, and was fully persuaded that what He had promised He was able to perform, so do we base our hope in God alone and hope against hope till the day breaks. We rest in *what God is*. I believe that this alone is true faith. Any faith that must be supported by the evidence of the senses is not real faith. "Jesus saith unto him, Thomas, because thou hast seen me, thou hast believed: blessed are they that have not seen, and yet have believed."

The testimony of faith is that, no matter how things look in this fallen world, all God's acts are wrought in perfect wisdom. The incarnation of the Eternal Son in human flesh was one of God's mighty deeds, and we may be sure that this awesome deed was done with a perfection possible only to the Infinite. "Without controversy great is the mystery of godliness: God was manifest in the flesh."

Atonement too was accomplished with the same flawless skill that marks all of God's acts. However little we understand it all, we know that Christ's expiatory work perfectly reconciled God and men and opened the kingdom of heaven to all believers. Our concern is not to explain but to proclaim. Indeed I wonder whether God could make us understand all that happened there at the cross. According to the apostle Peter not even angels know, however eagerly they may desire to look into these things.

The operation of the gospel, the new birth, the coming of the divine Spirit into human nature, the ultimate overthrow of evil, and the final establishment of Christ's righteous kingdom—all these have flowed and do flow out of God's infinite fullness of wisdom. The sharpest eyes of the holiest watcher in the blest company above cannot discover a flaw in the ways of God in bringing all this to fruition, nor can the pooled wisdom of seraphim and cherubim suggest how an improvement might be made in the divine procedure. "I know that, whatsoever

God doeth, it shall be for ever: nothing can be put to it, nor any thing taken from it: and God doeth it, that men should fear before him."

It is vitally important that we hold the truth of God's infinite wisdom as a tenet of our creed; but this is not enough. We must by the exercise of faith and by prayer bring it into the practical world of our day-by-day experience.

To believe actively that our Heavenly Father constantly spreads around us providential circumstances that work for our present good and our everlasting well-being brings to the soul a veritable benediction. Most of us go through life praying a little, planning a little, jockeying for position, hoping but never being quite certain of anything, and always secretly afraid that we will miss the way. This is a tragic waste of truth and never gives rest to the heart.

There is a better way. It is to repudiate our own wisdom and take instead the infinite wisdom of God. Our insistence upon seeing ahead is natural enough, but it is a real hindrance to our spiritual progress. God has charged Himself with full responsibility for our eternal happiness and stands ready to take over the management of our lives the moment we turn in faith to Him. Here is His promise: "And I will bring the blind by a way that they knew not; I will lead them in paths that they have not known: I will make darkness light before them, and crooked things straight. These things will I do unto them, and not forsake them."

111

Let Him lead thee blindfold onwards,
  Love needs not to know;
Children whom the Father leadeth
  Ask not where they go.
Though the path be all unknown,
Over moors and mountains lone.

Gerhard Tersteegen

God constantly encourages us to trust Him in the dark. "I will go before thee, and make the crooked places straight: I will break in pieces the gates of brass, and cut in sunder the bars of iron: and I will give thee the treasures of darkness, and hidden riches of secret places, that thou mayest know that I, the Lord, which call thee by thy name, am the God of Israel."

It is heartening to learn how many of God's mighty deeds were done in secret, away from the prying eyes of men or angels.

When God created the heavens and the earth, darkness was upon the face of the deep. When the Eternal Son became flesh, He was carried for a time in the darkness of the sweet virgin's womb. When He died for the life of the world, it was in the darkness, seen by no one at the last. When He arose from the dead, it was "very early in the morning." No one saw Him rise. It is as if God were saying, "What I am is all that need matter to you, for there lie your hope and your peace. I will do what I will do, and it will all come to light at last, but how I do it is My secret. Trust Me, and be not afraid."

With the goodness of God to desire our highest welfare, the wisdom of God to plan it, and the power of God to achieve it, what do we lack? Surely we are the most favored of all creatures.

> *In all our Maker's grand designs,*
> *Omnipotence, with wisdom, shines;*
> *His works, through all this wondrous frame,*
> *Declare the glory of His Name.*
>   Thomas Blacklock

———————•———————

CHAPTER 12

The Omnipotence of God

Our Heavenly Father, we have heard Thee say, "I am the Almighty God; walk before me, and be thou perfect." But unless Thou dost enable us by the exceeding greatness of Thy power how can we who are by nature weak and sinful walk in a perfect way? Grant that we may learn to lay hold on the working of the mighty power which wrought in Christ when Thou didst raise Him from the dead and set Him at Thine own right hand in the heavenly places. *Amen.*

I n the time of his vision John the Revelator heard as it were the voice of a great multitude and as the voice of many waters and as the voice of mighty thunderings sounding throughout the universe, and what the voice proclaimed was the sovereignty and omnipotence of God: "Alleluia: for the Lord God omnipotent reigneth."

Sovereignty and omnipotence must go together. One cannot exist without the other. To reign, God must have power, and to reign sovereignly, He must have all power.

And that is what *omnipotent* means, having all power. The word derives from the Latin and is identical in meaning with the more familiar *almighty* which we have from the Anglo-Saxon. This latter word occurs fifty-six times in our English Bible and is never used of anyone but God. He alone is almighty.

God possesses what no creature can: an incomprehensible plenitude of power, a potency that is absolute. This we know by divine revelation, but once known, it is recognized as being in full accord with reason. Grant that God is infinite and self-existent and we see at once that He must be all-powerful as well, and reason kneels to worship before the divine omnipotence.

"Power belongeth unto God," says the psalmist, and Paul the apostle declares that nature itself gives evidence of the eternal power of the Godhead (Rom. 1:20). From this knowledge we reason to the omnipotence of God this way: God has power. Since God is also infinite, whatever He has must be without limit; therefore God has limitless power, He is omnipotent. We see further that God the self-existent Creator is the source of all the power there is, and since a source must be at least equal to anything that emanates from it, God is of necessity equal to all the power there is, and this is to say again that He is omnipotent.

God has delegated power to His creatures, but being self-sufficient, He cannot relinquish anything of His perfections and, power being one of them, He has never surrendered the least iota of His power. He gives but He does not give away. All that He gives remains His own and returns to Him again. Forever He must remain what He has forever been, the Lord God omnipotent.

One cannot long read the Scriptures sympathetically without noticing the radical disparity between the outlook of men of the Bible and that of modern men. We are today suffering from a secularized mentality. Where the sacred writers saw God, we see the laws of nature. Their world was fully populated; ours is all but empty. Their world was alive and personal; ours is impersonal and dead. God ruled their world; ours is ruled by the laws of nature and we are always once removed from the presence of God.

And what are these laws of nature that have displaced God in the minds of millions? Law has two meanings. One is an external rule enforced by authority, such as the common rule against robbery and assault. The word is also used to denote the uniform way things act in the universe, but this second use of the word is erroneous. What we see in nature is simply the paths God's power and wisdom take through creation. Properly these are phenomena, not laws, but we call them laws by analogy with the arbitrary laws of society.

Science observes how the power of God operates, discovers a regular pattern somewhere, and fixes it as a "law." The uniformity of God's activities in His creation enables the scientist to predict the course of natural phenomena.

The trustworthiness of God's behavior in His world is the foundation of all scientific truth. Upon it the scientist rests his faith and from there he goes on to achieve great and useful things in such fields as those of navigation, chemistry, agriculture, and the medical arts.

Religion, on the other hand, goes back of nature to God. It is concerned not with the footprints of God along the paths of creation, but with the One who treads those paths. Religion is interested primarily in the One who is the source of all things, the master of every phenomenon. For this One philosophy has various names, the most horrendous that I have seen being that supplied by Rudolf Otto: "The absolute, the gigantic, never-resting, active world stress."[21] The Christian delights to remember that this "world stress" once said "I AM," and that the greatest teacher of them all directed His disciples to address Him as a person: "When ye pray, say, Our Father which art in heaven, Hallowed be thy name." The men of the Bible everywhere communed with this "gigantic absolute" in language as personal as speech affords, and with Him prophet and saint walked in a rapture of devotion, warm, intimate, and deeply satisfying.

Omnipotence is not a name given to the sum of all power, but an attribute of a personal God whom we Christians believe to be the Father of our Lord Jesus Christ and of all who believe in Him to life eternal. The worshiping man finds this knowledge a source of wonderful strength for his inner life. His faith rises to take the great leap upward into the fellowship of Him who can do whatever He wills to do, for whom nothing is hard or difficult because He possesses power absolute.

Since He has at His command all the power in the universe, the Lord God omnipotent can do anything as easily as anything else. All His acts are done without effort. He expends no energy that must be replenished. His self-sufficiency makes it unnecessary for Him to look outside of Himself for a renewal of strength. All the power required to do all that He wills to do lies in undiminished fullness in His own infinite being.

The Presbyterian pastor, A. B. Simpson, approaching middle age, broken in health, deeply despondent, and ready to quit the ministry, chanced to hear the simple Negro spiritual,

> *Nothing is too hard for Jesus,*
> *No man can work like Him.*

Its message sped like an arrow to his heart, carrying faith and hope and life for body and soul. He sought a place of retirement and after a season alone with God arose to his feet completely cured, and went forth in fullness of joy to found what has since become one of the largest foreign missionary societies in the world. For thirty-five years after this encounter with God, he labored prodigiously in the service of Christ. His faith in the God of limitless power gave him all the strength he needed to carry on.

Almighty One! I bend in dust before Thee;
  Even so veiled cherubs bend;
In calm and still devotion I adore Thee,
  All-wise, all-present Friend.

Thou to the earth its emerald robe hast given,
  Or curtained it in snow;
And the bright sun, and the soft moon in heaven,
  Before Thy presence bow.

Sir John Bowring

———————•———————

CHAPTER 13

The Divine Transcendence

O Lord our Lord, there is none like Thee in heaven above or in the earth beneath. Thine is the greatness and the dignity and the majesty. All that is in the heaven and the earth is Thine; Thine is the kingdom and the power and the glory forever, O God, and Thou art exalted as head over all. *Amen.*

When we speak of God as transcendent we mean of course that He is exalted far above the created universe, so far above that human thought cannot imagine it.

To think accurately about this, however, we must keep in mind that "far above" does not here refer to physical distance from the earth but to quality of being. We are concerned not with location in space nor with mere altitude, but with life.

God is spirit, and to Him magnitude and distance have no meaning. To us they are useful as analogies and illustrations, so God refers to them constantly when speaking down to our limited understanding. The words of God as found in Isaiah, "Thus saith the high and lofty One that inhabiteth eternity," give a distinct impression of altitude, but that is because we who dwell in a world of matter, space, and time tend to think in material terms and can grasp abstract ideas only when they are identified in some way with material things. In its struggle to free itself from the tyranny of the natural world, the human heart must learn to translate upward the language the Spirit uses to instruct us. It is spirit that gives significance to matter and apart from spirit nothing has any value at last. A little child strays from a party of sight-seers and becomes lost on a mountain, and immediately the whole mental perspective of the members of the party is changed. Rapt admiration for the grandeur of nature gives way to acute distress for the lost child. The group spreads out over the mountainside anxiously calling the child's name and searching eagerly into every secluded spot where the little one might chance to be hidden.

What brought about this sudden change? The tree-clad mountain is still there towering into the clouds in breath-taking beauty, but no one notices it now. All attention is focused upon the search for a curly-haired little girl not yet two years old and weighing less than thirty pounds. Though so new and so small, she is more precious to parents and friends than all the huge bulk of the vast and ancient mountain they had been admiring a few minutes before. And in their judgment the whole civilized world concurs, for the little girl can love and laugh and speak and pray, and the mountain cannot. It is the child's quality of being that gives it worth.

Yet we must not compare the being of God with any other as we just now compared the mountain with the child. We must not think of God as highest in an ascending order of beings, starting with the single cell and going on up from the fish to the bird to the animal to man to angel to cherub to God. This would be to grant God eminence, even pre-eminence, but that is not enough; we must grant Him *transcendence* in the fullest meaning of that word. Forever God stands apart, in light unapproachable. He is as high above an archangel as above a caterpillar, for the gulf that separates the archangel from the caterpillar is but finite, while the gulf between God and the archangel is infinite. The caterpillar and the archangel, though far removed from each other in the scale of created things, are nevertheless one in that they are alike created. They both belong in the category of that-which-is-not-God and are separated from God by infinitude itself.

Reticence and compulsion forever contend within the heart that would speak of God.

> *How shall polluted mortals dare*
> *To sing Thy glory or Thy grace?*
> *Beneath Thy feet we lie afar,*
> *And see but shadows of Thy face.*
>   Isaac Watts

Yet we console ourselves with the knowledge that it is God Himself who puts it in our hearts to seek Him and makes it possible in some measure to know Him, and He is pleased with even the feeblest effort to make Him known.

If some watcher or holy one who has spent his glad centuries by the sea of fire were to come to earth, how meaningless to him would be the ceaseless chatter of the busy tribes of men. How strange to him and how empty would sound the flat, stale, and profitless words heard in the average pulpit from week to week. And were such a one to speak on earth would he not speak of God? Would he not charm and fascinate his hearers with rapturous descriptions of the Godhead? And after hearing him could we ever again consent to listen to anything less than theology, the doctrine of God? Would we not thereafter demand of those who would presume to teach us that they speak to us from the mount of divine vision or remain silent altogether?

When the psalmist saw the transgression of the wicked his heart told him how it could be. "There is no fear of God before his eyes," he explained, and in so saying revealed to us the psychology of sin. When men no longer fear God, they transgress His laws without hesitation. The fear of consequences is no deterrent when the fear of God is gone.

In olden days men of faith were said to "walk in the fear of God" and to "serve the Lord with fear." However intimate their communion with God, however bold their prayers, at the base of their religious life was the conception of God as awesome and dreadful. This idea of God transcendent runs through the whole Bible and gives color and tone to the character of the saints. This fear of God was more than a natural apprehension of danger; it was a nonrational dread, an acute feeling of personal insufficiency in the presence of God the Almighty.

Wherever God appeared to men in Bible times the results were the same—an overwhelming sense of terror and dismay, a wrenching sensation of sinfulness and guilt. When God spoke, Abram stretched himself upon the ground to listen. When Moses saw the Lord in the burning bush, he hid his face in fear to look upon God. Isaiah's vision of God wrung from him the cry, "Woe is me!" and the confession, "I am undone; because I am a man of unclean lips."

Daniel's encounter with God was probably the most dreadful and wonderful of them all. The prophet lifted up his eyes and saw One whose "body also was like the beryl, and his face as the appearance of lightning, and his eyes as lamps of fire, and his arms and his feet like in colour to polished brass, and the voice of his words like the voice of a multitude." "I Daniel alone saw the vision," he afterwards wrote, "for the men that were with me saw not the vision; but a great quaking fell upon them, so that they fled to hide themselves. Therefore I was left alone, and saw this great vision, and there remained no strength in me: for my comeliness was turned in me into corruption, and I retained no strength. Yet heard I the voice of his words: and when I heard the voice of his words, then was I in a deep sleep on my face, and my face toward the ground."

These experiences show that a vision of the divine transcendence soon ends all controversy between the man and his God. The fight goes out of the man and he is ready with the conquered Saul to ask meekly, "Lord, what wilt thou have me to do?" Conversely, the self-assurance of modern Christians, the basic levity present in so many of our religious gatherings, the shocking disrespect shown for the Person of God, are evidence enough of deep blindness of heart. Many call themselves by the name of Christ, talk much about God, and pray to Him sometimes, but evidently do not know who He is. "The fear of the LORD is a fountain of life," but this healing fear is today hardly found among Christian men.

Once in conversation with his friend Eckermann, the poet Goethe turned to thoughts of religion and spoke of the abuse of the divine name. " People treat it," he said, "as if that incomprehensible and most high Being, who is even beyond the reach of thought, were only their equal. Otherwise they would not say 'the Lord God, the dear God, the good God.' This expression becomes to them, especially to the clergy, who have it daily in their mouths, a mere phrase, a barren name, to which no thought whatever is attached. If they were impressed by His greatness they would be dumb, and through veneration unwilling to name Him."[22]

> *Lord of all being, throned afar,*
> *Thy glory flames from sun and star;*
> *Center and soul of every sphere,*
> *Yet to each loving heart how near!*
>
> *Lord of all life, below, above,*
> *Whose light is truth, whose warmth is love,*
> *Before Thy ever-blazing throne*
> *We ask no luster of our own.*
>
> Oliver Wendell Holmes

CHAPTER 14

God's Omnipresence

Our Father, we know that Thou art present with us, but our knowledge is but a figure and shadow of truth and has little of the spiritual savor and inward sweetness such knowledge should afford. This is for us a great loss and the cause of much weakness of heart. Help us to make at once such amendment of life as is necessary before we can experience the true meaning of the words "In thy presence is fulness of joy." *Amen.*

The word *present*, of course, means *here, close to, next to,* and the prefix *omni* gives it universality. God is everywhere here, close to everything, next to everyone.

Few other truths are taught in the Scriptures with as great clarity as the doctrine of the divine omnipresence. Those passages supporting this truth are so plain that it would take considerable effort to misunderstand them. They declare that God is immanent in His creation, that there is no place in heaven or earth or hell where men may hide from His presence. They teach that God is at once far off and near, and that in Him men move and live and have their being. And what is equally convincing is that they everywhere compel us to assume that God is omnipresent to account for other facts they tell us about Him.

For instance, the Scriptures teach that God is infinite. This means that His being knows no limits. Therefore there can be no limit to His presence; He is omnipresent. In His infinitude He surrounds the finite creation and contains it. There is no place beyond Him for anything to be. God is our environment as the sea is to the fish and the air to the bird. "God is over all things," wrote Hildebert of Lavardin, "under all things; outside all; within but not enclosed; without but not excluded; above but not raised up; below but not depressed; wholly above, presiding; wholly beneath, sustaining; wholly within, filling."[23]

The belief that God is present within His universe cannot be held in isolation. It has practical implications in many areas of theological thought and bears directly upon certain religious problems, such, for instance, as the nature of the world. Thinking men of almost every age and culture have been concerned with the question of what kind of world this is. Is it a material world running by itself, or is it spiritual and run by unseen powers? Does this interlocking system explain itself or does its secret lie in mystery? Does the stream of existence begin and end in itself? Or is its source higher up and farther back in the hills?

Christian theology claims to have the answer to these questions. It does not speculate nor offer an opinion but presents its "Thus saith the Lord" as its authority. It declares positively that the world is spiritual: it originated in spirit, flows out of spirit, is spiritual in its essence, and is meaningless apart from the Spirit that inhabits it.

The doctrine of the divine omnipresence personalizes man's relation to the universe in which he finds himself. This great central truth gives meaning to all other truths and imparts supreme value to all his little life. God is present, near him, next to him, and this God sees him and knows him through and through. At this point faith begins, and while it may go on to include a thousand other wonderful truths, these all refer back to the truth that *God is*, and *God is here*. "He that cometh to God," says the Book of Hebrews, "must believe that he is." And Christ Himself said, "Ye believe in God, believe also. . . ." Whatever "also" may be added to the elementary belief in God is superstructure, and regardless of the heights to which it may rise, it continues to rest solidly upon the original foundation.

The teaching of the New Testament is that God created the world by the *Logos*, the Word, and the Word is identified with the second Person of the Godhead who was present in the world even before He became incarnate in human nature. The Word made all things and remained in His creation to uphold and sustain it and be at the same time a moral light enabling every man to distinguish good from evil. The universe operates as an orderly system, not by impersonal laws but by the creative voice of the immanent and universal Presence, the *Logos*.

Canon W. G. H. Holmes of India told of seeing Hindu worshipers tapping on trees and stones and whispering "Are you there? Are you there?" to the god they hoped might reside within. In complete humility the instructed Christian brings the answer to that question. God is indeed there. He is there as He is here and everywhere, not confined to tree or stone, but free in the universe, near to everything, next to everyone, and through Jesus Christ immediately accessible to every loving heart. The doctrine of the divine omnipresence decides this forever.

This truth is to the convinced Christian a source of deep comfort in sorrow and of steadfast assurance in all the varied experiences of his life. To him "the practice of the presence of God" consists not of projecting an imaginary object from within his own mind and then seeking to realize its presence; it is rather to recognize the real presence of the One whom all sound theology declares to be already there, an objective entity, existing apart from any apprehension of Him on the part of His creatures. The resultant experience is not visionary but real.

The certainty that God is always near us, present in all parts of His world, closer to us than our thoughts, should maintain us in a state of high moral happiness most of the time. But not all the time. It would be less than honest to promise every believer continual jubilee and less than realistic to expect it. As a child may cry out in pain even when sheltered in its mother's arms, so a Christian may sometimes know what it is to suffer even in the conscious presence of God. Though "always rejoicing," Paul admitted that he was sometimes sorrowful, and for our sakes Christ experienced strong crying and tears though He never left the bosom of the Father (John 1:18).

But all will be well. In a world like this tears have their therapeutic effects. The healing balm distilled from the garments of the enfolding Presence cures our ills before they become fatal. The knowledge that we are never alone calms the troubled sea of our lives and speaks peace to our souls.

That God is here both Scripture and reason declare. It remains only for us to learn to realize this in conscious experience. A sentence from a letter by Dr. Allen Fleece sums up the testimony of many others: "The knowledge that God is present is blessed, but to *feel* His presence is nothing less than sheer happiness.

> *God reveals His presence:*
> *Let us now adore Him,*
> *And with awe appear before Him.*
>
> *Him alone, God we own;*
> *He's our Lord and Saviour,*
> *Praise His name forever.*

God Himself is with us:
Whom the angelic legions
Serve with awe in heavenly regions.

Gerhard Tersteegen

CHAPTER 15

The Faithfulness of God

It is a good thing to give thanks unto Thee and to sing praises unto Thy name, O Most High, to show forth Thy loving-kindness in the morning and Thy faithfulness every night. As Thy Son while on earth was loyal to Thee, His Heavenly Father, so now in heaven He is faithful to us, His earthly brethren; and in this knowledge we press on with every confident hope for all the years and centuries yet to come. *Amen.*

As emphasized earlier, God's attributes are not isolated traits of His character but facets of His unitary being. They are not things-in-themselves; they are, rather, thoughts by which we think of God, aspects of a perfect whole, names given to whatever we know to be true of the Godhead.

To have a correct understanding of the attributes it is necessary that we see them all as one. We can think of them separately but they cannot be separated. "All attributes assigned to God cannot differ in reality, by reason of the perfect simplicity of God, although we in divers ways use of God divers words," says Nicholas of Cusa. "Whence, although we attribute to God sight, hearing, taste, smell, touch, sense, reason and intellect, and so forth, according to the divers significations of each word, yet in Him sight is not other than hearing, or tasting, or smelling, or touching, or feeling, or understanding. And so all theology is said to be stablished in a circle, because any one of His attributes is affirmed of another."[24]

In studying any attribute, the essential oneness of all the attributes soon becomes apparent. We see, for instance, that if God is self-existent He must be also self-sufficient; and if He has power He, being infinite, must have all power. If He possesses knowledge, His infinitude assures us that He possesses all knowledge. Similarly, His immutability presupposes His faithfulness. If He is unchanging, it follows that He could not be unfaithful, since that would require Him to change. Any failure within the divine character would argue imperfection and, since God is perfect, it could not occur. Thus the attributes explain each other and prove that they are but glimpses the mind enjoys of the absolutely perfect Godhead.

All of God's acts are consistent with all of His attributes. No attribute contradicts any other, but all harmonize and blend into each other in the infinite abyss of the Godhead. All that God does agrees with all that God is, and being and doing are one in Him. The familiar picture of God as often torn between His justice and His mercy is altogether false to the facts. To think of God as inclining first toward one and then toward another of His attributes is to imagine a God who is unsure of Himself, frustrated and emotionally unstable, which of course is to say that the one of whom we are thinking is not the true God at all but a weak, mental reflection of Him badly out of focus.

God, being who He is, cannot cease to be what He is, and being what He is, He cannot act out of character with Himself. He is at once faithful and immutable, so all His words and acts must be and must remain faithful. Men become unfaithful out of desire, fear, weakness, loss of interest, or because of some strong influence from without. Obviously none of these forces can affect God in any way. He is His own reason for all He is and does. He cannot be compelled from without, but ever speaks and acts from within Himself by His own sovereign will as it pleases Him.

I think it might be demonstrated that almost every heresy that has afflicted the church through the years has arisen from believing about God things that are not true, or from overemphasizing certain true things so as to obscure other things equally true. To magnify any attribute to the exclusion of another is to head straight for one of the dismal swamps of theology; and yet we are all constantly tempted to do just that.

For instance, the Bible teaches that God is love; some

have interpreted this in such a way as virtually to deny that He is just, which the Bible also teaches. Others press the Biblical doctrine of God's goodness so far that it is made to contradict His holiness. Or they make His compassion cancel out His truth. Still others understand the sovereignty of God in a way that destroys or at least greatly diminishes His goodness and love.

We can hold a correct view of truth only by daring to believe everything God has said about Himself. It is a grave responsibility that a man takes upon himself when he seeks to edit out of God's self-revelation such features as he in his ignorance deems objectionable. Blindness in part must surely fall upon any of us presumptuous enough to attempt such a thing. And it is wholly uncalled for. We need not fear to let the truth stand as it is written. There is no conflict among the divine attributes. God's being is unitary. He cannot divide Himself and act at a given time from one of His attributes while the rest remain inactive. All that God is must accord with all that God does. Justice must be present in mercy, and love in judgment. And so with all the divine attributes.

The faithfulness of God is a datum of sound theology but to the believer it becomes far more than that: it passes through the processes of the understanding and goes on to become nourishing food for the soul. For the Scriptures not only teach truth, they show also its uses for mankind. The inspired writers were men of like passion with us, dwelling in the midst of life. What they learned about God became to them a sword, a shield, a hammer; it became their life motivation, their good hope, and their confident expectation. From the objective facts of theology their hearts made how many thousand joyous deductions and personal applications! The Book of Psalms rings with glad thanksgiving for the faithfulness of God. The New Testament takes up the theme and celebrates the loyalty of God the Father and His Son Jesus Christ who before Pontius Pilate witnessed a good confession; and in the Apocalypse Christ is seen astride a white horse riding toward His triumph, and the names He bears are Faithful and True.

Christian song, too, celebrates the attributes of God, and among them the divine faithfulness. In our hymnody, at its best, the attributes become the wellspring from which flow rivers of joyous melody. Some old hymnbooks may yet be found in which the hymns have no names; a line in italics above each one indicates its theme, and the worshiping heart cannot but rejoice in what it finds: "God's glorious perfections celebrated." "Wisdom, majesty and goodness." "Omniscience." "Omnipotence and immutability." "Glory, mercy and grace." These are a few samples taken from a hymnbook published in 1849, but everyone familiar with Christian hymnody knows that the stream of sacred song takes its rise far back in the early years of the Church's existence. From the beginning belief in the perfection of God brought sweet assurance to believing men and taught the ages to sing.

Upon God's faithfulness rests our whole hope of future

blessedness. Only as He is faithful will His covenants stand and His promises be honored. Only as we have complete assurance that He is faithful may we live in peace and look forward with assurance to the life to come.

Every heart can make its own application of this truth and draw from it such conclusions as the truth suggests and its own needs bring into focus. The tempted, the anxious, the fearful, the discouraged may all find new hope and good cheer in the knowledge that our Heavenly Father is faithful. He will ever be true to His pledged word. The hard-pressed sons of the covenant may be sure that He will never remove His loving-kindness from them nor suffer His faithfulness to fail.

Happy the man whose hopes rely
On Israel's God; He made the sky,
   And earth, and seas, with all their train;
His truth forever stands secure;
He saves the oppressed, He feeds the poor,
   And none shall find His promise vain.
                                    Isaac Watts

CHAPTER 16

The Goodness of God

Do good in Thy good pleasure unto us, O Lord. Act toward us not as we deserve but as it becomes Thee, being the God Thou art. So shall we have nothing to fear in this world or in that which is to come *Amen.*

The word *good* means so many things to so many persons that this brief study of the divine goodness begins with a definition. The meaning may be arrived at only by the use of a number of synonyms, going out from and returning by different paths to the same place.

When Christian theology says that God is good, it is not the same as saying that He is righteous or holy. The holiness of God is trumpeted from the heavens and re-echoed on earth by saints and sages wherever God has revealed Himself to men; however, we are not at this time considering His holiness but His goodness, which is quite another thing.

The goodness of God is that which disposes Him to

be kind, cordial, benevolent, and full of good will toward men. He is tenderhearted and of quick sympathy, and His unfailing attitude toward all moral beings is open, frank, and friendly. By His nature He is inclined to bestow blessedness and He takes holy pleasure in the happiness of His people.

That God is good is taught or implied on every page of the Bible and must be received as an article of faith as impregnable as the throne of God. It is a foundation stone for all sound thought about God and is necessary to moral sanity. To allow that God could be other than good is to deny the validity of all thought and end in the negation of every moral judgment. If God is not good, then there can be no distinction between kindness and cruelty, and heaven can be hell and hell, heaven.

The goodness of God is the drive behind all the blessings He daily bestows upon us. God created us because He felt good in His heart and He redeemed us for the same reason.

Julian of Norwich, who lived six hundred years ago, saw clearly that the ground of all blessedness is the goodness of God. Chapter six of her incredibly beautiful and perceptive little classic, *Revelations of Divine Love*, begins, "This Shewing was made to learn our soul wisely to cleave to the Goodness of God." Then she lists some of the mighty deeds God has wrought in our behalf, and after each one she adds "of his Goodness." She saw that all our religious activities and every means of grace, however right and useful they may be, are nothing until we understand that the unmerited, spontaneous goodness of God is back of all and underneath all His acts.

Divine goodness, as one of God's attributes, is self-caused, infinite, perfect, and eternal. Since God is immutable He never varies in the intensity of His loving-kindness. He has never been kinder than He now is, nor will He ever be less kind. He is no respecter of persons but makes His sun to shine on the evil as well as on the good, and sends His rain on the just and on the unjust. The cause of His goodness is in Himself; the recipients of His goodness are all His beneficiaries without merit and without recompense.

With this agrees reason, and the moral wisdom that knows itself runs to acknowledge that there can be no merit in human conduct, not even in the purest and the best. Always God's goodness is the ground of our expectation. Repentance, though necessary, is not meritorious but a condition for receiving the gracious gift of pardon which God gives of His goodness. Prayer is not in itself meritorious. It lays God under no obligation nor puts Him in debt to any. He hears prayer because He is good, and for no other reason. Nor is faith meritorious; it is simply confidence in the goodness of God, and the lack of it is not a reflection upon God's holy character.

The whole outlook of mankind might be changed if we could all believe that we dwell under a friendly sky and that the God of heaven, though exalted in power and majesty, is eager to be friends with us.

But sin has made us timid and self-conscious, as well it might. Years of rebellion against God have bred in us a fear that cannot be overcome in a day. The captured rebel does not enter willingly the presence of the king he has so long fought unsuccessfully to overthrow. But if he is truly penitent he may come, trusting only in the loving-kindness of his Lord, and the past will not be held against him. Meister Eckhart encourages us to remember that, when we return to God, even if our sins were as great in number as all mankind's put together, still God would not count them against us, but would have as much confidence in us as if we had never sinned.

Now someone who in spite of his past sins honestly wants to become reconciled to God may cautiously inquire, "If I come to God, how will He act toward me? What kind of disposition has He? What will I find Him to be like?"

The answer is that He will be found to be exactly like Jesus. "He that hath seen me," said Jesus, "hath seen the Father." Christ walked with men on earth that He might show them what God is like and make known the true nature of God to a race that had wrong ideas about Him. This was only one of the things He did while here in the flesh, but this He did with beautiful perfection.

From Him we learn how God acts toward people. The hypocritical, the basically insincere, will find Him cold and aloof, as they once found Jesus; but the penitent will find Him merciful; the self-condemned will find Him generous and kind. To the frightened He is friendly, to the poor in spirit He is forgiving, to the ignorant, considerate; to the weak, gentle; to the stranger, hospitable.

By our own attitudes we may determine our reception by Him. Though the kindness of God is an infinite, overflowing fountain of cordiality, God will not force His attention upon us. If we would be welcomed as the Prodigal was, we must come as the Prodigal came; and when we so come, even though the Pharisees and the legalists sulk without, there will be a feast of welcome within, and music and dancing as the Father takes His child again to His heart.

The greatness of God rouses fear within us, but His goodness encourages us not to be afraid of Him. To fear and not be afraid—that is the paradox of faith.

O God, my hope, my heavenly rest,
My all of happiness below,
Grant my importunate request,
To me, to me, Thy goodness show;
Thy beatific face display,
The brightness of eternal day.

Before my faith's enlightened eyes,
Make all Thy gracious goodness pass;
Thy goodness is the sight I prize:
O might I see Thy smiling face:
Thy nature in my soul proclaim,
Reveal Thy love, Thy glorious name.

Charles Wesley

———————•———————

CHAPTER 17

The Justice of God

Our Father, we love Thee for Thy justice. We acknowledge that Thy judgments are true and righteous altogether. Thy justice upholds the order of the universe and guarantees the safety of all who put their trust in Thee. We live because Thou art just—and merciful. Holy, holy, holy, Lord God Almighty, righteous in all Thy ways and holy in all Thy works. Amen.

I n the inspired Scriptures justice and righteousness are scarcely to be distinguished from each other. The same word in the original becomes in English *justice* or *righteousness*, almost, one would suspect, at the whim of the translator.

The Old Testament asserts God's justice in language clear and full, and as beautiful as may be found anywhere in the literature of mankind. When the destruction of Sodom was announced, Abraham interceded for the righteous within the city, reminding God that he knew He would act like Himself in the human emergency.

"That be far from thee to do after this manner, to slay the righteous with the wicked: and that the righteous should be as the wicked, that be far from thee: Shall not the Judge of all the earth do right?"

The concept of God held by the psalmists and prophets of Israel was that of an all-powerful ruler, high and lifted up, reigning in equity. "Clouds and darkness are round about him: righteousness and judgment are the habitation of his throne." Of the long-awaited Messiah it was prophesied that when He came He should judge the people with righteousness and the poor with judgment. Holy men of tender compassion, outraged by the inequity of the world's rulers, prayed, "O Lord God, to whom vengeance belongeth; O God, to whom vengeance belongeth, shew thyself. Lift up thyself, thou judge of the earth: render a reward to the proud. LORD, how long shall the wicked, how long shall the wicked triumph?" And this is to be understood not as a plea for personal vengeance but as a longing to see moral equity prevail in human society.

Such men as David and Daniel acknowledged their own unrighteousness in contrast to the righteousness of God, and as a result their penitential prayers gained great power and effectiveness. "O LORD, righteousness belongeth unto thee, but unto us confusion of faces." And when the long-withheld judgment of God begins to fall upon the world, John sees the victorious saints standing upon a sea of glass mingled with fire. In their hands they hold harps of God; the song they sing is the song of Moses and the Lamb, and the theme of their song is the divine justice. "Great and marvellous are thy works, Lord God Almighty; just and true are thy ways, thou King of saints. Who shall not fear thee, O Lord, and glorify thy name? for thou alone art holy: for all nations shall come and worship before thee; for thy judgments are made manifest."

Justice embodies the idea of moral equity, and iniquity is the exact opposite; it is *in*-equity, the absence of equality from human thoughts and acts. Judgment is the application of equity to moral situations and may be favorable or unfavorable according to whether the one under examination has been equitable or inequitable in heart and conduct.

It is sometimes said, "Justice requires God to do this," referring to some act we know He will perform. This is an error of thinking as well as of speaking, for it postulates a principle of justice outside of God which compels Him to act in a certain way. Of course there is no such principle. If there were it would be superior to God, for only a superior power can compel obedience. The truth is that there is not and can never be anything outside of the nature of God which can move Him in the least degree. All God's reasons come from within His uncreated being. Nothing has entered the being of God from eternity, nothing has been removed, and nothing has been changed.

Justice, when used of God, is a name we give to the way God is, nothing more; and when God acts justly He is not doing so to conform to an independent criterion, but simply acting like Himself in a given situation. As gold is an element in itself and can never change nor compromise but is gold wherever it is found, so God is God, always, only, fully God, and can never be other than He is. Everything in the universe is good to the degree it conforms to the nature of God and evil as it fails to do so. God is His own self-existent principle of moral equity, and when He sentences evil men or rewards the righteous, He simply acts like Himself from within, uninfluenced by anything that is not Himself.

All this seems, but only seems, to destroy the hope of justification for the returning sinner. The Christian philosopher and saint, Anselm, Archbishop of Canterbury, sought a solution to the apparent contradiction between the justice and the mercy of God. "How dost Thou spare the wicked," he inquired of God, "if Thou art all just and supremely just?"[25] Then he looked straight at God for the answer, for he knew that it lies in what God is. Anselm's findings may be paraphrased this way: God's being is unitary; it is not composed of a number of parts working harmoniously, but simply one. There is nothing in His justice which forbids the exercise of His mercy. To think of God as we sometimes think of a court where a kindly judge, compelled by law, sentences a man to death with tears and apologies, is to think in a manner wholly unworthy of the true God. God is never at cross-purposes with Himself. No attribute of God is in conflict with another.

God's compassion flows out of His goodness, and goodness without justice is not goodness. God spares us because He is good, but He could not be good if He were not just. When God punishes the wicked, Anselm concludes, it is just because it is consistent with their deserts; and when He spares the wicked it is just because it is compatible with His goodness; so God does what becomes Him as the supremely good God. This is reason seeking to understand, not that it may believe but because it already believes.

A simpler and more familiar solution for the problem of how God can be just and still justify the unjust is found in the Christian doctrine of redemption. It is that, through the work of Christ in atonement, justice is not violated but satisfied when God spares a sinner. Redemptive theology teaches that mercy does not become effective toward a man until justice has done its work. The just penalty for sin was exacted when Christ our Substitute died for us on the cross. However unpleasant this may sound to the ear of the natural man, it has ever been sweet to the ear of faith. Millions have been morally and spiritually transformed by this message, have lived lives of great moral power, and died at last peacefully trusting in it.

This message of justice discharged and mercy operative is more than a pleasant theological theory; it announces a fact made necessary by our deep human need.

Because of our sin we are all under sentence of death, a judgment which resulted when justice confronted our moral situation. When infinite equity encountered our chronic and willful in-equity, there was violent war between the two, a war which God won and must always win. But when the penitent sinner casts himself upon Christ for salvation, the moral situation is reversed. Justice confronts the changed situation and pronounces the believing man just. Thus justice actually goes over to the side of God's trusting children. This is the meaning of those daring words of the apostle John: "If we confess our sins, he is faithful and just to forgive us our sins, and to cleanse us from all unrighteousness."

But God's justice stands forever against the sinner in utter severity. The vague and tenuous hope that God is too kind to punish the ungodly has become a deadly opiate for the consciences of millions. It hushes their fears and allows them to practice all pleasant forms of iniquity while death draws every day nearer and the command to repent goes unregarded. As responsible moral beings we dare not so trifle with our eternal future.

> *Jesus, Thy blood and righteousness*
> *My beauty are, my glorious dress;*
> *'Midst flaming worlds, in these arrayed,*
> *With joy shall I lift up my head.*

Bold shall I stand in Thy great day;
For who aught to my charge shall lay?
Fully absolved through these I am—From
sin and fear, from guilt and shame.

Count N. L. von Zinzendorf

CHAPTER 18

The Mercy of God

Holy Father, Thy wisdom excites our admiration, Thy power fills us with fear, Thy omnipresence turns every spot of earth into holy ground; but how shall we thank Thee enough for Thy mercy which comes down to the lowest part of our need to give us beauty for ashes, the oil of joy for mourning, and for the spirit of heaviness a garment of praise? We bless and magnify Thy mercy, through Jesus Christ our Lord. *Amen.*

When through the blood of the everlasting covenant we children of the shadows reach at last our home in the light, we shall have a thousand strings to our harps, but the sweetest may well be the one tuned to sound forth most perfectly the mercy of God.

For what right will we have to be there? Did we not by our sins take part in that unholy rebellion which rashly sought to dethrone the glorious King of creation? And did we not in times past walk according to the course of this world, according to the evil prince of the power of the air, the spirit that now works in the sons of disobedience? And did we not all at once live in the lusts of our flesh? And were we not by nature the children of wrath, even as others? But we who were one time enemies and alienated in our minds through wicked works shall then see God face to face and His name shall be in our foreheads. We who earned banishment shall enjoy communion; we who deserve the pains of hell shall know the bliss of heaven. And all through the tender mercy of our God, whereby the Dayspring from on high hath visited us.

> *When all Thy mercies, O my God,*
> *My rising soul surveys,*
> *Transported with the view, I'm lost*
> *In wonder, love, and praise.*
>
> Joseph Addison

Mercy is an attribute of God, an infinite and inexhaustible energy within the divine nature which disposes God to be actively compassionate. Both the Old and the New Testaments proclaim the mercy of God, but the Old has more than four times as much to say about it as the New.

We should banish from our minds forever the common but erroneous notion that justice and judgment characterize the God of Israel, while mercy and grace belong to the Lord of the Church. Actually there is in principle no difference between the Old Testament and the New. In the New Testament Scriptures there is a fuller development of redemptive truth, but one God speaks in both dispensations, and what He speaks agrees with what He is. Wherever and whenever God appears to men, He acts like Himself. Whether in the Garden of Eden or the Garden of Gethsemane, God is merciful as well as just. He has always dealt in mercy with mankind and will always deal in justice when His mercy is despised. Thus He did in antediluvian times; thus when Christ walked among men; thus He is doing today and will continue always to do for no other reason than that He is God.

If we could remember that the divine mercy is not a temporary mood but an attribute of God's eternal being, we would no longer fear that it will someday cease to be. Mercy never began to be, but from eternity was; so it will never cease to be. It will never be more since it is itself infinite; and it will never be less because the infinite cannot suffer diminution. Nothing that has occurred or will occur in heaven or earth or hell can change the tender mercies of our God. Forever His mercy stands, a boundless, overwhelming immensity of divine pity and compassion.

As judgment is God's justice confronting moral inequity, so mercy is the goodness of God confronting human suffering and guilt. Were there no guilt in the world, no pain and no tears, God would yet be infinitely merciful; but His mercy might well remain hidden in His heart, unknown to the created universe. No voice would be raised to celebrate the mercy of which none felt the need. It is human misery and sin that call forth the divine mercy.

"Kyrie eleison! Christe eleison!" the Church has pleaded through the centuries; but if I mistake not I hear in the voice of her pleading a note of sadness and despair. Her plaintive cry, so often repeated in that tone of resigned dejection, compels one to infer that she is praying for a boon she never actually expects to receive. She may go on dutifully to sing of the greatness of God and to recite the creed times beyond number, but her plea for mercy sounds like a forlorn hope and no more, as if mercy were a heavenly gift to be longed for but never really enjoyed.

Could our failure to capture the pure joy of mercy consciously experienced be the result of our unbelief or our ignorance, or both? It was so once in Israel. "I bear them record," Paul testified of Israel, "that they have a zeal of God, but not according to knowledge." They failed because there was at least one thing they did not know, one thing that would have made the difference. And of Israel in the wilderness the Hebrew writer says, "But the word preached did not profit them, not being mixed with faith in them that heard it." To receive mercy we must first know that God is merciful. And it is not enough to believe that He once showed mercy to Noah or Abraham or David and will again show mercy in some happy future day. We must believe that God's mercy is boundless, free and, through Jesus Christ our Lord, available to us now in our present situation.

We may plead for mercy for a lifetime in unbelief, and at the end of our days be still no more than sadly hopeful that we shall somewhere, sometime, receive it. This is to starve to death just outside the banquet hall in which we have been warmly invited. Or we may, if we will, lay hold on the mercy of God by faith, enter the hall, and sit down with the bold and avid souls who will not allow diffidence and unbelief to keep them from the feast of fat things prepared for them.

> *Arise, my soul, arise;*
> *Shake off thy guilty fears;*
> *The bleeding Sacrifice*
> *In my behalf appears:*
> *Before the throne my Surety stands,*
> *My name is written on His hands.*
>
> *My God is reconciled;*
> *His pardoning voice I hear:*
> *He owns me for His child;*
> *I can no longer fear:*
> *With confidence I now draw nigh,*
> *And "Father, Abba, Father," cry.*

Charles Wesley

———————•———————

CHAPTER 19

The Grace of God

God of all grace, whose thoughts toward us are ever thoughts of peace and not of evil, give us hearts to believe that we are accepted in the Beloved; and give us minds to admire that perfection of moral wisdom which found a way to preserve the integrity of heaven and yet receive us there. We are astonished and marvel that one so holy and dread should invite us into Thy banqueting house and cause love to be the banner over us. We cannot express the gratitude we feel, but look Thou on our hearts and read it there. *Amen.*

I n God mercy and grace are one; but as they reach us they are seen as two, related but not identical.

As mercy is God's goodness confronting human misery and guilt, so grace is His goodness directed toward human debt and demerit. It is by His grace that God imputes merit where none previously existed and declares no debt to be where one had been before.

Grace is the good pleasure of God that inclines Him to bestow benefits upon the undeserving. It is a self-existent principle inherent in the divine nature and appears to us as a self-caused propensity to pity the wretched, spare the guilty, welcome the outcast, and bring into favor those who were before under just disapprobation. Its use to us sinful men is to save us and make us sit together in heavenly places to demonstrate to the ages the exceeding riches of God's kindness to us in Christ Jesus.

We benefit eternally by God's being just what He is. Because He is what He is, He lifts up our heads out of the prison house, changes our prison garments for royal robes, and makes us to eat bread continually before Him all the days of our lives.

Grace takes its rise far back in the heart of God, in the awful and incomprehensible abyss of His holy being; but the channel through which it flows out to men is Jesus Christ, crucified and risen. The apostle Paul, who beyond all others is the exponent of grace in redemption, never disassociates God's grace from God's crucified Son. Always in his teachings the two are found together, organically one and inseparable.

A full and fair summation of Paul's teaching on this subject is found in his Epistle to the Ephesians: "Having predestinated us unto the adoption of children by Jesus Christ to himself, according to the good pleasure of his will, to the praise of the glory of his grace, wherein he hath made us accepted in the beloved. In whom we have redemption through his blood, the forgiveness of sins, according to the riches of his grace."

John also in the Gospel that bears his name identifies Christ as the medium through which grace reaches mankind: "For the law was given by Moses, but grace and truth came by Jesus Christ."

But right here it is easy to miss the path and go far astray from the truth; and some have done this. They have compelled this verse to stand by itself, unrelated to other Scriptures bearing on the doctrine of grace, and have made it teach that Moses knew only law and Christ knows only grace. So the Old Testament is made to be a book of law and the New Testament a book of grace. The truth is quite otherwise.

The law was given to men through Moses, but it did not originate with Moses. It had existed in the heart of God from before the foundation of the world. On Mount Sinai it became the legal code for the nation of Israel; but the moral principles it embodies are eternal. There never was a time when the law did not represent the will of God for mankind nor a time when the violation of it did not bring its own penalty, though God was patient and sometimes "winked" at wrongdoing because of the ignorance of the people. Paul's close-knit arguments in the third and fifth chapters of his Epistle to the Romans make this very clear. The spring of Christian morality is the love of Christ, not the law of Moses; nevertheless there has been no abrogation of the principles of morality contained in the law. No privileged class exists exempt from that righteousness which the law enjoins.

The Old Testament is indeed a book of law, but not of law only. Before the great flood Noah "found grace in the eyes of the LORD," and after the law was given God said to Moses, "Thou hast found grace in my sight." And how could it be otherwise? God will always be Himself, and grace is an attribute of His holy being. He can no more hide His grace than the sun can hide its brightness. Men may flee from the sunlight to dark and musty caves of the earth, but they cannot put out the sun. So men may in any dispensation despise the grace of God, but they cannot extinguish it.

Had the Old Testament times been times of stern, unbending law alone the whole complexion of the early world would have been vastly less cheerful than we find it to be in the ancient writings. There could have been no Abraham, friend of God; no David, man after God's own heart; no Samuel, no Isaiah, no Daniel. The eleventh chapter of Hebrews, that Westminster Abbey of the spiritually great of the Old Testament, would stand dark and tenantless. Grace made sainthood possible in Old Testament days just as it does today.

No one was ever saved other than by grace, from Abel to the present moment. Since mankind was banished from the eastward Garden, none has ever returned to the divine favor except through the sheer goodness of God. And wherever grace found any man it was always by Jesus Christ. Grace indeed came by Jesus Christ, but it did not wait for His birth in the manger or His death on the cross before it became operative. Christ is the Lamb slain from the foundation of the world. The first man in human history to be reinstated in the fellowship of God came through faith in Christ. In olden times men looked forward to Christ's redeeming work; in later times they gaze back upon it, but always they came and they come by grace, through faith.

We must keep in mind also that the grace of God is infinite and eternal. As it had no beginning, so it can have no end, and being an attribute of God, it is as boundless as infinitude.

Instead of straining to comprehend this as a theological truth, it would be better and simpler to compare God's grace with our need. We can never know the enormity of our sin, neither is it necessary that we should. What we can know is that "where sin abounded, grace did much more abound."

To "abound" in sin: that is the worst and the most we could or can do. The word *abound* defines the limit of our finite abilities; and although we feel our iniquities rise over us like a mountain, the mountain, nevertheless, has definable boundaries: it is so large, so high, it weighs only this certain amount and no more. But who shall define the limitless grace of God? Its "much more" plunges our thoughts into infinitude and confounds them there. All thanks be to God for grace abounding.

We who feel ourselves alienated from the fellowship of God can now raise our discouraged heads and look up.

Through the virtues of Christ's atoning death the cause of our banishment has been removed. We may return as the Prodigal returned, and be welcome. As we approach the Garden, our home before the Fall, the flaming sword is withdrawn. The keepers of the tree of life stand aside when they see a son of grace approaching.

> *Return, O wanderer, now return,*
> *   And seek thy Father's face;*
> *Those new desires which in thee burn*
> *   Were kindled by His grace.*
>
> *Return, O wanderer, now return,*
> *   And wipe the falling tear:*
> *Thy Father calls,—no longer mourn;*
> *   'Tis love invites thee near.*

William Benco Collyer

CHAPTER 20

The Love of God

Our Father which art in heaven, we Thy children are often troubled in mind, hearing within us at once the affirmations of faith and the accusations of conscience. We are sure that there is in us nothing that could attract the love of One as holy and as just as Thou art. Yet Thou hast declared Thine unchanging love for us in Christ Jesus. If nothing in us can win Thy love, nothing in the universe can prevent Thee from loving us. Thy love is uncaused and undeserved. Thou art Thyself the reason for the love wherewith we are loved. Help us to believe the intensity, the eternity of the love that has found us. Then love will cast out fear; and our troubled hearts will be at peace, trusting not in what we are but in what Thou hast declared Thyself to be. *Amen.*

The apostle John, by the Spirit, wrote, "God is love," and some have taken his words to be a definitive statement concerning the essential nature of God. This is a great error. John was by those words stating a fact, but he was not offering a definition.

Equating love with God is a major mistake which has produced much unsound religious philosophy and has brought forth a spate of vaporous poetry completely out of accord with the Holy Scriptures and altogether of another climate from that of historic Christianity.

Had the apostle declared that love is what God is, we would be forced to infer that God is what love is. If literally God is love, then literally love is God, and we are in all duty bound to worship love as the only God there is. If love is equal to God then God is only equal to love, and God and love are identical. Thus we destroy the concept of personality in God and deny outright all His attributes save one, and that one we substitute for God. The God we have left is not the God of Israel; He is not the God and Father of our Lord Jesus Christ; He is not the God of the prophets and the apostles; He is not the God of the saints and reformers and martyrs, nor yet the God of the theologians and hymnists of the church.

For our souls' sake we must learn to understand the Scriptures. We must escape the slavery of words and give loyal adherence to meanings instead. Words should express ideas, not originate them. We say that God is love; we say that God is light; we say that Christ is truth; and we mean the words to be understood in much the same way that words are understood when we say of a man, "He is kindness itself." By so saying we are not stating that kindness and the man are identical, and no one understands our words in that sense.

The words "God is love" mean that love is an essential attribute of God. Love is something true of God but it is not God. It expresses the way God is in His unitary being, as do the words holiness, justice, faithfulness, and truth. Because God is immutable He always acts like Himself, and because He is a unity He never suspends one of His attributes in order to exercise another.

From God's other known attributes we may learn much about His love. We can know, for instance, that because God is self-existent, His love had no beginning; because He is eternal, His love can have no end; because He is infinite, it has no limit; because He is holy, it is the quintessence of all spotless purity; because He is immense, His love is an incomprehensibly vast, bottomless, shoreless sea before which we kneel in joyful silence and from which the loftiest eloquence retreats confused and abashed.

Yet if we would know God and for others' sakes tell what we know, we must try to speak of His love. All Christians have tried, but none has ever done it very well. I can no more do justice to that awesome and wonder-filled theme than a child can grasp a star. Still, by reaching toward the star the child may call attention to it and even indicate the direction one must look to see it. So, as I stretch my heart toward the high, shining love of God, someone who has not before known about it may be encouraged to look up and have hope.

We do not know, and we may never know, what love *is*, but we can know how it manifests itself, and that is enough for us here. First we see it showing itself as good will. Love wills the good of all and never wills harm or evil to any. This explains the words of the apostle John: "There is no fear in love; but perfect love casteth out fear." Fear is the painful emotion that arises at the thought that we may be harmed or made to suffer. This fear persists while we are subject to the will of someone who does not desire our well-being. The moment we come under the protection of one of good will, fear is cast out. A child lost in a crowded store is full of fear because it sees the strangers around it as enemies. In its mother's arms a moment later all the terror subsides. The known good will of the mother casts out fear.

The world is full of enemies, and as long as we are subject to the possibility of harm from these enemies, fear is inevitable. The effort to conquer fear without removing the causes is altogether futile. The heart is wiser than the apostles of tranquillity. As long as we are in the hands of chance, as long as we look for hope to the law of averages, as long as we must trust for survival to our ability to outthink or outmaneuver the enemy, we have every good reason to be afraid. And fear hath torment.

To know that love is of God and to enter into the secret place leaning upon the arm of the Beloved—this and only this can cast out fear. Let a man become convinced that nothing can harm him and instantly for him all fear goes out of the universe. The nervous reflex, the natural revulsion to physical pain may be felt sometimes, but the deep torment of fear is gone forever. God is love and God is sovereign. His love disposes Him to desire our everlasting welfare and His sovereignty enables Him to secure it. Nothing can hurt a good man.

> *The body they may kill:*
> *God's truth abideth still,*
>   *His kingdom is forever.*
>   Martin Luther

God's love tells us that He is friendly and His Word assures us that He is our friend and wants us to be His friends. No man with a trace of humility would first think that he is a friend of God; but the idea did not originate with men. Abraham would never have said, "I am God's friend," but God Himself said that Abraham was His friend. The disciples might well have hesitated to claim friendship with Christ, but Christ said to them, "Ye are my friends." Modesty may demur at so rash a thought, but audacious faith dares to believe the Word and claim friendship with God. We do God more honor by believing what He has said about Himself and having the courage to come boldly to the throne of grace than by hiding in self-conscious humility among the trees of the garden.

Love is also an emotional identification. It considers nothing its own but gives all freely to the object of its affection. We see this constantly in our world of men and women. A young mother, thin and tired, nurses at her breast a plump and healthy baby, and far from complaining, the mother gazes down at her child with eyes shining with happiness and pride. Acts of self-sacrifice are common to love. Christ said of Himself, "Greater love hath no man than this, that a man lay down his life for his friends."

It is a strange and beautiful eccentricity of the free God that He has allowed His heart to be emotionally identified with men. Self-sufficient as He is, He wants our love and will not be satisfied till He gets it. Free as He is, He has let His heart be bound to us forever. "Herein is love, not that we loved God, but that he loved us, and sent his Son to be the propitiation for our sins." "For our soul is so specially loved of Him that is highest," says Julian of Norwich, "that it overpasseth the knowing of all creatures: that is to say, there is no creature that is made that may know how much and how sweetly and how tenderly our Maker loveth us. And therefore we may with grace and His help stand in spiritual beholding, with everlasting marvel of this high, overpassing, inestimable Love that Almighty God hath to us of His Goodness."[26]

Another characteristic of love is that it takes pleasure in its object. God enjoys His creation. The apostle John says frankly that God's purpose in creation was His own pleasure. God is happy in His love for all that He has made. We cannot miss the feeling of pleasure in God's delighted references to His handiwork. Psalm 104 is a divinely inspired nature poem almost rhapsodic in its happiness, and the delight of God is felt throughout it. "The glory of the LORD shall endure for ever: the LORD shall rejoice in his works."

The Lord takes peculiar pleasure in His saints. Many think of God as far removed, gloomy, and mightily displeased with everything, gazing down in a mood of fixed apathy upon a world in which He has long ago lost interest; but this is to think erroneously. True, God hates sin and can never look with pleasure upon iniquity, but where men seek to do God's will He responds in genuine affection. Christ in His atonement has removed the bar to the divine fellowship. Now in Christ all believing souls are objects of God's delight. "The LORD thy God in the midst of thee is mighty; he will save, he will rejoice over thee with joy; he will rest in his love, he will joy over thee with singing."

According to the Book of Job, God's work of creation was done to musical accompaniment. "Where wast thou," God asks, "when I laid the foundations of the earth . . . when the morning stars sang together, and all the sons of God shouted for joy?" John Dryden carried the idea a bit further than this, but not, perhaps, too far to be true:

> *From harmony, from heavenly harmony,*
> *This universal frame began:*
> *When nature underneath a heap*
> *Of jarring atoms lay,*

And could not heave her head,
The tuneful voice was heard from high,
"Arise, ye more than dead!"
Then cold, and hot, and moist, and dry,
In order to their stations leap,
And Music's power obey.
From harmony, from heavenly harmony,
This universal frame began:
From harmony to harmony
Through all the compass of the notes it ran,
The diapason closing full in Man.

From "A Song for St. Cecilia's Day"

Music is both an expression and a source of pleasure, and the pleasure that is purest and nearest to God is the pleasure of love. Hell is a place of no pleasure because there is no love there. Heaven is full of music because it is the place where the pleasures of holy love abound. Earth is the place where the pleasures of love are mixed with pain, for sin is here, and hate and ill will. In such a world as ours love must sometimes suffer, as Christ suffered in giving Himself for His own. But we have the certain promise that the causes of sorrow will finally be abolished and the new race enjoy forever a world of selfless, perfect love.

It is of the nature of love that it cannot lie quiescent. It is active, creative, and benign. "God commendeth his love toward us, in that, while we were sinners, Christ died for us." "God so loved the world, that he gave his only begotten Son." So it must be where love is; love must ever give to its own, whatever the cost.

The apostles rebuked the young churches sharply because a few of their members had forgotten this and had allowed their love to spend itself in personal enjoyment while their brethren were in need. "But whoso hath this world's good, and seeth his brother have need, and shutteth up his bowels of compassion from him, how dwelleth the love of God in him?" So wrote that John who has been known to the centuries as "the Beloved."

The love of God is one of the great realities of the universe, a pillar upon which the hope of the world rests. But it is a personal, intimate thing, too. God does not love populations, He loves people. He loves not masses, but men. He loves us all with a mighty love that has no beginning and can have no end.

In Christian experience there is a highly satisfying love content that distinguishes it from all other religions and elevates it to heights far beyond even the purest and noblest philosophy. This love content is more than a thing; it is God Himself in the midst of His Church singing over His people. True Christian joy is the heart's harmonious response to the Lord's song of love.

> *Thou hidden love of God, whose height,*
> *Whose depth unfathomed, no man knows,*
> *I see from far Thy beauteous light,*

Inly I sigh for Thy repose;
My heart is pained, nor can it be
At rest till it finds rest in Thee.

Gerhard Tersteegen

CHAPTER 21

The Holiness of God

Glory be to God on high. We praise Thee, we bless Thee, we worship Thee, for Thy great glory. Lord, I uttered that I understood not; things too wonderful for me which I knew not. I heard of Thee by the hearing of the ear, but now mine eye seeth Thee and I abhor myself in dust and ashes. O Lord, I will lay my hand upon my mouth. Once have I spoken, yea, twice, but I will proceed no further.

But while I was musing the fire burned. Lord, I must speak of Thee, lest by my silence I offend against the generation of Thy children. Behold, Thou has chosen the foolish things of the world to confound the wise, and the weak things of the world to confound the mighty. O Lord, forsake me not. Let me show forth Thy strength unto this generation and Thy power to everyone that is to come. Raise up prophets and seers in Thy Church who shall magnify Thy glory and through Thine almighty Spirit restore to Thy people the knowledge of the holy. *Amen.*

The moral shock suffered by us through our mighty break with the high will of heaven has left us all with a permanent trauma affecting every part of our nature.

There is disease both in ourselves and in our environment.

The sudden realization of his personal depravity came like a stroke from heaven upon the trembling heart of Isaiah at the moment when he had his revolutionary vision of the holiness of God. His pain-filled cry, "Woe is me! for I am undone; because I am a man of unclean lips, and I dwell in the midst of a people of unclean lips: for mine eyes have seen the King, the LORD of hosts," expresses the feeling of every man who has discovered himself under his disguises and has been confronted with an inward sight of the holy whiteness that is God. Such an experience cannot but be emotionally violent.

Until we have seen ourselves as God sees us, we are not likely to be much disturbed over conditions around us as long as they do not get so far out of hand as to threaten our comfortable way of life. We have learned to live with unholiness and have come to look upon it as the natural and expected thing. We are not disappointed that we do not find all truth in our teachers or faithfulness in our politicians or complete honesty in our merchants or full trustworthiness in our friends. That we may continue to exist we make such laws as are necessary to protect us from our fellow men and let it go at that.

Neither the writer nor the reader of these words is qualified to appreciate the holiness of God. Quite literally a new channel must be cut through the desert of our minds to allow the sweet waters of truth that will heal our great sickness to flow in. We cannot grasp the true meaning of the divine holiness by thinking of someone or something very pure and then raising the concept to the highest degree we are capable of. God's holiness is not simply the best we know infinitely bettered. We know nothing like the divine holiness. It stands apart, unique, unapproachable, incomprehensible, and unattainable. The natural man is blind to it. He may fear God's power and admire His wisdom, but His holiness he cannot even imagine.

Only the Spirit of the Holy One can impart to the human spirit the knowledge of the holy. Yet as electric power flows only through a conductor, so the Spirit flows through truth and must find some measure of truth in the mind before He can illuminate the heart. Faith wakes at the voice of truth but responds to no other sound. "Faith cometh by hearing, and hearing by the word of God." Theological knowledge is the medium through which the Spirit flows into the human heart, yet there must be humble penitence in the heart before truth can produce faith. The Spirit of God is the Spirit of truth. It is possible to have some truth in the mind without having the Spirit in the heart, but it is never possible to have the Spirit apart from truth.

In his penetrating study of the holy, Rudolf Otto makes a strong case for the presence in the human mind of something he names the "numinous," by which, apparently, he means a sense that there is in the world a vague, incomprehensible Something, the *Mysterium Tremendum*, the awesome Mystery, surrounding and enfolding the universe. This is an It, an awful Thing, and can never be intellectually conceived, only sensed and felt in the depths of the human spirit. It remains as a permanent religious instinct, a feeling for that unnamed, undiscoverable Presence that "runs quicksilverlike through creation's veins" and sometimes stuns the mind by confronting it with a supernatural, suprarational manifestation of itself. The man thus confronted is brought down and overwhelmed and can only tremble and be silent.

This nonrational dread, this feeling for the uncreated Mystery in the world, is back of all religion. The pure religion of the Bible, no less than the basest animism of the naked tribesman, exists only because this basic instinct is present in human nature. Of course, the difference between the religion of an Isaiah or a Paul and that of the animist is that one has truth and the other has not; he has only the "numinous" instinct. He "feels after" an unknown God, but an Isaiah and a Paul have found the true God through His own self-disclosure in the inspired Scriptures.

The feeling for mystery, even for the Great Mystery, is basic in human nature and indispensable to religious faith, but it is not enough. Because of it men may whisper, "That awful Thing," but they do not cry, "Mine Holy One!" In the Hebrew and Christian Scriptures God carries forward His self-revelation and gives it personality and moral content. This awful Presence is shown to be not a Thing but a moral Being with all the warm qualities of genuine personality. More than this, He is the absolute quintessence of moral excellence, infinitely perfect in righteousness, purity, rectitude, and incomprehensible holiness. And in all this He is uncreated, self-sufficient, and beyond the power of human thought to conceive or human speech to utter.

Through the self-revelation of God in the Scriptures and the illumination of the Holy Spirit the Christian gains everything and loses nothing. To his idea of God there are added the twin concepts of personality and moral character, but there remains the original sense of wonder and fear in the presence of the world-filling Mystery. Today his heart may leap up with the happy cry, "Abba Father, my Lord and my God!" Tomorrow he may kneel with the delighted trembling to admire and adore the High and Lofty One that inhabiteth eternity.

Holy is the way God is. To be holy He does not conform to a standard. He is that standard. He is absolutely holy with an infinite, incomprehensible fullness of purity that is incapable of being other than it is. Because He is holy, His attributes are holy; that is, whatever we think of as belonging to God must be thought of as holy.

God is holy and He has made holiness the moral condition necessary to the health of His universe. Sin's temporary presence in the world only accents this. Whatever is holy is healthy; evil is a moral sickness that must end ultimately in death. The formation of the language itself suggests this, the English word *holy* deriving from the Anglo-Saxon *halig, hal,* meaning, "well, whole."

Since God's first concern for His universe is its moral

health, that is, its holiness, whatever is contrary to this is necessarily under His eternal displeasure. To preserve His creation God must destroy whatever would destroy it. When He arises to put down iniquity and save the world from irreparable moral collapse, He is said to be angry. Every wrathful judgment in the history of the world has been a holy act of preservation. The holiness of God, the wrath of God, and the health of the creation are inseparably united. God's wrath is His utter intolerance of whatever degrades and destroys. He hates iniquity as a mother hates the polio that take the life of her child.

God is holy with an absolute holiness that knows no degrees, and this He cannot impart to His creatures. But there is a relative and contingent holiness which He shares with angels and seraphim in heaven and with redeemed men on earth as their preparation for heaven. This holiness God can and does impart to His children. He shares it with them by imputation and by impartation, and because He has made it available to them through the blood of the Lamb, He requires it of them. To Israel first and later to His Church God spoke, saying, "Be ye holy; for I am holy." He did not say "Be ye as holy as I am holy," for that would be to demand of us absolute holiness, something that belongs to God alone. Before the uncreated fire of God's holiness angels veil their faces. Yea, the heavens are not clean, and the stars are not pure in His sight. No honest man can say "I am holy," but neither is any honest man willing to ignore the solemn words of the inspired writer, "Follow peace with all men, and holiness, without which no man shall see the Lord."

Caught in this dilemma, what are we Christians to do? We must like Moses cover ourselves with faith and humility while we steal a quick look at the God whom no man can see and live. The broken and the contrite heart He will not despise. We must hide our unholiness in the wounds of Christ as Moses hid himself in the cleft of the rock while the glory of God passed by. We must take refuge from God in God. Above all we must believe that God sees us perfect in His Son while He disciplines and chastens and purges us that we may be partakers of His holiness.

By faith and obedience, by constant meditation on the holiness of God, by loving righteousness and hating iniquity, by a growing acquaintance with the Spirit of holiness, we can acclimate ourselves to the fellowship of the saints on earth and prepare ourselves for the eternal companionship of God and the saints above. Thus, as they say when humble believers meet, we will have a heaven to go to heaven in.

> *How dread are Thine eternal years,*
> *O everlasting Lord!*
> *By prostrate spirits day and night*
> *Incessantly adored!*
>
> *How beautiful, how beautiful*
> *The sight of Thee must be,*

Thine endless wisdom, boundless power,
  And awful purity!

Oh how I fear Thee, living God!
  With deepest, tenderest fears,
And worship Thee with trembling hope,
  And penitential tears.

Frederick W. Faber

CHAPTER 22

The Sovereignty of God

Who wouldst not fear Thee, O Lord God of Hosts, most high and most terrible? For Thou art Lord alone. Thou has made heaven and the heaven of heavens, the earth and all things that are therein, and in Thy hand is the soul of every living thing. Thou sittest king upon the flood; yea, Thou sittest king forever. Thou art a great king over all the earth. Thou art clothed with strength; honor and majesty are before Thee. *Amen.*

God's sovereignty is the attribute by which He rules His entire creation, and to be sovereign God must be all-knowing, all-powerful, and absolutely free. The reasons are these:

Were there even one datum of knowledge, however small, unknown to God, His rule would break down at that point. To be Lord over all the creation, He must possess all knowledge. And were God lacking one infinitesimal modicum of power, that lack would end His reign and undo His kingdom; that one stray atom of power would belong to someone else and God would be a limited ruler and hence not sovereign.

Furthermore, His sovereignty requires that He be absolutely free, which means simply that He must be free to do whatever He wills to do anywhere at any time to carry out His eternal purpose in every single detail without interference. Were He less than free He must be less than sovereign.

To grasp the idea of unqualified freedom requires a vigorous effort of the mind. We are not psychologically conditioned to understand freedom except in its imperfect forms. Our concepts of it have been shaped in a world where no absolute freedom exists. Here each natural object is dependent upon many other objects, and that dependence limits its freedom.

Wordsworth at the beginning of his "Prelude" rejoiced that he had escaped the city where he had long been pent up and was "now free, free as a bird to settle where I will." But to be free as a bird is not to be free at all. The naturalist knows that the supposedly free bird actually lives its entire life in a cage made of fears, hungers, and instincts; it is limited by weather conditions, varying air pressures, the local food supply, predatory beasts, and that strangest of all bonds, the irresistible compulsion to stay within the small plot of land and air assigned it by birdland comity. The freest bird is, along with every other created thing, held in constant check by a net of necessity. Only God is free.

God is said to be absolutely free because no one and no thing can hinder Him or compel Him or stop Him. He is able to do as He pleases always, everywhere, forever. To be thus free means also that He must possess universal authority. That He has unlimited power we know from the Scriptures and may deduce from certain other of His attributes. But what about His authority?

Even to discuss the authority of Almighty God seems a bit meaningless, and to question it would be absurd. Can we imagine the Lord God of Hosts having to request permission of anyone or to apply for anything to a higher body? To whom would God go for permission? Who is higher than the Highest? Who is mightier than the Almighty? Whose position antedates that of the Eternal? At whose throne would God kneel? Where is the greater one to whom He must appeal? "Thus saith the LORD the King of Israel, and his redeemer the LORD of hosts; I am the first, and I am the last; and beside me there is no God."

The sovereignty of God is a fact well established in the Scriptures and declared aloud by the logic of truth. But admittedly it raises certain problems which have not to this time been satisfactorily solved. These are mainly two.

The first is the presence in the creation of those things which God cannot approve, such as evil, pain, and death. If God is sovereign He could have prevented their coming into existence. Why did He not do so?

The *Zend-Avesta*, sacred book of Zoroastrianism, loftiest of the great non-Biblical religions, got around this difficulty neatly enough by postulating a theological dualism. There were two Gods, Ormazd and Ahriman, and these between them created the world. The good Ormazd made all good things, and the evil Ahriman made the rest. It was quite simple. Ormazd had no sovereignty to worry about, and apparently did not mind sharing his prerogatives with another.

For the Christian this explanation will not do, for it flatly contradicts the truth taught so emphatically throughout the whole Bible, that there is one God and that He alone created the heaven and the earth and all the things that are therein. God's attributes are such as to make impossible the existence of another God. The Christian admits that he does not have the final answer to the riddle of permitted evil. But he knows what that answer is not. And he knows that the *Zend-Avesta* does not have it either.

While a complete explanation of the origin of sin eludes us, there are a few things we do know. In His sovereign wisdom God has permitted evil to exist in carefully restricted areas of His creation, a kind of fugitive outlaw whose activities are temporary and limited in scope. In doing this God has acted according to His infinite wisdom and goodness. More than that no one knows at present; and more than that no one needs to know. The name of God is sufficient guarantee of the perfection of His works.

Another real problem created by the doctrine of the divine sovereignty has to do with the will of man. If God rules His universe by His sovereign decrees, how is it possible for man to exercise free choice? And if he cannot exercise freedom of choice, how can he be held responsible for his conduct? Is he not a mere puppet whose actions are determined by a behind-the-scenes God who pulls the strings as it pleases Him?

The attempt to answer these questions has divided the Christian church neatly into two camps which have borne the names of two distinguished theologians, Jacobus Arminius and John Calvin. Most Christians are content to get into one camp or the other and deny either sovereignty to God or free will to man. It appears possible, however, to reconcile these two positions without doing violence to either, although the effort that follows may prove deficient to partisans of one camp or the other.

Here is my view: God sovereignly decreed that man should be free to exercise moral choice, and man from the beginning has fulfilled that decree by making his choice between good and evil. When he chooses to do evil, he does not thereby countervail the sovereign will of God but fulfills it, inasmuch as the eternal decree decided not which choice the man should make but that he should be free to make it. If in His absolute freedom God has willed to give man limited freedom, who is there to stay His hand or say, "What doest thou?" Man's will is free because God is sovereign. A God less than sovereign could not bestow moral freedom upon His creatures. He would be afraid to do so.

Perhaps a homely illustration might help us to understand. An ocean liner leaves New York bound for Liverpool. Its destination has been determined by proper authorities. Nothing can change it. This is at least a faint picture of sovereignty.

On board the liner are several scores of passengers. These are not in chains, neither are their activities determined for them by decree. They are completely free to move about as they will. They eat, sleep, play, lounge about on the deck, read, talk, altogether as they please; but all the while the great liner is carrying them steadily onward toward a predetermined port.

Both freedom and sovereignty are present here and they do not contradict each other. So it is, I believe, with man's freedom and the sovereignty of God. The mighty liner of God's sovereign design keeps its steady course over the sea of history. God moves undisturbed and unhindered toward the fulfillment of those eternal purposes which He purposed in Christ Jesus before the world began. We do not know all that is included in those purposes, but enough has been disclosed to furnish us with a broad outline of things to come and to give us good hope and firm assurance of future well-being.

We know that God will fulfill every promise made to the prophets; we know that sinners will some day be cleansed out of the earth; we know that a ransomed company will enter into the joy of God and that the righteous will shine forth in the kingdom of their Father; we know that God's perfections will yet receive universal acclamation, that all created intelligences will own Jesus Christ Lord to the glory of God the Father, that the present imperfect order will be done away, and a new heaven and a new earth be established forever.

Toward all this God is moving with infinite wisdom and perfect precision of action. No one can dissuade Him from His purposes; nothing turn Him aside from His plans. Since He is omniscient, there can be no unforeseen circumstances, no accidents. As He is sovereign, there can be no countermanded orders, no breakdown in authority; and as He is omnipotent, there can be no want of power to achieve His chosen ends. God is sufficient unto Himself for all these things.

In the meanwhile things are not as smooth as this quick outline might suggest. The mystery of iniquity doth already work. Within the broad field of God's sovereign, permissive will the deadly conflict of good with evil continues with increasing fury. God will yet have His way in the whirlwind and the storm, but the storm and the whirlwind are here, and as responsible beings we must make our choice in the present moral situation.

Certain things have been decreed by the free determination of God, and one of these is the law of choice and consequences. God has decreed that all who willingly commit themselves to His Son Jesus Christ in the obedience of faith shall receive eternal life and become sons of God. He has also decreed that all who love darkness and continue in rebellion against the high authority of heaven shall remain in a state of spiritual alienation and suffer eternal death at last.

Reducing the whole matter to individual terms, we arrive at some vital and highly personal conclusions. In the moral conflict now raging around us whoever is on God's side is on the winning side and cannot lose; whoever is on the other side is on the losing side and cannot win. Here there is no chance, no gamble. There is freedom to choose which side we shall be on but no freedom to negotiate the results of the choice once it is made. By the mercy of God we may repent a wrong choice and alter the consequences by making a new and right choice. Beyond that we cannot go.

The whole matter of moral choice centers around Jesus Christ. Christ stated it plainly: "He that is not with me is against me," and "No man cometh unto the Father, but by me." The gospel message embodies three distinct elements: an announcement, a command, and a call. It announces the good news of redemption accomplished in mercy; it commands all men everywhere to repent, and it calls all men to surrender to the terms of grace by believing in Jesus Christ as Lord and Saviour.

We must all choose whether we will obey the gospel or turn away in unbelief and reject its authority. Our choice is our own, but the consequences of the choice have already been determined by the sovereign will of God, and from this there is no appeal.

The Lord descended from above,
　　And bowed the heavens most high,
And underneath His feet He cast
　　The darkness of the sky.

On cherubim and seraphim
　　Full royally He rode,
And on the wings of mighty winds
　　Came flying all abroad.

He sat serene upon the floods,
　　Their fury to restrain;
And He, as sovereign Lord and King,
　　For evermore shall reign.

Psalm paraphrase,
by Thomas Sternhold

CHAPTER 23

The Open Secret

When viewed from the perspective of eternity, the most critical need of this hour may well be that the Church should be brought back from her long Babylonian captivity and the name of God be glorified in her again as of old. Yet we must not think of the Church as an anonymous body, a mystical religious abstraction. We Christians are the Church and whatever we do is what the Church is doing. The matter, therefore, is for each of us a personal one. Any forward step in the Church must begin with the individual.

What can we plain Christians do to bring back the departed glory? Is there some secret we may learn? Is there a formula for personal revival we can apply to the present situation, to our own situation? The answer to these questions is yes.

Yet the answer may easily disappoint some persons, for it is anything but profound. I bring no esoteric cryptogram, no mystic code to be painfully deciphered. I appeal to no hidden law of the unconscious, no occult knowledge meant only for the few. The secret is an open one which the wayfaring man may read. It is simply the old and ever-new counsel: Acquaint thyself with God. To regain her lost power the Church must see heaven opened and have a transforming vision of God.

But the God we must see is not the utilitarian God who is having such a run of popularity today, whose chief claim to men's attention is His ability to bring them success in their various undertakings and who for that reason is being cajoled and flattered by everyone who wants a favor. The God we must learn to know is the Majesty in the heavens, God the Father Almighty, Maker of heaven and earth, the only wise God our Saviour. He it is that sitteth upon the circle of the earth, who stretched out the heavens as a curtain and spreadeth them out as a tent to dwell in, who bringeth out His starry host by number and calleth them all by name through the greatness of His power, who seeth the works of man as vanity, who putteth no confidence in princes and asks no counsel of kings.

Knowledge of such a Being cannot be gained by study alone. It comes by a wisdom the natural man knows nothing of, neither can know, because it is spiritually discerned. To know God is at once the easiest and the most difficult thing in the world. It is easy because the knowledge is not won by hard mental toil, but is something freely given. As sunlight falls free on the open field, so the knowledge of the holy God is a free gift to men who are open to receive it. But this knowledge is difficult because there are conditions to be met and the obstinate nature of fallen man does not take kindly to them.

Let me present a brief summary of these conditions as taught by the Bible and repeated through the centuries by the holiest, sweetest saints the world has ever known:

First, we must forsake our sins. The belief that a holy God cannot be known by men of confirmed evil lives is not new to the Christian religion. The Hebrew book, *The Wisdom of Solomon*, which antedates Christianity by many years, has the following passage: "Love righteousness, ye that be judges of the earth: think of the Lord with a good heart, and in simplicity of heart seek him. For he will be found of them that tempt him not; and showeth himself unto such as do not distrust him. For froward thoughts separate from God: and his power, when it is tried, reproveth the unwise. For unto a malicious soul wisdom shall not enter; nor dwell in the body that is subject to sin. For the holy spirit of discipline will flee deceit, and remove from thoughts that are without understanding, and will not abide when unrighteousness cometh in." This same thought is found in various sayings throughout the inspired Scriptures, the best known probably being the words of Christ, "Blessed are the pure in heart: for they shall see God."

Second, there must be an utter committal of the whole life to Christ in faith. This is what it means to "believe in Christ." It involves a volitional and emotional attachment to Him accompanied by a firm purpose to obey Him in all things. This requires that we keep His commandments, carry our cross, and love God and our fellow men.

Third, there must be a reckoning of ourselves to have died unto sin and to be alive unto God in Christ Jesus, followed by a throwing open of the entire personality to the inflow of the Holy Spirit. Then we must practice whatever self-discipline is required to walk in the Spirit, and trample under our feet the lusts of the flesh.

Fourth, we must boldly repudiate the cheap values of the fallen world and become completely detached in spirit from everything that unbelieving men set their hearts upon, allowing ourselves only the simplest enjoyments of nature which God has bestowed alike upon the just and the unjust.

Fifth, we must practice the art of long and loving meditation upon the majesty of God. This will take some effort, for the concept of majesty has all but disappeared from the human race. The focal point of man's interest is now himself. Humanism in its various forms has displaced theology as the key to the understanding of life. When the nineteenth-century poet Swinburne wrote, "Glory to Man in the highest! for man is the master of things," he gave to the modern world its new Te Deum. All this must be reversed by a deliberate act of the will and kept so by a patient effort of the mind.

God is a Person and can be known in increasing degrees of intimate acquaintance as we prepare our hearts for the wonder. It may be necessary for us to alter our former beliefs about God as the glory that gilds the Sacred Scriptures dawns over our interior lives. We may also need to break quietly and graciously with the lifeless textualism that prevails among the gospel churches, and to protest the frivolous character of much that passes for Christianity among us. By this we may for the time lose friends and gain a passing reputation for being holier-than-thou; but no man who permits the expectation of unpleasant consequences to influence him in a matter like this is fit for the kingdom of God.

Sixth, as the knowledge of God becomes more wonderful, greater service to our fellow men will become for us imperative. This blessed knowledge is not given to be enjoyed selfishly. The more perfectly we know God the more we will feel the desire to translate the new-found knowledge into deeds of mercy toward suffering humanity. The God who gave all to us will continue to give all *through* us as we come to know Him better.

Thus far we have considered the individual's personal relation to God, but like the ointment of a man's right hand, which by its fragrance "betrayeth itself," any intensified knowledge of God will soon begin to affect those around us in the Christian community. And we must seek purposefully to share our increasing light with the fellow members of the household of God.

This we can best do by keeping the majesty of God in full focus in all our public services. Not only our private prayers should be filled with God, but our witnessing, our singing, our preaching, our writing should center around the Person of our holy, holy Lord and extol continually the greatness of His dignity and power. There is a glorified Man on the right hand of the Majesty in heaven faithfully representing us there. We are left for a season among men; let us faithfully represent Him here.

NOTES

1. Nicholas of Cusa, *The Vision of God*. E. P. Dutton & Sons, New York, 1928. p. 60.

2. Ibid. pp. 58–59.

3. Richard Rolle, *The Amending of Life*. John M. Watkins, London, 1922. pp. 83–84.

4. *The Cloud of Unknowing*. John M. Watkins, London, 1946.

5. Michael de Molinos, *The Spiritual Guide*. Methune & Co., Ltd., London, sixth edition, 1950. p. 56.

6. Ibid. pp. 56–57.

7. Julian of Norwich, *Revelations of Divine Love*. Methune & Co., Ltd., London, seventh edition, 1920. pp. 14–15.

8. Thomas Traherne, *Centuries of Meditations*. P. J. and A. E. Dobell, London, 1948. p. 6.

9. The Athanasian Creed.

10. Thomas Carlyle, *Heroes and Hero Worship*. Henry Altemus Co., Philadelphia. pp. 14–15.

11. Michael de Molinos, *op. cit.* p. 58.

12. St. Anselm, *Proslogium*. Open Court Publishing Co., LaSalle, Ill., 1903. p. 6.

13. Novatian, *On the Trinity*. Macmillan Co., New York, 1919. p. 25.

14. Michael de Molinos, *op. cit.* p. 58.

15. Julian of Norwich, *op. cit.* p. 27.

16. Nicholas of Cusa, *op. cit.* pp. 48, 49, 50.

17. Tennyson, *In Memoriam*.

18. St. Anselm, *op. cit.* p. 3.

19. Novatian, *op. cit.* pp. 26–27.

20. St. Anselm, *op. cit.* pp. 24–25.

21. Rudolf Otto, *The Idea of the Holy*. Oxford University Press, New York, 1958. p. 24.

22. Johann Peter Eckermann, *Conversations with Eckermann*. M. Walter Dunn, Washington and London, 1901. p. 45.

23. *A New Dictionary of Quotations*, Selected and Edited by H. L. Mencken. Alfred A. Knopf, New York, 1942. pp. 462–463.

24. Nicholas of Cusa, *op. cit.* p. 12.

25. St. Anselm, *op. cit.* p. 14.

26. Julian of Norwich, *op. cit.* p. 58.

SOURCES OF BIBLICAL QUOTATIONS

Page	Line	Source
70	15–16	Phil. 2:13
73	2	Ps. 90:2
73	24–25	Rev. 4:8
74	23–24	Isa. 46:9–10
75	16–17	Ps. 90:1
75	23–24	Ps. 90:12
76	3	Eccles. 3:11 ASV
77	5–7	Tim. 1:10
86	8–9	Rom. 5:20
86	16	John 3:16
93	1–4	II Cor. 3:18
94	4–5	Col. 3:10
94	17–18	Heb. 10:9
96	24–25	Matt. 11:28
97	2–3	Mal. 3:6
99	13–17	Isa. 40:13–14
99–100	10, 1	Rom. 11:34
100	25–28	Isa. 40:28
101	1	Mal. 3:6
101	5	Titus 1:2
101	6	Luke 1:37
102	7–8	I Cor. 2:11
102	18–19	Ps. 90:8
102	21–25	Ps. 139:7, 11–12
103	8–11	Isa. 54:10
105–106	14–17, 1–2	Dan. 2:20–22
106	3–5	Rev. 7:12
106	13	Ps. 147:5
106	24	I Tim. 1:17
108	14–16	Gen. 1:31
109	5–7	Rom. 8:20
109–110	28, 1–2	John 20:29
110	8–9	I Tim. 3:16
110–111	28, 1–3	Eccles. 3:14
111	24–28	Isa. 42:16
112	9–14	Isa. 45:2–3

Page	Line	Source
112	23–24	Luke 24:1
115	14	Rev. 19:6
116	14	Ps. 62:11
118	15	Exod. 3:14
118	17–18	Luke 11:2
122	2–3	Isa. 57:15
124	21–22	Ps. 36:1
125	15–17	Isa. 6:5
125–126	20–28, 1–5	Dan. 10:6–9
126	9–10	Acts 9:6
126	16–17	Prov. 14:27
131	15–16	Heb. 11:6
131	17	John 14:1
133	4	II Cor. 6:10
144	18–19	John 14:9
148	1–4	Gen. 18:25
148	7–9	Ps. 97:2
148	13–17	Ps. 94:1–3
148	24–25	Dan. 9:7
149	3–8	Rev. 15:3–4
152	11–13	John 1:9
158	13–15	Rom. 10:2
158	18–20	Heb. 4:2
162	22–28	Eph. 1:5–7
163	3–4	John 1:17
164	2–3	Gen. 6:8
164	4	Exod. 33:17
165	15–16	Rom. 5:20
167	14	I John 4:8
170	4	I John 4:18
171	17	John 15:14
172	5–7	John 15:13
173	3–4	Ps. 104:31
173	14–17	Zeph. 3:17
173	19–22	Job 38:4, 7
174–175	26–27, 1	Rom. 5:8

Page	Line	Source
175	1–2	John 3:16
175	7–10	I John 3:17
178	5–8	Isa. 6:5
179	15–16	Rom. 10:17
180	23	Hab. 1:12
182	22	I Pet. 1:16
183	1–2	Heb. 12–14
187	16–18	Isa. 44:6
189	25	Dan. 4:35
192	16–17	Matt. 12:30
192	17–18	John 14:6
197	23–24	Matt. 5:8

The Pursuit
of God

FOREWORD

T*he Pursuit of God* was the fruit of A. W. Tozer's spiritual exploration into the essence of God's nature. What resulted from the efforts of this obscure pastor from the South side of Chicago has left a profound mark on the evangelical church. The 1948 publication of this book thrust Tozer into a respected position of spiritual leadership that he maintained for the remainder of his life. Tozer's ministry became a spiritual oasis for those of the "fellowship of the burning heart," to use a phrase he delighted in.

I was fifteen when I first discovered *The Pursuit of God*. I have read it twenty times or more. Each time I read it my soul is ministered to in a fresh way. The discovery of *The Pursuit of God* also started me on a journey into the life of this intriguing man.

Tozer's walk with God was a priority with him and he allowed nothing to interfere. It was the basis of his attraction to the Christian mystics. Their absorption in the daily practice of the presence of God was a stimulus for him and he delighted in their spiritual fellowship. He could forgive anyone almost anything if he discovered they had pure intent toward God.

Dr. Tozer's prayer life was quite remarkable. His regular habit was to sprawl on his study floor, facedown, and worship God. Often, according to his own testimony, he would lie in silent, wordless worship of God, usually oblivious to his surroundings. Such prayer and worship marked the foundation of his study and preparation for public ministry.

The desire to worship God and to inspire others to a deeper awareness of God are clearly evident in *The Pursuit of God*. For the person thirsting for the things of God without distracting embellishments, this book will become a faithful companion. There are some books that can be enjoyed with one reading, others are enhanced by many readings. *The Pursuit of God* is one of the latter.

REV. JAMES L. SNYDER
March 1993

TOZER'S LEGACY

Quietness of soul, the fruit of truly seeking God, is seldom found in twentieth-century Christians. Far too many have come to accept turbulence of soul as the norm and have ceased to seek God with their whole hearts. Some have fled the cities to cloistered retreats in the hope of finding this quietness, only to discover their hearts still restless. One unusual American minister who found for his own soul the secret of quietness and articulated his discovery to the Christian community was A. W. Tozer. He came upon this closer walk with God in the bustle and noise of the city of Chicago. Tozer never enjoyed the luxury of a cloistered life. Born in a poor home in the hills of western Pennsylvania, he had known hardship from as long as he could remember. Forced by his home situation to forfeit an education, Tozer entered the ministry without either high school or college training.

A. W. Tozer came to Christ at the age of seventeen, after hearing a lay preacher speaking at a street meeting in Akron, Ohio. He joined the Methodist church and became an active witness for Christ. A dingy corner of the basement of the family home became his private prayer chamber. There, at the very beginning of his Christian life, Tozer established what was to be a lifelong practice of waiting on God.

Having become a lay preacher, Tozer found himself in disfavor with his church and decided to join with The Christian and Missionary Alliance where he found opportunity to use his gifts. His preaching ability soon made a place for him. In 1919 the district superintendent assigned Tozer to pastor the Alliance church in Nutter Fort, West Virginia. After subsequent pastorates in Toledo and Indianapolis, he accepted a call in 1928 to Southside Alliance Church in Chicago, Illinois. His ministry in that congregation continued for thirty-one years. Avenue Road Alliance Church in Toronto, Ontario, Canada, was the last pastorate he served.

For many of the years he pastored the Chicago congregation, Tozer also preached on the Moody Bible Institute radio station WMBI. Thousands of lay people and pastors listened regularly to his rich exposition of Bible truth given on "Talks from a Pastor's Study."

His literary skills were soon recognized by his own denomination and eventually by the whole evangelical church community. In 1950 the General Council of The Christian and Missionary Alliance elected him editor of *The Alliance Witness* (now *Alliance Life*), a position he held until his death.

Aiden W. Tozer educated himself by years of diligent study and a constant prayerful seeking of the mind of God. With Tozer, seeking truth and seeking God were one and the same thing. For example, when he felt he needed an understanding of the great English works of Shakespeare, he read them through on his knees, asking God to help him understand their meaning. This procedure was typical of his method of self-education.

With no teacher but the Holy Spirit and good books, A. W. Tozer became a theologian, a scholar and a master craftsman in the use of the English language. There are not many quotes in his writings, for he had so assimilated all he had read that he could freely write in simple but attractive language the principles of truth he had discovered across these years of anointed study. The evangelical mystics were his favorite study. The longings of his own heart were satisfied by what he learned from the men and women who kept the light of spiritual reality burning in a time when apostasy and spiritual darkness seemed almost universal.

Much of the strong meat in *The Pursuit of God* came out of the crucible of Tozer's own personal experience. The chapter titled "The Blessedness of Possessing Nothing" reflected his desperate struggle to turn his only daughter over to God. The battle for him was intense and devastating, but when full surrender came, a new and glorious release became his. He had learned to know God in the school of practical experience.

Since the first edition of *The Pursuit of God* was published in 1948, millions of copies have been printed and distributed in several languages around the world. While all of Tozer's writings are well received, *The Pursuit of God* continues to be the most popular.

The writing of this book was for A. W. Tozer a deep spiritual experience. Dr. David J. Fant Jr., one of his biographers, describes the process:

> Tozer literally wrote *The Pursuit of God* [while] on his knees. Perhaps that explains its power and the blessing that has rested on it.

Perhaps the continued usefulness of this book can be attributed to the writer's great spiritual discovery that to seek God does not narrow one's life, but brings it, rather, to the level of highest possible fulfillment.

A. W. Tozer was something of a twentieth-century prophet calling the modern church back to the practice of godliness and to that level of spiritual reality enjoyed by serious seekers after God from the days of the apostles. In the legacy of his writings, none speaks more clearly to our deepest heart need than *The Pursuit of God*.

PREFACE

In this hour of all-but-universal darkness, one cheering gleam appears: Within the fold of conservative Christianity there are to be found increasing numbers of persons whose religious lives are marked by a growing hunger after God Himself. They are eager for spiritual realities and will not be put off with words, nor will they be content with correct "interpretations" of truth. They are athirst for God, and they will not be satisfied till they have drunk deep at the Fountain of Living Water.

This is the only real harbinger of revival that I have been able to detect anywhere on the religious horizon. It may be the cloud the size of a man's hand for which a few saints here and there have been looking. It can result in a resurrection of life for many souls and a recapture of that radiant wonder that should accompany faith in Christ, that wonder that has all but fled the church of God in our day.

But this hunger must be recognized by our religious leaders. Current evangelicalism has (to change the figure) laid the altar and divided the sacrifice into parts, but now seems satisfied to count the stones and rearrange the pieces with never a care that there is not a sign of fire upon the top of lofty Carmel. But God be thanked that there are a few who care. They are those who, while they love the altar and delight in the sacrifice, are yet unable to reconcile themselves to the continued absence of fire. They desire God above all. They are athirst to taste for themselves the "piercing sweetness" of the love of Christ about whom all the holy prophets did write and the psalmists did sing.

There is today no lack of Bible teachers to set forth correctly the principles of the doctrines of Christ, but too many of these seem satisfied to teach the fundamentals of the faith year after year, strangely unaware that there is in their ministry no manifest Presence, nor anything unusual in their personal lives. They minister constantly to believers who feel within their breasts a longing which their teaching simply does not satisfy.

I trust I speak in charity, but the lack in our pulpits is real. Milton's terrible sentence applies to our day as accurately as it did to his: "The hungry sheep look up, and are not fed." It is a solemn thing, and no small scandal in the kingdom, to see God's children starving while actually seated at the Father's table. The truth of Wesley's words is established before our eyes:

> Orthodoxy, or right opinion, is, at best, a very slender part of religion. Though right tempers cannot subsist without right opinions, yet right opinions may subsist without right tempers. There may be a right opinion of God without either love or one right temper toward Him. Satan is a proof of this.

Thanks to our splendid Bible societies and to other effective agencies for dissemination of the Word, there are today many millions of people who hold "right opinions," probably more than ever before in the history of the church. Yet I wonder if there was ever a time when true spiritual worship was at a lower ebb. To great sections of the church the art of worship has been lost entirely, and in its place has come that strange and foreign thing called the "program." This word has been borrowed from the stage and applied with sad wisdom to the type of public service which now passes for worship among us.

Sound Bible exposition is an imperative *must* in the church of the Living God. Without it no church can be a New Testament church in any strict meaning of that term. But exposition may be carried on in such a way as to leave the hearers devoid of any true spiritual nourishment whatever. For it is not mere words that nourish the soul, but God Himself, and unless and until the hearers find God in personal experience they are not the better for having heard the truth. The Bible is not an end in itself, but a means to bring men to an intimate and satisfying knowledge of God, that they may enter into Him, that they may delight in His Presence, may taste and know the inner sweetness of the very God Himself in the core and center of their hearts.

This book is a modest attempt to aid God's hungry children so to find Him. Nothing here is new except in the sense that it is a discovery which my own heart has made of spiritual realities most delightful and wonderful to me. Others before me have gone much farther into these holy mysteries than I have done, but if my fire is not large it is yet real, and there may be those who can light their candle at its flame.

A. W. TOZER
Chicago, Illinois
June 16, 1948

—————————•—————————

CHAPTER 1

Following Hard
after God

My soul followeth hard after thee:
thy right hand upholdeth me.

PSALM 63:8

C hristian theology teaches the doctrine of prevenient grace, which, briefly stated, means that before a man can seek God, God must first have sought the man.

Before a sinful man can think a right thought of God, there must have been a work of enlightenment done within him. Imperfect it may be, but a true work none-theless, and the secret cause of all desiring and seeking and praying which may follow.

We pursue God because, and only because, He has first put an urge within us that spurs us to the pursuit. "No man can come to me," said our Lord, "except the Father which hath sent me draw him" (John 6:44), and it is by this prevenient *drawing* that God takes from us every vestige of credit for the act of coming. The impulse to pursue God originates with God, but the outworking of that impulse is our following hard after Him. All the time we are pursuing Him we are already in His hand: "Thy right hand upholdeth me."

In this divine "upholding" and human "following" there is no contradiction. All is of God, for as von Hügel teaches, *God is always previous.* In practice, however (that is, where God's previous working meets man's present response), man must pursue God. On our part there must be positive reciprocation if this secret drawing of God is to eventuate in identifiable experience of the Divine. In the warm language of personal feeling, this is stated in Psalm 42:1–2: "As the hart panteth after the water brooks, so panteth my soul after thee, O God. My soul thirsteth for God, for the living God: when shall I come and appear before God?" This is deep calling unto deep, and the longing heart will understand it.

The doctrine of justification by faith—a biblical truth, and a blessed relief from sterile legalism and unavailing self-effort—has in our time fallen into evil company and been interpreted by many in such a manner as actually to bar men from the knowledge of God. The whole transaction of religious conversion has been made mechanical and spiritless. Faith may now be exercised without a jar to the moral life and without embarrassment to the Adamic ego. Christ may be "received" without creating any special love for Him in the soul of the receiver. The man is "saved," but he is not hungry nor thirsty after God. In fact, he is specifically taught to be satisfied and is encouraged to be content with little.

The modern scientist has lost God amid the wonders of His world; we Christians are in real danger of losing God amid the wonders of His Word. We have almost forgotten that God is a person and, as such, can be cultivated as any person can. It is inherent in personality to be able to know other personalities, but full knowledge of one personality by another cannot be achieved in one encounter. It is only after long and loving mental intercourse that the full possibilities of both can be explored.

All social intercourse between human beings is a response of personality to personality, grading upward from the most casual brush between man and man to the fullest, most intimate communion of which the human soul is capable. Religion, so far as it is genuine, is in essence the response of created personalities to the creating personality, God. "This is life eternal, that they might know thee the only true God, and Jesus Christ, whom thou hast sent" (John 17:3).

God is a person, and in the deep of His mighty nature He thinks, wills, enjoys, feels, loves, desires and suffers as any other person may. In making Himself known to us He stays by the familiar pattern of personality. He communicates with us through the avenues of our minds, our wills and our emotions. The continuous and unembarrassed interchange of love and thought between God and the soul of the redeemed man is the throbbing heart of New Testament religion.

This intercourse between God and the soul is known to us in conscious personal awareness. It is personal: it does not come through the body of believers, as such, but is known to the individual, and to the body through the individuals who compose it. It is conscious: it does not stay below the threshold of consciousness and work there unknown to the soul (as, for instance, infant baptism is thought by some to do), but comes within the field of awareness where the man can know it as he knows any other fact of experience.

You and I are in little (our sins excepted) what God is in large. Being made in His image we have within us the capacity to know Him. In our sins we lack only the power. The moment the Spirit has quickened us to life in regeneration our whole being senses its kinship to God and leaps up in joyous recognition. That is the heavenly birth without which we cannot see the kingdom of God. It is, however, not an end but an inception, for now begins the glorious pursuit, the heart's happy exploration of the infinite riches of the Godhead. That is where we begin, I say, but where we stop no man has yet discovered, for there is in the awful and mysterious depths of the Triune God neither limit nor end.

Shoreless Ocean, who can sound Thee?
Thine own eternity is round Thee, Majesty divine!

To have found God and still to pursue Him is the soul's paradox of love, scorned indeed by the too easily satisfied religionist, but justified in happy experience by the children of the burning heart. St. Bernard stated this holy paradox in a musical quatrain that will be instantly understood by every worshiping soul:

We taste Thee, O Thou Living Bread
And long to feast upon Thee still:
We drink of Thee, the Fountainhead,
And thirst our souls from Thee to fill.

Come near to the holy men and women of the past and you will soon feel the heat of their desire after God. They mourned for Him, they prayed and wrestled and sought for Him day and night, in season and out, and when they had found Him the finding was all the sweeter for the long seeking. Moses used the fact that he knew God as an argument for knowing Him better. "Now therefore, I pray thee, if I have found grace in thy sight, shew me now thy way, that I may know thee, that I may find grace in thy sight" (Exodus 33:13); and from there he rose to make the daring request, "I beseech thee, shew me thy glory" (33:18). God was frankly pleased by this display of ardor, and the next day called Moses into the mount, and there in solemn procession made all His glory pass before him.

David's life was a torrent of spiritual desire, and his psalms ring with the cry of the seeker and the glad shout of the finder. Paul confessed the mainspring of his life to be his burning desire after Christ. "That I may know him" (Philippians 3:10), was the goal of his heart, and to this he sacrificed everything. "Yea doubtless, and I count all things but loss for the excellency of the knowledge of Christ Jesus my Lord: for whom I have suffered the loss of all things, and do count them but dung, that I may win Christ" (3:8).

Hymnody is sweet with the longing after God, the God whom, while the singer seeks, he knows he has already found. "His track I see and I'll pursue," sang our fathers only a short generation ago, but that song is heard no more in the great congregation. How tragic that we in this dark day have had our seeking done for us by our teachers. Everything is made to center upon the initial act of "accepting" Christ (a term, incidentally, which is not found in the Bible) and we are not expected thereafter to crave any further revelation of God to our souls. We have been snared in the coils of a spurious logic which insists that if we have found Him, we need no more seek Him. This is set before us as the last word in orthodoxy, and it is taken for granted that no Bible-taught Christian ever believed otherwise. Thus the whole testimony of the worshiping, seeking, singing church on that subject is crisply set aside. The experiential heart-theology of a grand army of fragrant saints is rejected in favor of a smug interpretation of Scripture which would certainly have sounded strange to an Augustine, a Rutherford, or a Brainerd.

In the midst of this great chill there are some, I rejoice to acknowledge, who will not be content with shallow logic. They will admit the force of the argument, and then turn away with tears to hunt some lonely place and pray, "O God, show me Thy glory." They want to taste, to touch with their hearts, to see with their inner eyes the wonder that is God.

I want deliberately to encourage this mighty longing after God. The lack of it has brought us to our present low estate. The stiff and wooden quality about our religious lives is a result of our lack of holy desire. Complacency is a deadly foe of all spiritual growth. Acute desire must be present or there will be no manifestation of Christ to His people. He waits to be wanted. Too bad that with many of us He waits so long, so very long, in vain. Every age has its own characteristics. Right now we are in an age of religious complexity. The simplicity which is in Christ is rarely found among us. In its stead are programs, methods, organizations and a world of nervous activities which occupy time and attention but can never satisfy the longing of the heart. The shallowness of our inner experience, the hollowness of our worship and that servile imitation of the world which marks our promotional methods all testify that we, in this day, know God only imperfectly, and the peace of God scarcely at all.

If we would find God amid all the religious externals, we must first determine to find Him, and then proceed in the way of simplicity. Now, as always, God discovers Himself to "babes" and hides Himself in thick darkness from the wise and the prudent. We must simplify our approach to Him. We must strip down to essentials (and they will be found to be blessedly few). We must put away all effort to impress, and come with the guileless candor of childhood. If we do this, without doubt God will quickly respond.

When religion has said its last word, there is little that we need other than God Himself. The evil habit of seeking *God-and* effectively prevents us from finding God in full revelation. In the *and* lies our great woe. If we omit the *and* we shall soon find God, and in Him we shall find that for which we have all our lives been secretly longing.

We need not fear that in seeking God only we may narrow our lives or restrict the motions of our expanding hearts. The opposite is true. We can well afford to make God our All, to concentrate, to sacrifice the many for the One.

The author of the quaint old English classic *The Cloud of Unknowing* teaches us how to do this.

Lift up thine heart unto God with a meek stirring of love; and mean Himself, and none of His goods. And thereto, look thee loath to think on aught but God

Himself. So that nought work in thy wit, nor in thy will, but only God Himself. This is the work of the soul that most pleaseth God.

Again, he recommends that in prayer we practice a further stripping down of everything, even of our theology. "For it sufficeth enough, a naked intent direct unto God without any other cause than Himself." Yet underneath all his thinking lay the broad foundation of New Testament truth, for he explains that by "Himself" he means "God that made thee, and bought thee, and that graciously called thee, to thy degree." And he is all for simplicity: If we would have religion "lapped and folden in one word, for that thou shouldest have better hold thereupon, take thee but a little word of one syllable: for so it is better than of two, for even the shorter it is the better it accordeth with the work of the Spirit. And such a word is this word GOD or this word LOVE."

When the Lord divided Canaan among the tribes of Israel, Levi received no share of the land. God said to him simply, "I am thy part and thine inheritance," and by those words made him richer than all his brethren, richer than all the kings and rajas who have ever lived in the world. And there is a spiritual principle here, a principle still valid for every priest of the Most High God.

The man who has God for his treasure has all things in One. Many ordinary treasures may be denied him, or if he is allowed to have them, the enjoyment of them will be so tempered that they will never be necessary to his happiness. Or if he must see them go, one after one, he will scarcely feel a sense of loss, for having the Source of all things he has in One all satisfaction, all pleasure, all delight. Whatever he may lose he has actually lost nothing, for he now has it all in One, and he has it purely, legitimately and forever.

O God, I have tasted Thy goodness, and it has both satisfied me and made me thirsty for more. I am painfully conscious of my need of further grace.

I am ashamed of my lack of desire. O God, the Triune God, I want to want Thee; I long to be filled with longing; I thirst to be made more thirsty still.

Show me Thy glory, I pray Thee, that so I may know Thee indeed. Begin in mercy a new work of love within me. Say to my soul, "Rise up, my love, my fair one, and come away." Then give me grace to rise and follow Thee up from this misty lowland where I have wandered so long.

In Jesus' name
Amen.

———————•———————

CHAPTER 2

The Blessedness of Possessing Nothing

Blessed are the poor in spirit:
for theirs is the kingdom of heaven.

MATTHEW 5:3

B efore the Lord God made man upon the earth, He first prepared for him a world of useful and pleasant things for his sustenance and delight. In the Genesis account of the creation these are simply "things." They were made for man's use, but they were meant always to be external to the man and subservient to him. In the deep heart of the man was a shrine where none but God was worthy to come. Within him was God; without, a thousand gifts which God had showered upon him.

But sin has introduced complications and has made those very gifts of God a potential source of ruin to the soul.

Our woes began when God was forced out of His central shrine and things were allowed to enter. Within the human heart things have taken over. Men have now by nature no peace within their hearts, for God is crowned there no longer, but there in the moral dusk, stubborn and aggressive usurpers fight among themselves for first place on the throne.

This is not a mere metaphor, but an accurate analysis of our real spiritual trouble. There is within the human heart a tough, fibrous root of fallen life whose nature is to possess, always to possess. It covets things with a deep and fierce passion. The pronouns *my* and *mine* look innocent enough in print, but their constant and universal use is significant. They express the real nature of the old Adamic man better than a thousand volumes of theology could do. They are verbal symptoms of our deep disease. The roots of our hearts have grown down into things, and we dare not pull up one rootlet lest we die. Things have become necessary to us, a development never originally intended. God's gifts now take the place of God, and the whole course of nature is upset by the monstrous substitution.

Our Lord referred to this tyranny of things when He said to His disciples,

> *If any man will come after me, let him deny himself, and take up his cross, and follow me. For whosoever will save his life shall lose it: and whosoever*

will lose his life for my sake shall find it.
MATTHEW 16:24–25

Breaking this truth into fragments for our better understanding, it would seem that there is within each of us an enemy which we tolerate at our peril. Jesus called it "life" and "self," or as we would say, the *self-life*. Its chief characteristic is its possessiveness; the words *gain* and *profit* suggest this. To allow this enemy to live is, in the end, to lose everything. To repudiate it and give up all for Christ's sake is to lose nothing at last, but to preserve everything unto life eternal. And possibly also a hint is given here as to the only effective way to destroy this foe: It is by the cross. "Let him take up his cross, and follow me" (see Matthew 16:24).

The way to deeper knowledge of God is through the lonely valleys of soul poverty and abnegation of all things. The blessed ones who possess the kingdom are they who have repudiated every external thing and have rooted from their hearts all sense of possessing. These are the "poor in spirit." They have reached an inward state paralleling the outward circumstances of the common beggar in the streets of Jerusalem. That is what the word *poor* as Christ used it actually means. These blessed poor are no longer slaves to the tyranny of things. They have broken the yoke of the oppressor; and this they have done not by fighting but by surrendering. Though free from all sense of possessing, they yet possess all things. "Theirs is the kingdom of heaven."

Let me exhort you to take this seriously. It is not to be understood as mere Bible teaching to be stored away in the mind along with an inert mass of other doctrines. It is a marker on the road to greener pastures, a path chiseled against the steep sides of the mount of God. We dare not try to bypass it if we would follow on in this holy pursuit. We must ascend a step at a time. If we refuse one step, we bring our progress to an end.

As is frequently true, this New Testament principle of spiritual life finds its best illustration in the Old Testament. In the story of Abraham and Isaac we have a dramatic picture of the surrendered life as well as an excellent commentary on the first Beatitude.

Abraham was old when Isaac was born, old enough to have been his grandfather, and the child became at once the delight and idol of his heart. From the moment he first stooped to take the tiny form awkwardly in his arms, he was an eager love slave of his son. God went out of His way to comment on the strength of this affection. And it is not hard to understand. The baby represented everything sacred to his father's heart: the promises of God, the covenants, the hopes of the years and the long messianic dream. As he watched him grow from babyhood to young manhood, the heart of the old man was knit closer and closer with the life of his son, till at last the relationship bordered upon the perilous. It was then that God stepped in to save both father and son from the consequences of an uncleansed love. "Take now thy son," said God to Abraham, "thine only son Isaac, whom thou lovest, and get thee into the land of Moriah; and offer him there for a burnt offering upon one of the mountains which I will tell thee of" (Genesis 22:2). The sacred writer spares us a close-up of the agony that night on the slopes near Beersheba when the aged man had it out with his God, but respectful imagination may view in awe the bent form wrestling convulsively alone under the stars. Possibly not again until One greater than Abraham wrestled in the garden of Gethsemane did such mortal pain visit a human soul. If only the man himself might have been allowed to die. That would have been a thousand times easier, for he was old now, and to die would have been no great ordeal for one who had walked so long with God. Besides, it would have been a last, sweet pleasure to let his dimming vision rest upon the figure of his stalwart son who would live to carry on the Abrahamic line and fulfill in himself the promises of God made long before in Ur of the Chaldees.

How should he slay the lad! Even if he could get the consent of his wounded and protesting heart, how could he reconcile the act with the promise, "In Isaac shall thy seed be called"? This was Abraham's trial by fire, and he did not fail in the crucible. While the stars still shone like sharp white points above the tent where the sleeping Isaac lay, and long before the gray dawn had begun to lighten the east, the old saint had made up his mind. He would offer his son as God had directed him to do, and then *trust God to raise him from the dead*. This, says the writer to the Hebrews, was the solution his aching heart found sometime in the dark night, and he rose "early in the morning" to carry out the plan. It is beautiful to see that, while he erred as to God's method, he had correctly sensed the secret of His great heart. And the solution accords well with the New Testament Scripture, "Whosoever will lose . . . for my sake shall find" (Matthew 16:25).

God let the suffering old man go through with it up to the point where He knew there would be no retreat, and then forbade him to lay a hand upon the boy. To the wondering patriarch He now says in effect, "It's all right, Abraham. I never intended that you should actually slay the lad. I only wanted to remove him from the temple of your heart that I might reign unchallenged there. I wanted to correct the perversion that existed in your love. Now you may have the boy, sound and well. Take him and go back to your tent. Now I know that thou fearest God, seeing that thou hast not withheld thy son, thine only son, from Me."

Then heaven opened and a voice was heard saying to him,

> *By myself have I sworn, saith the LORD, for because thou hast done this thing, and hast not withheld thy son, thine only son: that in blessing I will bless thee,*

*and in multiplying I will multiply thy seed as the
stars of the heaven, and as the sand which is upon
the sea shore; and thy seed shall possess the gate of his
enemies; and in thy seed shall all the nations of the
earth be blessed; because thou hast obeyed my voice.*

GENESIS 22:16–18

The old man of God lifted his head to respond to the
Voice, and stood there on the mount strong and pure
and grand, a man marked out by the Lord for special
treatment, a friend and favorite of the Most High. Now
he was a man wholly surrendered, a man utterly obedient, a man who possessed nothing. He had concentrated
his all in the person of his dear son and God had taken
it from him. God could have begun out on the margin
of Abraham's life and worked inward to the center. He
chose rather to cut quickly to the heart and have it over
in one sharp act of separation. In dealing thus, He practiced an economy of means and time. It hurt cruelly, but
it was effective.

I have said that Abraham possessed nothing. Yet was
not this poor man rich? Everything he had owned before
was his still to enjoy: sheep, camels, herds, and goods
of every sort. He had also his wife and his friends, and
best of all he had his son Isaac safe by his side. He had
everything, *but he possessed nothing*. There is the spiritual
secret. There is the sweet theology of the heart which can
be learned only in the school of renunciation. The books

on systematic theology overlook this, but the wise will understand.

After that bitter and blessed experience I think the words *my* and *mine* never again had the same meaning for Abraham. The sense of possession which they connote was gone from his heart. Things had been cast out forever. They had now become external to the man. His inner heart was free from them. The world said, "Abraham is rich," but the aged patriarch only smiled. He could not explain it, but he knew that he owned nothing, that his real treasures were inward and eternal.

There can be no doubt that this possessive clinging to things is one of the most harmful habits in the life. Because it is natural, it is rarely recognized for the evil that it is. But its outworkings are tragic.

We are often hindered from giving up our treasures to the Lord out of fear for their safety. This is especially true when those treasures are loved relatives and friends. But we need have no such fears. Our Lord came not to destroy but to save. Everything is safe which we commit to Him, and nothing is really safe which is not so committed.

Our gifts and talents should also be turned over to Him. They should be recognized for what they are, God's loan to us, and should never be considered in any sense our own. We have no more right to claim credit for special abilities than for blue eyes or strong muscles. "For who maketh thee to differ from another? and what hast thou that thou didst not receive?" (1 Corinthians 4:7).

The Christian who is alive enough to know himself even slightly will recognize the symptoms of this possession malady, and will grieve to find them in his own heart. If the longing after God is strong enough within him, he will want to do something about the matter. Now, what should he do?

First of all, he should put away all defense and make no attempt to excuse himself either in his own eyes or before the Lord. Whoever defends himself will have himself for his defense, and he will have no other. But let him come defenseless before the Lord and he will have for his defender no less than God Himself. Let the inquiring Christian trample under foot every slippery trick of his deceitful heart and insist upon frank and open relations with the Lord.

Then he should remember that this is holy business. No careless or casual dealings will suffice. Let him come to God fully determined to be heard. Let him insist that God accept his all, that He take things out of his heart and Himself reign there in power. It may be he will need to become specific, to name things and people by their names one by one. If he will become drastic enough, he can shorten the time of his travail from years to minutes and enter the good land long before his slower brethren who coddle their feelings and insist upon caution in their dealing with God.

Let us never forget that a truth such as this cannot be learned by rote as one would learn the facts of physical science. They must be *experienced* before we can really know them. We must, in our hearts, live through Abraham's harsh and bitter experiences if we would know the blessedness which follows them. The ancient curse will not go out painlessly; the tough old miser within us will not lie down and die in obedience to our command. He must be torn out of our heart like a plant from the soil; he must be extracted in agony and blood like a tooth from the jaw. He must be expelled from our soul by violence, as Christ expelled the money changers from the temple. And we shall need to steel ourselves against his piteous begging, and to recognize it as springing out of self-pity, one of the most reprehensible sins of the human heart.

If we would indeed know God in growing intimacy, we must go this way of renunciation. And if we are set upon the pursuit of God, He will sooner or later bring us to this test. Abraham's testing was, at the time, not known to him as such, yet if he had taken some course other than the one he did, the whole history of the Old Testament would have been different. God would have found his man, no doubt, but the loss to Abraham would have been tragic beyond the telling. So we will be brought one by one to the testing place, and we may never know when we are there. At that testing place there will be no dozen possible choices for us—just one and an alternative —but our whole future will be conditioned by the choice we make.

Father, I want to know Thee, but my cowardly heart fears to give up its toys. I cannot part with them without inward bleeding, and I do not try to hide from Thee the terror of the parting. I come trembling, but I do come. Please root from my heart all those things which I have cherished so long and which have become a very part of my living self, so that Thou mayest enter and dwell there without a rival.

Then shalt Thou make the place of Thy feet glorious.

Then shall my heart have no need of the sun to shine in it, for Thyself wilt be the light of it, and there shall be no night there.

In Jesus' name.

Amen.

———————•———————

CHAPTER 3

Removing the Veil

*Having therefore, brethren, boldness to enter
into the holiest by the blood of Jesus.*

HEBREWS 10:19

Among the famous sayings of the church fathers, none is better known than Augustine's, "Thou hast formed us for Thyself, and our hearts are restless till they find rest in Thee."

The great saint states here in few words the origin and interior history of the human race. God made us for Himself—this is the only explanation that satisfies the heart of a thinking man, whatever his wild reason may say. Should faulty education and perverse reasoning lead a man to conclude otherwise, there is little that any Christian can do for him. For such a man I have no message. My appeal is addressed to those who have been previously taught in secret by the wisdom of God. I speak to thirsty hearts whose longings have been wakened by the touch of God within them, and such as they need no reasoned proof. Their restless hearts furnish all the proof they need.

God formed us for Himself. *The Shorter Catechism,* "Agreed upon by the Reverend Assembly of Divines at Westminster," as the old *New England Primer* has it, asks the ancient questions *what* and *why* and answers them in one short sentence hardly matched in any uninspired work. "*Question:* What is the chief end of man? *Answer:* Man's chief end is to glorify God and enjoy Him forever." With this agree the four and twenty elders who fall on their faces to worship Him that liveth forever and ever, saying, "Thou art worthy, O Lord, to receive glory and honour and power: for thou hast created all things, and for thy pleasure they are and were created" (Revelation 4:11).

God formed us for His pleasure, and so formed us that we, as well as He, can, in divine communion, enjoy the sweet and mysterious mingling of kindred personalities. He meant us to see Him and live with Him and draw our life from His smile. But we have been guilty of that "foul revolt" of which Milton speaks when describing the rebellion of Satan and his hosts. We have broken with God. We have ceased to obey Him or love Him, and in guilt and fear have fled as far as possible from His presence.

Yet, who can flee from His presence when the heaven and the heaven of heavens cannot contain Him? when as the wisdom of Solomon testifies, "the Spirit of the

Lord filleth the world"? The omnipresence of the Lord is one thing and is a solemn fact necessary to His perfection. The manifest Presence is another thing altogether, and from that Presence we have fled, like Adam, to hide among the trees of the garden, or like Peter, to shrink away crying, "Depart from me; for I am a sinful man, O Lord" (Luke 5:8).

So the life of man on the earth is a life away from the Presence, wrenched loose from that "blissful center," which is our right and proper dwelling place, our first estate, which we kept not, the loss of which is the cause of our unceasing restlessness.

The whole work of God in redemption is to undo the tragic effects of that foul revolt, and to bring us back again into right and eternal relationship with Himself. This requires that our sins be disposed of satisfactorily, that a full reconciliation be effected and the way opened for us to return again into conscious communion with God and to live again in the Presence as before. Then by His prevenient working within us He moves us to return. This first comes to our notice when our restless hearts feel a yearning for the presence of God and we say within ourselves, "I will arise and go to my Father." That is the first step, and as the Chinese sage Lao-tze has said, "The journey of a thousand miles begins with a first step."

The interior journey of the soul from the wilds of sin into the enjoyed presence of God is beautifully illustrated in the Old Testament tabernacle. The returning sinner first entered the outer court where he offered a blood sacrifice on the brazen altar and washed himself in the laver that stood near it. Then he passed through a veil into the holy place where no natural light could come, but the golden candlestick which spoke of Jesus, the Light of the World, threw its soft glow over all. There also was the shewbread to tell of Jesus, the Bread of Life, and the altar of incense, a figure of unceasing prayer.

Though the worshiper had enjoyed so much, still he had not yet entered the presence of God. Another veil separated from the Holy of Holies where above the mercy seat dwelt the very God Himself in awful and glorious manifestation. While the tabernacle stood, only the high priest could enter there, and that but once a year, with blood which he offered for his sins and the sins of the people. It was this last veil which was rent when our Lord gave up the ghost on Calvary, and the sacred writer explains that this rending of the veil opened the way for every worshiper in the world to come by the new and living way straight into the divine Presence.

Everything in the New Testament accords with this Old Testament picture. Ransomed men need no longer pause in fear to enter the Holy of Holies. *God wills that we should push on into His presence and live our whole life there.* This is to be known to us in conscious experience. It is more than a doctrine to be held; it is a life to be enjoyed every moment of every day.

This Flame of the Presence was the beating heart of the

Levitical order. Without it all the appointments of the tabernacle were characters of some unknown language, having no meaning for Israel or for us. The greatest fact of the tabernacle was that *Jehovah was there*; a Presence was waiting within the veil.

Similarly, the presence of God is the central fact of Christianity. At the heart of the Christian message is God Himself waiting for His redeemed children to push in to conscious awareness of His presence. That type of Christianity which happens now to be the vogue knows this Presence only in theory. It fails to stress the Christian's privilege of present realization. According to its teachings we are in the presence of God positionally, and nothing is said about the need to experience that Presence actually. The fiery urge that drove men like McCheyne is wholly missing. And the present generation of Christians measures itself by this imperfect rule. Ignoble contentment takes the place of burning zeal. We are satisfied to rest in our judicial possessions and, for the most part, we bother ourselves very little about the absence of personal experience.

Who is this within the veil who dwells in fiery manifestations? It is none other than God Himself.

"One God, the Father Almighty, Maker of heaven and earth, and of all things visible and invisible." It is "one Lord Jesus Christ, the only begotten Son of God; begotten of His Father before all worlds, God

of God, Light of Light, Very God of Very God; begotten, not made; being of one substance with the
Father."

And it is "the Holy Ghost, the Lord and Giver of life,
Who proceedeth from the Father and the Son, Who
with the Father and the Son together is worshiped
and glorified." Yet this holy Trinity is one God, for

"we worship one God in Trinity, and Trinity in Unity;
neither confounding the Persons, nor dividing the
Substance. For there is one Person of the Father,
another of the Son, and another of the Holy Ghost.
But the Godhead of the Father, of the Son, and of
the Holy Ghost, is all one: the glory equal and the
majesty co-eternal."

So in part run the ancient creeds, and so the inspired
Word declares.

Behind the veil is God, that God after whom the world,
with strange inconsistency, has felt, "if haply they might
. . . find him" (Acts 17:27). He has discovered Himself to
some extent in nature, but more perfectly in the incarnation. Now He waits to show Himself in ravishing fullness
to the humble of soul and the pure in heart.

The world is perishing for lack of the knowledge of
God and the church is famishing for want of His presence. The instant cure of most of our religious ills would

be to enter the Presence in spiritual experience, to become suddenly aware that we are in God and God is in us. This would lift us out of our pitiful narrowness and cause our hearts to be enlarged. This would burn away the impurities from our lives as the bugs and fungi were burned away by the fire that dwelt in the bush.

What a broad world to roam in, what a sea to swim in is this God and Father of our Lord Jesus Christ. He is *eternal*. He antedates time and is wholly independent of it. Time began in Him and will end in Him. To it He pays no tribute and from it He suffers no change.

He is *immutable*. He has never changed and can never change in any smallest measure. To change He would need to go from better to worse or from worse to better. He cannot do either, for being perfect He cannot become more perfect, and if He were to become less perfect He would be less than God.

He is *omniscient*. He knows in one free and effortless act all matter, all spirit, all relationships, all events. He has no past and He has no future. He *is*, and none of the limiting and qualifying terms used of creatures can apply to Him.

Love and mercy and righteousness are His, and *holiness* so ineffable that no comparisons or figures will avail to express it. Only fire can give even a remote conception of it. In fire He appeared at the burning bush; in the pillar of fire He dwelt through all the long wilderness journey. The fire that glowed between the wings of the cherubim in the holy place was called the Shekinah, the Presence, through the years of Israel's glory, and when the old had given place to the new, He came at Pentecost as a fiery flame and rested upon each disciple.

Spinoza wrote of the intellectual love of God, and he had a measure of truth there. But the highest love of God is not intellectual, it is spiritual. God is Spirit and only the spirit of a man can know Him really. In the deep spirit of a man the fire must glow or his love is not the true love of God. The great of the kingdom have been those who loved God more than others did. We all know who they have been and gladly pay tribute to the depth and sincerity of their devotion. We have but to pause for a moment and their names come trooping past us, smelling of myrrh and aloes and cassia out of the ivory palaces.

Frederick Faber was one whose soul panted after God as the roe deer pants after the water brook, and the measure in which God revealed Himself to his seeking heart set the good man's whole life afire with a burning adoration rivaling that of the seraphim before the throne. His love for God extended to the three Persons of the Godhead equally, yet he seemed to feel for each One a special kind of love reserved for Him alone. Of God the Father he sings:

> *Only to sit and think of God Oh what a joy it is!*
> *To think the thought, to breathe the Name;*
> *Earth has no higher bliss.*

> *Father of Jesus, love's reward!*
> *What rapture it will be, Prostrate before Thy*
> *throne to lie,*
> *And gaze and gaze on Thee!*

His love for the Person of Christ was so intense that it threatened to consume him. It burned within him as a sweet and holy madness and flowed from his lips like molten gold. In one of his sermons he says,

Wherever we turn in the church of God, there is Jesus. He is the beginning, middle and end of everything to us. . . . There is nothing good, nothing holy, nothing beautiful, nothing joyous which He is not to His servants. No one need to be poor, because, if he chooses, he can have Jesus for his own property and possession. No one need be downcast, for Jesus is the joy of heaven, and it is His joy to enter into sorrowful hearts. We can exaggerate about many things; but we can never exaggerate our obligation to Jesus or the compassionate abundance of the love of Jesus to us. All our lives long we might talk of Jesus, and yet we should never come to an end of the sweet things that might be said of Him. Eternity will not be long enough to learn all He is, or to praise Him for all He has done, but then, that matters not; for we shall be always with Him, and we desire nothing more.

And addressing our Lord directly he says to Him:

I love Thee so, I know not how
My transports to control;
Thy love is like a burning fire
Within my very soul.

Faber's blazing love extended also to the Holy Spirit. Not only in his theology did he acknowledge His deity and full equality with the Father and the Son, but he celebrated it constantly in his songs and in his prayers. He literally pressed his forehead to the ground in his eager, fervid worship of the Third Person of the Godhead. In one of his great hymns to the Holy Spirit he sums up his burning devotion thus:

O Spirit, beautiful and dread!
My heart is fit to break
With love of all Thy tenderness
For us poor sinners' sake.

I have risked the tedium of quotation that I might show by pointed example what I have set out to say, viz., that God is so vastly wonderful, so utterly and completely delightful that He can, without anything other than Himself, meet and overflow the deepest demands of our total nature, mysterious and deep as that nature is. Such worship as Faber knew (and he is but one of a great company which no man can number) can never come from a mere doctrinal knowledge of God. Hearts that are "fit to break" with love for the Godhead are those who have been in the Presence and have looked with opened eye upon the majesty of Deity. Men of the breaking hearts had a quality about them not known to nor understood by common men. They habitually spoke with spiritual authority. They had been in the presence of God and they reported what they saw there.

They were prophets, not scribes, for the scribe tells us what he has read, and the prophet tells what he has seen. The distinction is not an imaginary one. Between the scribe who has read and the prophet who has seen there is a difference as wide as the sea. We are overrun today with orthodox scribes, but the prophets, where are they? The hard voice of the scribe sounds over evangelicalism, but the church waits for the tender voice of the saint who has penetrated the veil and has gazed with inward eye upon the wonder that is God. And yet, thus to penetrate, to push in sensitive living experience into the holy Presence, is a privilege open to every child of God. With the veil removed by the rending of Jesus' flesh, with nothing on God's side to prevent us from entering, why do we tarry without? Why do we consent to abide all our days just outside the Holy of Holies and never enter at all to look upon God? We hear the Bridegroom say, "Let me see thy countenance, let me hear thy voice; for sweet is thy voice, and thy countenance is comely" (Song of Solomon

2:14). We sense that the call is for us, but still we fail to draw near, and the years pass and we grow old and tired in the outer courts of the tabernacle. What hinders us?

The answer usually given, simply that we are "cold," will not explain all the facts. There is something more serious than coldness of heart, something that may be back of that coldness and be the cause of its existence. What is it? What but the presence of a veil in our hearts? A veil not taken away as the first veil was, but which remains there still shutting out the light and hiding the face of God from us. It is the veil of our fleshly, fallen nature living on, unjudged within us, uncrucified and unrepudiated. It is the close-woven veil of the self-life which we have never truly acknowledged, of which we have been secretly ashamed, and which for these reasons we have never brought to the judgment of the cross. It is not too mysterious, this opaque veil, nor is it hard to identify. We have but to look into our own hearts and we shall see it there, sewn and patched and repaired it may be, but there nevertheless, an enemy to our lives and an effective block to our spiritual progress.

This veil is not a beautiful thing and it is not a thing about which we commonly care to talk. But I am addressing the thirsting souls who are determined to follow God, and I know they will not turn back because the way leads temporarily through the blackened hills. The urge of God within them will assure their continuing pursuit. They will face the facts however unpleasant and endure the cross for the joy set before them. So I am bold to name the threads out of which this inner veil is woven.

It is woven of the fine threads of the self-life, the hyphenated sins of the human spirit. They are not something we *do*, they are something we *are*, and therein lies both their subtlety and their power.

To be specific, the self-sins are self-righteousness, self-pity, self-confidence, self-sufficiency, self-admiration, self-love and a host of others like them. They dwell too deep within us and are too much a part of our natures to come to our attention till the light of God is focused upon them. The grosser manifestations of these sins—egotism, exhibitionism, self-promotion—are strangely tolerated in Christian leaders, even in circles of impeccable orthodoxy. They are so much in evidence as actually, for many people, to become identified with the gospel. I trust it is not a cynical observation to say that they appear these days to be a requisite for popularity in some sections of the church visible. Promoting self under the guise of promoting Christ is currently so common as to excite little notice.

One should suppose that proper instruction in the doctrines of man's depravity and the necessity for justification through the righteousness of Christ alone would deliver us from the power of the self-sins, but it does not work that way. Self can live unrebuked at the very altar. It can watch the bleeding Victim die and not be in the least affected by what it sees. It can fight for the faith of the reformers and preach eloquently the creed of salvation by grace and gain strength by its efforts. To tell the truth, it seems actually to feed upon orthodoxy and is more at home in a Bible conference than in a tavern. Our very state of longing after God may afford it an excellent condition under which to thrive and grow.

Self is the opaque veil that hides the face of God from us. It can be removed only in spiritual experience, never by mere instruction. We may as well try to instruct leprosy out of our system. There must be a work of God in destruction before we are free. We must invite the cross to do its deadly work within us. We must bring our self-sins to the cross for judgment. We must prepare ourselves for an ordeal of suffering in some measure like that through which our Savior passed when He suffered under Pontius Pilate.

Let us remember that when we talk of the rending of the veil we are speaking in a figure, and the thought of it is poetical, almost pleasant, but in actuality there is nothing pleasant about it. In human experience that veil is made of living spiritual tissue; it is composed of the sentient, quivering stuff of which our whole beings consist, and to touch it is to touch us where we feel pain. To tear it away is to injure us, to hurt us and make us bleed. To say otherwise is to make the cross no cross and death no death at all. It is never fun to die. To rip through the dear and tender stuff of which life is made can never be anything but deeply painful. Yet that is what the cross did to Jesus and it is what the cross would do to every man to set him free.

Let us beware of tinkering with our inner life, hoping ourselves to rend the veil. God must do everything for us. Our part is to yield and trust. We must confess, forsake, repudiate the self-life, and then reckon it crucified. But we must be careful to distinguish lazy "acceptance" from the real work of God. We must insist upon the work being done. We dare not rest content with a neat doctrine of self-crucifixion. That is to imitate Saul and spare the best of the sheep and the oxen.

Insist that the work be done in very truth and it will be done. The cross is rough and it is deadly, but it is effective. It does not keep its victim hanging there forever. There comes a moment when its work is finished and the suffering victim dies. After that is resurrection glory and power, and the pain is forgotten for joy that the veil is taken away and we have entered in actual spiritual experience the presence of the living God.

Lord, how excellent are Thy ways, and how devious and dark are the ways of man. Show us how to die, that we may rise again to newness of life.

Rend the veil of our self-life from the top down as Thou didst rend the veil of the Temple. We would draw near in full assurance of faith.

We would dwell with Thee in daily experience here on this earth so that we may be accustomed to the glory when we enter Thy heaven to dwell with Thee there.

In Jesus' name.

Amen.

CHAPTER 4

———————•———————

Apprehending God

O taste and see.

PSALM 34:8

C anon Holmes of India, more than twenty-five years ago, called attention to the inferential character of the average man's faith in God. To most people God is an inference, not a reality. He is a deduction from evidence which they consider adequate, but He remains personally unknown to the individual. "He *must* be," they say, "therefore we believe He is." Others do not go even so far as this; they know of Him only by hearsay. They have never bothered to think the matter out for themselves, but have heard about Him from others, and have put belief in Him into the back of their minds along with various odds and ends that make up their total creed. To many others, God is but an ideal, another name for goodness or beauty or truth; or He is law or life or the creative impulse back of the phenomena of existence.

These notions about God are many and varied, but they who hold them have one thing in common: they do not know God in personal experience. The possibility of intimate acquaintance with Him has not entered their minds. While admitting His existence they do not think of Him as being knowable in the sense that we know things or people.

Christians, to be sure, go further than this, at least in theory. Their creed requires them to believe in the personality of God and they have been taught to pray, "Our Father which art in heaven" (Luke 11:2). Now personality and fatherhood carry with them the idea of the possibility of personal acquaintance. This is admitted, I say, in theory, but for millions of Christians, nevertheless, God is no more real than He is to the non-Christian. They go through life trying to love an ideal and be loyal to a mere principle.

Over against all this cloudy vagueness stands the clear scriptural doctrine that God can be known in personal experience. A loving Personality dominates the Bible, walking among the trees of the garden and breathing fragrance over every scene. Always a living Person is present, speaking, pleading, loving, working and manifesting Himself whenever and wherever His people have the receptivity necessary to receive the manifestation.

The Bible assumes as a self-evident fact that men can know God with at least the same degree of immediacy as they know any other person or thing that comes within the field of their experience. The same terms are used to express the knowledge of God as are used to express knowledge of physical things. "O *taste* and *see* that the LORD is good" (Psalm 34:8, emphasis added). "All thy garments *smell* of myrrh, and aloes, and cassia, out of the ivory palaces" (45:8). "My sheep *hear* my voice" (John 10:27, emphasis added). "Blessed are the pure in heart: for they shall *see* God" (Matthew 5:8, emphasis added). These are but four of countless such passages from the Word of God. And more important than any proof text is the fact that the whole import of Scripture is toward this belief.

What can all this mean except that we have in our hearts organs by means of which we can know God as certainly as we know material things through our familiar five senses? We apprehend the physical world by exercising the faculties given us for that purpose, and we possess spiritual faculties by means of which we can know God and the spiritual world if we will obey the Spirit's urge and begin to use them.

That a saving work must first be done in the heart is taken for granted here. The spiritual faculties of the unregenerate man lie asleep in his nature, unused, and for every purpose dead. That is the stroke that has fallen upon us by sin. They may be quickened to active life again by the operation of the Holy Spirit in regeneration. That is one of the immeasurable benefits that comes to us through Christ's atoning work on the cross.

But why do the very ransomed children of God themselves know so little of that habitual, conscious communion with God that Scripture offers? The answer is because of our chronic unbelief. Faith enables our spiritual sense to function. Where faith is defective the result will be inward insensibility and numbness toward spiritual things. This is the condition of vast numbers of Christians today. No proof is necessary to support that statement. We have but to converse with the first Christian we meet or enter the first church we open to acquire all the proof we need.

A spiritual kingdom lies all about us, enclosing us, embracing us, altogether within reach of our inner selves, waiting for us to recognize it. God Himself is here waiting our response to His presence. This eternal world will come alive to us the moment we begin to reckon upon its reality.

I have just now used two words that demand definition. Or if definition is impossible, I must at least make clear what I mean when I use them. They are *reckon* and *reality*.

What do I mean by *reality*? I mean that which has existence apart from any idea any mind may have of it, and would exist if there were no mind anywhere to entertain a thought of it. That which is real has being in itself. It does not depend upon the observer for its validity.

I am aware that there are those who love to poke fun at the plain man's idea of reality. They are the idealists who spin endless proofs that nothing is real outside of the mind. They are the relativists who like to show that there are no fixed points in the universe from which we can measure anything. They smile down upon us from their lofty intellectual peaks and settle us to their own satisfaction by fastening upon us the reproachful term "absolutist." The Christian is not put out of countenance by this show of contempt. He can smile right back at them, for he knows that there is only One who is Absolute, that is God. But he knows also that the Absolute One has made this world for man's use, and while there is nothing fixed or real in the last meaning of the words (the meaning as applied to God), *for every purpose of human life we are permitted to act as if there were.* And every man does act thus except the mentally sick. These unfortunates also have trouble with reality, but they are consistent; they insist upon living in accordance with their ideas of things. They are honest, and it is their very honesty that constitutes them a social problem.

The idealists and relativists are not mentally sick. They prove their soundness by living their lives according to the very notions of reality they in theory repudiate and by counting upon the very fixed points that they prove are not there. They could earn a lot more respect for their notions if they were willing to live by them; but this they are careful not to do. Their ideas are brain-deep, not life-deep. Wherever life touches them they repudiate their theories and live like other men.

The Christian is too sincere to play with ideas for their

own sake. He takes no pleasure in the mere spinning of gossamer webs for display. All his beliefs are practical. They are geared into his life. By them he lives or dies, stands or falls for this world and for all time to come. From the insincere man he turns away.

The sincere, plain man knows that the world is real. He finds it here when he wakes to consciousness, and he knows that he did not think it into being. It was here waiting for him when he came, and he knows that when he prepares to leave this earthly scene it will be here still to bid him goodbye as he departs. By the deep wisdom of life he is wiser than a thousand men who doubt. He stands upon the earth and feels the wind and rain in his face, and he knows that they are real. He sees the sun by day and the stars by night. He sees the hot lightning play out of the dark thundercloud. He hears the sounds of nature and the cries of human joy and pain. These he knows are real. He lies down on the cool earth at night and has no fear that it will prove illusory or fail him while he sleeps. In the morning the firm ground will be under him, the blue sky above him and the rocks and trees around him as when he closed his eyes the night before. So he lives and rejoices in a world of reality.

With his five senses he engages this real world. All things necessary to his physical existence he apprehends by the faculties with which he has been equipped by the God who created him and placed him in such a world as this.

Now by our definition also God is real. He is real in the absolute and final sense that nothing else is. All other reality is contingent upon His. The great Reality is God, the Author of that lower and dependent reality that makes up the sum of created things, including ourselves. God has objective existence independent of and apart from any notions we may have concerning Him. The worshiping heart does not create its Object. It finds Him here when it wakes from its mortal slumber in the morning of its regeneration.

Another word that must be cleared up is *reckon*. This does not mean to visualize or imagine. Imagination is not faith. The two are not only different from, but stand in sharp opposition to, each other. Imagination projects unreal images out of the mind and seeks to attach reality to them. Faith creates nothing; it simply reckons upon that which is already there.

God and the spiritual world are real. We can reckon upon them with as much assurance as we reckon upon the familiar world around us. Spiritual things are there (or rather we should say here) inviting our attention and challenging our trust.

Our trouble is that we have established bad thought habits. We habitually think of the visible world as real and doubt the reality of any other. We do not deny the existence of the spiritual world but we doubt that it is real in the accepted meaning of the word.

The world of sense intrudes upon our attention day

and night for the whole of our lifetime. It is clamorous, insistent and self-demonstrating. It does not appeal to our faith; it is here, assaulting our five senses, demanding to be accepted as real and final. But sin has so clouded the lenses of our hearts that we cannot see that other reality, the City of God, shining around us. The world of sense triumphs. The visible becomes the enemy of the invisible, the temporal, of the eternal. That is the curse inherited by every member of Adam's tragic race.

At the root of the Christian life lies belief in the invisible. The object of the Christian's faith is unseen reality.

Our uncorrected thinking, influenced by the blindness of our natural hearts and the intrusive ubiquity of visible things, tends to draw a contrast between the spiritual and the real—but actually no such contrast exists. The antithesis lies elsewhere—between the real and the imaginary, between the spiritual and the material, between the temporal and the eternal; but between the spiritual and the real, never. The spiritual is real.

If we would rise into that region of light and power plainly beckoning us through the Scriptures of truth, we must break the evil habit of ignoring the spiritual. We must shift our interest from the seen to the unseen. For the great unseen Reality is God. "He that cometh to God must believe that he is, and that he is a rewarder of them that diligently seek him" (Hebrews 11:6). This is basic in the life of faith. From there we can rise to unlimited heights. "Ye believe in God," said our Lord Jesus Christ, "believe also in me" (John 14:1). Without the first there can be no second.

If we truly want to follow God, we must seek to be other-worldly. This I say knowing well that word has been used with scorn by the sons of this world and applied to the Christian as a badge of reproach. So be it. Every man must choose his world. If we who follow Christ, with all the facts before us and knowing what we are about, deliberately choose the kingdom of God as our sphere of interest, I see no reason why anyone should object. If we lose by it, the loss is our own; if we gain, we rob no one by so doing. The "other world," which is the object of this world's disdain and the subject of the drunkard's mocking song, is our carefully chosen goal and the object of our holiest longing.

But we must avoid the common fault of pushing the "other world" into the future. It is not future, but present. It parallels our familiar physical world, and the doors between the two worlds are open. "Ye are come," says the writer to the Hebrews (and the tense is plainly present),

> *unto mount Sion, and unto the city of the living God, the heavenly Jerusalem, and to an innumerable company of angels, to the general assembly and church of the firstborn, which are written in heaven, and to God the Judge of all, and to the spirits of just men made perfect, and to Jesus the mediator of the*

new covenant, and to the blood of sprinkling, that
speaketh better things than that of Abel.

HEBREWS 12:22–24

All these things are contrasted with "the mount that might be touched" (12:18) and "the sound of a trumpet, and the voice of words" (12:19) that might be heard. May we not safely conclude that, as the realities of Mount Sinai were apprehended by the senses, so the realities of Mount Zion are to be grasped by the soul? And this not by any trick of the imagination but in downright actuality. The soul has eyes with which to see and ears with which to hear. Feeble they may be from long disuse, but by the life-giving touch of Christ they are now alive and capable of sharpest sight and most sensitive hearing.

As we begin to focus upon God, the things of the spirit will take shape before our inner eyes. Obedience to the word of Christ will bring an inward revelation of the Godhead (John 14:21–23). It will give acute perception enabling us to see God even as is promised to the pure in heart. A new God-consciousness will seize upon us and we shall begin to taste and hear and inwardly feel God, who is our life and our all. There will be seen the constant shining of "the true Light, which lighteth every man that cometh into the world" (John 1:9). More and more, as our faculties grow sharper and more sure, God will become to us the great All, and His presence the glory and wonder of our lives.

*O God, quicken to life every power within me, that I may
lay hold on eternal things. Open my eyes that I may see; give
me acute spiritual perception; enable me to taste Thee and
know that Thou art good. Make heaven more real to
me than any earthly thing has ever been.
Amen.*

CHAPTER 5

The Universal Presence

Whither shall I go from thy spirit?
or whither shall I flee from thy presence?

PSALM 139:7

In all Christian teaching certain basic truths are found, hidden at times, and rather assumed than asserted, but necessary to all truth as the primary colors are found in and necessary to the finished painting. Such a truth is the divine immanence.

God dwells in His creation and is everywhere indivisibly present in all His works. This is boldly taught by prophet and apostle and is accepted by Christian theology generally. That is, it appears in the books, but for some reason it has not sunk into the average Christian's heart so as to become a part of his believing self. Christian teachers shy away from its full implications and, if they mention it at all, mute it down till it has little meaning. I would guess the reason for this to be the fear of

269

being charged with pantheism. But the doctrine of the divine Presence is definitely not pantheism. Pantheism's error is too palpable to deceive anyone. It is that God is the sum of all created things. Nature and God are one, so that whoever touches a leaf or a stone touches God. That is, of course, to degrade the glory of the incorruptible Deity and, in an effort to make all things divine, banish all divinity from the world entirely.

The truth is that while God dwells in His world He is separated from it by a gulf forever impassable. However closely He may be identified with the work of His hands, they are and must eternally be other than He, and He is and must be antecedent to and independent of them. He is transcendent above all His works even while He is immanent within them.

What does the divine immanence mean in direct Christian experience? It means simply that *God is here*. Wherever we are, God is here. There is no place, there can be no place, where He is not. Ten million intelligences standing at as many points in space and separated by incomprehensible distances can each one say with equal truth, God is here. No point is nearer to God than any other point. It is exactly as near to God from any place as it is from any other place. No one is in mere distance any further from or any nearer to God than any other person.

These are truths believed by every instructed Christian. It remains for us to think on them and pray over them until they begin to glow within us.

"In the beginning God . . ." (Genesis 1:1). Not matter, for matter is not self-causing. It requires an antecedent cause, and God is that Cause. Not law, for law is but a name for the course which all creation follows. That course had to be planned, and the Planner is God. Not mind, for mind also is a created thing and must have a Creator back of it. In the beginning God, the uncaused Cause of matter, mind and law. There we must begin.

Adam sinned and, in his panic, frantically tried to do the impossible; he tried to hide from the presence of God. David also must have had wild thoughts of trying to escape from the Presence, for he wrote, "Whither shall I go from thy spirit? or whither shall I flee from thy presence?" (Psalm 139:7). Then he proceeded through one of his most beautiful psalms to celebrate the glory of the divine immanence. "If I ascend up into heaven, thou art there: if I make my bed in hell, behold, thou art there. If I take the wings of the morning, and dwell in the uttermost parts of the sea; even there shall thy hand lead me, and thy right hand shall hold me" (139:8–10). And he knew that God's *being* and God's *seeing* are the same, that the seeing Presence had been with him even before he was born, watching the mystery of unfolding life. Solomon exclaimed, "But will God indeed dwell on the earth? behold, the heaven and heaven of heavens cannot contain thee; how much less this house that I have builded" (1 Kings 8:27). Paul assured the Athenians that "he be not far from every one of us: for in him we live, and move, and have our being" (Acts 17:27–28).

If God is present at every point in space, if we cannot go where He is not, cannot even conceive of a place where He is not, why then has not that Presence become the one universally celebrated fact of the world? The patriarch Jacob, "in the waste howling wilderness" (Deuteronomy 32:10), gave the answer to that question. He saw a vision of God and cried out in wonder, "Surely the LORD is in this place; and I knew it not" (Genesis 28:16). Jacob had never been for one small division of a moment outside the circle of that all-pervading Presence. But he knew it not. That was his trouble, and it is ours. Men do not know that God is here. What a difference it would make if they knew.

The Presence and the manifestation of the Presence are not the same. There can be the one without the other. God is here when we are wholly unaware of it. He is manifest only when and as we are aware of His presence. On our part, there must be surrender to the Spirit of God, for His work is to show us the Father and the Son. If we cooperate with Him in loving obedience, God will manifest Himself to us, and that manifestation will be the difference between a nominal Christian life and a life radiant with the light of His face.

Always, everywhere God is present, and always He seeks to discover Himself to each one. He would reveal not only that He is, but what He is as well. He did not have to be persuaded to reveal Himself to Moses. "And the LORD descended in the cloud, and stood with him there, and proclaimed the name of the LORD" (Exodus 34:5). He not only made a verbal proclamation of His nature but He revealed His very Self to Moses so that the skin of Moses's face shone with the supernatural light. It will be a great moment for some of us when we begin to believe that God's promise of self-revelation is literally true, that He promised much, but no more than He intends to fulfill.

Our pursuit of God is successful just because He is forever seeking to manifest Himself to us. The revelation of God to any man is not God coming from a distance once upon a time to pay a brief and momentous visit to the man's soul. Thus to think of it is to misunderstand it all. The approach of God to the soul or of the soul to God is not to be thought of in spatial terms at all. There is no idea of physical distance involved in the concept. It is not a matter of miles but of experience.

To speak of being near to or far from God is to use language in a sense always understood when applied to our ordinary human relationships. A man may say, "I feel that my son is coming nearer to me as he gets older," and yet that son has lived by his father's side since he was born and has never been away from home more than a day or so in his entire life. What then can the father mean? Obviously he is speaking of experience. He means that the boy is coming to know him more intimately and with deeper understanding, that the barriers of thought and feeling between the two are disappearing, that father and son are becoming more closely united in mind and heart.

So when we sing, "Draw me nearer, nearer, nearer, blessed Lord," we are not thinking of the nearness of place, but of the nearness of relationship. It is for increasing degrees of awareness that we pray, for a more perfect consciousness of the divine Presence. We need never shout across the spaces to an absent God. He is nearer than our own soul, closer than our most secret thoughts.

Why do some persons "find" God in a way that others do not? Why does God manifest His presence to some and let multitudes of others struggle along in the half light of imperfect Christian experience? Of course, the will of God is the same for all. He has no favorites within His household. All He has ever done for any of His children He will do for all of His children. The difference lies not with God but with us.

Pick at random a score of great saints whose lives and testimonies are widely known. Let them be Bible characters or well-known Christians of post-biblical times. You will be struck instantly with the fact that the saints were not alike. Sometimes the unlikenesses were so great as to be positively glaring. How different, for example, was Moses from Isaiah; how different was Elijah from David; how unlike each other were John and Paul, St. Francis and Luther, Finney and Thomas à Kempis. The differences are as wide as human life itself—differences of race, nationality, education, temperament, habit and personal qualities. Yet they all walked, each in his day, upon a high road of spiritual living far above the common way.

Their differences must have been incidental and in the eyes of God of no significance. In some vital quality they must have been alike. What was it?

I venture to suggest that the one vital quality they had in common was spiritual receptivity. Something in them was open to heaven, something that urged them Godward. Without attempting anything like a profound analysis, I shall say simply that they had spiritual awareness and that they went on to cultivate it until it became the biggest thing in their lives. They differed from the average person in that when they felt the inward longing they *did something about it*. They acquired the lifelong habit of spiritual response. They were not disobedient to the heavenly vision. As David put it neatly, "When thou saidst, Seek ye my face; my heart said unto thee, Thy face, LORD, will I seek" (Psalm 27:8).

As with everything good in human life, back of this receptivity is God. The sovereignty of God is here, and is felt even by those who have not placed particular stress upon it theologically. The pious Michelangelo confessed this in a sonnet:

> *My unassisted heart is barren clay,*
> *That of its native self can nothing feed:*
> *Of good and pious works Thou are the seed,*
> *That quickens only where Thou sayest it may:*

Unless Thou show to us Thine own true way
No man can find it: Father! Thou must lead.

These words will repay study as the deep and serious testimony of a great Christian.

Important as it is that we recognize God working in us, I would yet warn against a too-great preoccupation with the thought. It is a sure road to sterile passivity. God will not hold us responsible to understand the mysteries of election, predestination and the divine sovereignty. The best and safest way to deal with these truths is to raise our eyes to God and in deepest reverence say, "O Lord, Thou knowest." Those things belong to the deep and mysterious profound of God's omniscience. Prying into them may make theologians, but it will never make saints.

Receptivity is not a single thing; rather, it is a compound, a blending of several elements within the soul. It is an affinity for, a bent toward, a sympathetic response to, a desire to have. From this it may be gathered that it can be present in degrees, that we may have little or more, depending upon the individual. It may be increased by exercise or destroyed by neglect. It is not a sovereign and irresistible force which comes upon us as a seizure from above. It is a gift of God, indeed, but one which must be recognized and cultivated as any other gift if we are to realize the purpose for which it was given.

Failure to see this is the cause of a very serious breakdown in modern evangelicalism. The idea of cultivation and exercise, so dear to the saints of old, has now no place in our total religious picture. It is too slow, too common. We now demand glamour and fast-flowing dramatic action. A generation of Christians reared among push buttons and automatic machines is impatient of slower and less direct methods of reaching their goals. We have been trying to apply machine-age methods to our relations with God. We read our chapter, have our short devotions and rush away, hoping to make up for our deep inward bankruptcy by attending another gospel meeting or listening to another thrilling story told by a religious adventurer lately returned from afar.

The tragic results of this spirit are all about us: shallow lives, hollow religious philosophies, the preponderance of the element of fun in gospel meetings, the glorification of men, trust in religious externalities, quasireligious fellowships, salesmanship methods, the mistaking of dynamic personality for the power of the Spirit. These and such as these are the symptoms of an evil disease, a deep and serious malady of the soul.

For this great sickness that is upon us no one person is responsible, and no Christian is wholly free from blame. We have all contributed directly or indirectly, to this sad state of affairs. We have been too blind to see, or too timid to speak out, or too self-satisfied to desire anything better than the poor, average diet with which others appear satisfied. To put it differently, we have accepted one another's notions, copied one another's lives and made one another's experiences the model for our own. And for a generation the trend has been downward. Now we have reached a low place of sand and burnt wire grass and, worst of all, we have made the Word of Truth conform to our experience and accepted this low plane as the very pasture of the blessed.

It will require a determined heart and more than a little courage to wrench ourselves loose from the grip of our times and return to biblical ways. But it can be done. Every now and then in the past Christians have had to do it. History has recorded several large-scale returns led by such men as St. Francis, Martin Luther, and George Fox. Unfortunately, there seems to be no Luther or Fox on the horizon at present. Whether or not another such return may be expected before the coming of Christ is a question upon which Christians are not fully agreed, but that is not of too great importance to us now.

What God in His sovereignty may yet do on a world scale I do not claim to know. But what He will do for the plain man or woman who seeks His face I believe I do know and can tell others. Let any man turn to God in earnest, let him begin to exercise himself unto godliness, let him seek to develop his powers of spiritual receptivity by trust and obedience and humility, and the results will exceed anything he may have hoped in his leaner and weaker days.

Any man who by repentance and a sincere return to God will break himself out of the mold in which he has been held, and will go to the Bible itself for his spiritual standards, will be delighted with what he finds there.

Let us say it again: The universal Presence is a fact. God is here. The whole universe is alive with His life. And He is no strange or foreign God, but the familiar Father of our Lord Jesus Christ whose love has for these thousands of years enfolded the sinful race of men. And always He is trying to get our attention, to reveal Himself to us, to communicate with us. We have within us the ability to know Him if we will but respond to His overtures. (And this we call pursuing God!) We will know Him in increasing degree as our receptivity becomes more perfect by faith and love and practice.

O God and Father, I repent of my sinful preoccupation with visible things. The world has been too much with me. Thou hast been here and I knew it not.

I have been blind to Thy presence. Open my eyes that I may behold Thee in and around me.

For Christ's sake.

Amen.

CHAPTER 6

The Speaking Voice

*In the beginning was the Word, and the Word
was with God, and the Word was God.*

JOHN 1:1

An intelligent, plain man, untaught in the truths of Christianity, coming upon this text, would likely conclude that John meant to teach that it is the nature of God to speak, to communicate His thoughts to others. And he would be right. A word is a medium by which thoughts are expressed, and the application of the term to the eternal Son leads us to believe that self-expression is inherent in the Godhead, that God is forever seeking to speak Himself out to His creation. The whole Bible supports this idea. God is speaking. Not God spoke, but *God is speaking.* He is, by His nature, continuously articulate. He fills the world with His speaking voice.

One of the great realities with which we have to deal is the voice of God in His world. The briefest and only satisfying cosmogony is this: "He spake, and it was done" (Psalm 33:9). The *why* of natural law is the loving voice of God immanent in His creation. And this word of God which brought all worlds into being cannot be understood to mean the Bible, for it is not a written or printed word at all, but the expression of the will of God is the breath of God filling the world with living potentiality. The voice of God is the most powerful force in nature, indeed the only force in nature, for all energy is here only because the power-filled Word is being spoken.

The Bible is the written Word of God, and because it is written it is confined and limited by the necessities of ink and paper and leather. The voice of God, however, is alive and free as the sovereign God is free. "The words that I speak unto you, they are spirit, and they are life" (John 6:63). The life is in the speaking words. God's word in the Bible can have power only because it corresponds to God's word in the universe. It is the present Voice which makes the written Word all powerful. Otherwise it would lie locked in slumber within the covers of a book.

We take a low and primitive view of things when we conceive of God at the creation coming into physical contact with things, shaping and fitting and building like a carpenter. The Bible teaches otherwise: "By the word of the LORD were the heavens made; and all the host of them by the breath of his mouth. . . . For he spake, and it was done; he commanded, and it stood fast" (Psalm 33:6, 9). "Through faith we understand that the worlds were framed by the word of God" (Hebrews 11:3). Again we must remember that God is referring here not to His written Word, but to His speaking Voice. His world-filling Voice is meant, that Voice which antedates the Bible by uncounted centuries, that Voice which has not been silent since the dawn of creation, but is sounding still throughout the full far reaches of the universe.

The Word of God is quick and powerful. In the beginning He spoke to nothing, and it became *something*. Chaos heard it and became order; darkness heard it and became light. "And God said . . . and it was so" (Genesis 1:9). These twin phrases, as cause and effect, occur throughout the Genesis story of creation. The *said* accounts for the *so*. The *so* is the *said* put into the continuous present.

God is here and He is speaking—these truths are back of all other Bible truths; without them there could be no revelation at all. God did not write a book and send it by messenger to be read at a distance by unaided minds. He spoke a Book and lives in His spoken words, constantly speaking His words and causing the power of them to persist across the years. God breathed on clay and it became a man; He breathes on men and they become clay. "Return, ye children of men" (Psalm 90:3) was the word spoken at the Fall by which God decreed the death of every man, and no added word has He needed to speak. The sad procession of mankind across the face of the earth from birth to the grave is proof that His original word was enough.

We have not given sufficient attention to that deep utterance in the book of John, "That was the true Light, which lighteth every man that cometh into the world" (1:9). Shift the punctuation around as we will, the truth is still there: The Word of God affects the hearts of all men as light in the soul. In the hearts of all men the light shines, the Word sounds, and there is no escaping them. Something like this would of necessity be so if God is alive and in His world. And John says that it is so. Even those persons who have never heard of the Bible have still been preached to with sufficient clarity to remove every excuse from their hearts forever. "Which shew the work of the law written in their hearts, their conscience also bearing witness, and their thoughts the mean while accusing or else excusing one another" (Romans 2:15). "For the invisible things of him from the creation of the world are clearly seen, being understood by the things that are made, even his eternal power and Godhead; so that they are without excuse" (1:20).

This universal Voice of God was by the ancient Hebrews often called Wisdom, and was said to be everywhere sounding and searching throughout the earth, seeking some response from the sons of men. The eighth chapter of Proverbs begins, "Doth not wisdom cry? and understanding put forth her voice?" The writer then pictures wisdom as a beautiful woman standing "in the top of high places, by the way in the places of the paths" (8:2). She sounds her voice from every quarter so that no one may miss hearing it. "Unto you, O men, I call; and my voice is to the sons of man" (8:4). Then she pleads for the simple and the foolish to give ear to her words. It is spiritual responses for which this Wisdom of God is pleading, a response which she has always sought and is but rarely able to secure. The tragedy is that our eternal welfare depends upon our hearing and we have trained our ears not to hear.

This universal Voice has ever sounded, and it has often troubled men even when they did not understand the source of their fears. Could it be that this Voice distilling like a living mist upon the hearts of men has been the undiscovered cause of the troubled conscience and the longing for immortality confessed by millions since the dawn of recorded history? We need not fear to face up to this. The speaking Voice is a fact. How men have reacted to it is for any observer to note.

When God spoke out of heaven to our Lord, self-centered men who heard it explained it by natural causes, saying, "It thundered." This habit of explaining the Voice by appeals to natural law is at the very root of modern science. In the living, breathing cosmos there is a mysterious Something, too wonderful, too awful for any mind to understand. The believing man does not claim to understand. He falls to his knees and whispers, "God." The man of earth kneels also, but not to worship. He kneels to examine, to search, to find the cause and the how of things. Just now we happen to be living in a secular age.

Our thought habits are those of the scientist, not those of the worshiper. We are more likely to explain than to adore. "It thundered," we exclaim, and go our earthly way. But still the Voice sounds and searches. The order and life of the world depend upon that Voice, but men are mostly too busy or too stubborn to give attention.

Every one of us has had experiences which we have not been able to explain—a sudden sense of loneliness, or a feeling of wonder or awe in the face of the universal vastness. Or we have had a fleeting visitation of light like an illumination from some other sun, giving us in a quick flash an assurance that we are from another world, that our origins are divine. What we saw there, or felt, or heard, may have been contrary to all that we had been taught in the schools and at wide variance with all our former beliefs and opinions. We were forced to suspend our acquired doubts while, for a moment, the clouds were rolled back and we saw and heard for ourselves. Explain such things as we will, I think we have not been fair to the facts until we allow at least the possibility that such experiences may arise from the presence of God in the world and His persistent effort to communicate with mankind. Let us not dismiss such an hypothesis too flippantly.

It is my own belief (and here I shall not feel bad if no one follows me) that every good and beautiful thing which man has produced in the world has been the result of his faulty and sin-blocked response to the creative Voice sounding over the earth. The moral philosophers who dreamed their high dreams of virtue, the religious thinkers who speculated about God and immortality, the poets and artists who created out of common stuff pure and lasting beauty: How can we explain them? It is not enough to say simply, "It was genius."

What then is genius? Could it be that a genius is a man haunted by the speaking Voice, laboring and striving like one possessed to achieve ends which he only vaguely understands? That the great man may have missed God in his labors, that he may even have spoken or written against God does not destroy the idea I am advancing. God's redemptive revelation in Scripture is necessary to saving faith and peace with God. Faith in a risen Savior is necessary if the vague stirrings toward immortality are to bring us to restful and satisfying communion with God. To me this is a plausible explanation of all that is best out of Christ. But you can be a good Christian and not accept my thesis.

The Voice of God is a friendly Voice. No one need fear to listen to it unless he has already made up his mind to resist it. The blood of Jesus has covered not only the human race but all creation as well. "And, having made peace through the blood of his cross, by him to reconcile all things unto himself; by him, I say, whether they be things in earth, or things in heaven" (Colossians 1:20). We may safely preach a friendly heaven. The heavens as well as the earth are filled with the good will of Him that dwelt in the bush. The perfect blood of atonement secures this forever.

Whoever will listen will hear the speaking heaven. This is definitely not the hour when men take kindly to an exhortation to listen, for listening is not today a part of popular religion. We are at the opposite end of the pole from there. Religion has accepted the monstrous heresy that noise, size, activity and bluster make a man dear to God. But we may take heart. To a people caught in the tempest of the last great conflict God says, "Be still, and know that I am God" (Psalm 46:10), and still He says it, as if He means to tell us that our strength and safety lie not in noise but in silence.

It is important that we get still to wait on God. And it is best that we get alone, preferably with our Bible outspread before us. Then if we will we may draw near to God and begin to hear Him speak to us in our hearts. I think for the average person the progression will be something like this: First a sound as of a Presence walking in the garden. Then a Voice, more intelligible, but still far from clear. Then the happy moment when the Spirit begins to illuminate the Scriptures, and that which had been only a sound, or at best a voice, now becomes an intelligible word, warm and intimate and clear as the word of a dear friend. Then will come life and light, and best of all, ability to see and rest in and embrace Jesus Christ as Savior and Lord and All.

The Bible will never be a living Book to us until we are convinced that God is articulate in His universe. To jump from a dead, impersonal world to a dogmatic Bible is too much for most people. They may admit that they should accept the Bible as the Word of God, and they may try to think of it as such, but they find it impossible to believe that the words there on the page are actually for them. A man may say, "These words are addressed to me," and yet in his heart not feel and know that they are. He is the victim of a divided psychology. He tries to think of God as mute everywhere else and vocal only in a book.

I believe that much of our religious unbelief is due to a wrong conception of and a wrong feeling for the Scriptures of Truth. A silent God suddenly began to speak in a book and when the book was finished lapsed back into silence again forever. Now we read the book as the record of what God said when He was for a brief time in a speaking mood. With notions like that in our heads how can we believe? The facts are that God is not silent, has never been silent. It is the nature of God to speak. The second Person of the Holy Trinity is called the Word. The Bible is the inevitable outcome of God's continuous speech. It is the infallible declaration of His mind for us put into our familiar human words. I think a new world will arise out of the religious mists when we approach our Bible with the idea that it is not only a book which was once spoken, but a book which is *now speaking*. The prophets habitually said, "Thus *saith* the LORD." They meant their hearers to understand that God's speaking is in the continuous present. We may use the past tense properly to indicate that at a certain time a certain word of God was spoken, but a word of God once spoken continues to be spoken, as a child once born continues to be alive, or a world once created continues to exist. And those are but imperfect illustrations, for children die and worlds burn out, but the Word of our God endureth forever.

If you would follow on to know the Lord, come at once to the open Bible expecting it to speak to you. Do not come with the notion that it is a thing which you may push around at your convenience. It is more than a thing; it is a voice, a word, the very Word of the living God.

Lord, teach me to listen. The times are noisy and my ears are weary with the thousand raucous sounds which continuously assault them. Give me the spirit of the boy Samuel when he said to Thee, "Speak, for Thy servant heareth." Let me hear Thee speaking in my heart. Let me get used to the sound of Thy voice, that its tones may be familiar when the sounds of earth die away and the only sound will be the music of Thy speaking voice.

Amen.

CHAPTER 7

The Gaze of the Soul

*Looking unto Jesus the author
and finisher of our faith.*

HEBREWS 12:2

L et us think of our intelligent, plain man mentioned in chapter 6 coming for the first time to the reading of the Scriptures. He approaches the Bible without any previous knowledge of what it contains. He is wholly without prejudice; he has nothing to prove and nothing to defend.

Such a man will not have to read long until his mind begins to observe certain truths standing out from the page. They are the spiritual principles behind the record of God's dealings with men, and woven into the writings of holy men as they "were moved by the Holy Ghost" (2 Peter 1:21). As he reads on he might want to number these truths as they become clear to him and make a brief summary under each number. These summaries will be the tenets of his biblical creed. Further reading will not affect these points except to enlarge and strengthen them. Our man is finding out what the Bible actually teaches.

High up on the list of things which the Bible teaches will be the doctrine of *faith*. The place of weighty importance which the Bible gives to faith will be too plain for him to miss. He will very likely conclude that faith is all-important in the life of the soul. "Without faith it is impossible to please [God]" (Hebrews 11:6). Faith will get me anything, take me anywhere in the kingdom of God, but without faith there can be no approach to God, no forgiveness, no deliverance, no salvation, no communion, no spiritual life at all.

By the time our friend has reached the eleventh chapter of Hebrews the eloquent encomium which is there pronounced upon faith will not seem strange to him. He will have read Paul's powerful defense of faith in his Roman and Galatian epistles. Later, if he goes on to study church history, he will understand the amazing power in the teachings of the Reformers as they showed the central place of faith in the Christian religion.

Now if faith is so vitally important, if it is an indispensable must in our pursuit of God, it is perfectly natural that we should be deeply concerned over whether or not we possess this most precious gift. And our minds being what they are, it is inevitable that sooner or later we should get around to inquiring after the nature of faith. What *is* faith? would lie close to the question, Do I *have* faith? and would demand an answer if it were anywhere to be found.

Almost all who preach or write on the subject of faith have much the same things to say concerning it. They tell us that it is believing a promise, that it is taking God at His word, that it is reckoning the Bible to be true and stepping out upon it. The rest of the book or sermon is usually taken up with stories of persons who have had their prayers answered as a result of their faith. These answers are mostly direct gifts of a practical and temporal nature such as health, money, physical protection or success in business. Or if the teacher is of a philosophic turn of mind he may take another course and lose us in a welter of metaphysics or snow us under with psychological jargon as he defines and redefines, paring the slender hair of faith thinner and thinner till it disappears in gossamer shavings at last. When he is finished we get up disappointed and go out "by that same door where in we went." Surely there must be something better than this.

In Scripture there is practically no effort made to define faith. Outside of a brief fourteen-word definition in Hebrews 11:1, I know of no biblical definition. Even there faith is defined functionally, not philosophically; that is, it is a statement of what faith is *in operation, not* what it is *in essence*. It assumes the presence of faith and shows what it results in, rather than what it is. We will be wise to go just that far and attempt to go no further. We are told from whence it comes and by what means:

"Faith . . . is the gift of God" (Ephesians 2:8) and "Faith cometh by hearing, and hearing by the word of God" (Romans 10:17). This much is clear, and, to paraphrase Thomas à Kempis, "I had rather exercise faith than know the definition thereof."

From here on, when the words "faith is" or their equivalent occur in this chapter I ask that they be understood to refer to what faith is in operation as exercised by a believing man. Right here we drop the notion of definition and think about faith as it may be experienced in action. The complexion of our thoughts will be practical, not theoretical.

In a dramatic story in the book of Numbers (21:4–9) faith is seen in action. Israel became discouraged and spoke against God, and the Lord sent fiery serpents among them. "And they bit the people; and much people of Israel died" (21:6). Then Moses sought the Lord for them and He heard and gave them a remedy against the bite of the serpents. He commanded Moses to make a serpent of brass and put it upon a pole in sight of all the people, "and it shall come to pass, that every one that is bitten, when he looketh upon it, shall live" (21:8). Moses obeyed, "and it came to pass, that if a serpent had bitten any man, when he beheld the serpent of brass, he lived" (21:9).

In the New Testament this important bit of history is interpreted for us by no less an authority than our Lord Jesus Christ Himself. He is explaining to His hearers how they may be saved. He tells them that it is by believing.

Then to make it clear He refers to this incident in the book of Numbers. "As Moses lifted up the serpent in the wilderness, even so must the Son of man be lifted up: that whosoever believeth in him should not perish, but have eternal life" (John 3:14–15).

Our plain man, in reading this, would make an important discovery. He would notice that *look* and *believe* are synonymous terms. "Looking" on the Old Testament serpent is identical with "believing" on the New Testament Christ. That is, the *looking* and the *believing* are the same thing. And he would understand that, while Israel looked with their external eyes, believing is done with the heart. I think he would conclude that *faith is the gaze of a soul upon a saving God.*

When he had seen this he would remember passages he had read before, and their meaning would come flooding over him. "They looked unto him, and were lightened: and their faces were not ashamed" (Psalm 34:5). "Unto thee lift I up mine eyes, O thou that dwellest in the heavens. Behold, as the eyes of servants look unto the hand of their masters, and as the eyes of a maiden unto the hand of her mistress; so our eyes wait upon the LORD our God, until that he have mercy upon us" (123:1–2). Here the man seeking mercy looks straight at the God of mercy and never takes his eyes away from Him till He grants mercy. And our Lord Himself looked always at God. "Looking up to heaven, he blessed, and brake, and gave the loaves to his disciples" (Matthew 14:19). Indeed,

Jesus taught that He wrought His works by always keeping His inward eyes upon His Father. His power lay in His continuous look at God (John 5:19–21).

In full accord with the few texts we have quoted is the whole tenor of the inspired Word. It is summed up for us in the Hebrew epistle when we are instructed to run life's race "looking unto Jesus the author and finisher of our faith" (Hebrews 12:2). From all this we learn that faith is not a once-done act, but a continuous gaze of the heart at the Triune God.

Believing, then, is directing the heart's attention to Jesus. It is lifting the mind to "Behold the Lamb of God" (John 1:29), and never ceasing that beholding for the rest of our lives. At first this may be difficult, but it becomes easier as we look steadily at His wondrous person, quietly and without strain. Distractions may hinder, but once the heart is committed to Him, after each brief excursion away from Him, the attention will return again and rest upon Him like a wandering bird coming back to its window.

I would emphasize this one committal, this one great volitional act which establishes the heart's intention to gaze forever upon Jesus. God takes this intention for our choice and makes what allowances He must for the thousand distractions which beset us in this evil world. He knows that we have set the direction of our hearts toward Jesus, and we can know it too, and comfort ourselves with the knowledge that a habit of soul is forming which will become, after a while, a sort of spiritual reflex requiring no more conscious effort on our part.

Faith is the least self-regarding of the virtues. It is by its very nature scarcely conscious of its own existence. Like the eye which sees everything in front of it and never sees itself, faith is occupied with the Object upon which it rests and pays no attention to itself at all. While we are looking at God we do not see ourselves—blessed riddance. The man who has struggled to purify himself and has had nothing but repeated failures will experience real relief when he stops tinkering with his soul and looks away to the perfect One. While he looks at Christ, the very things he has so long been trying to do will be getting done within him. It will be God working in him to will and to do.

Faith is not in itself a meritorious act; the merit is in the One toward Whom it is directed. Faith is a redirecting of our sight, a getting out of the focus of our own vision and getting God into focus. Sin has twisted our vision inward and made it self-regarding. Unbelief has put self where God should be, and is perilously close to the sin of Lucifer who said, "I will set my throne above the throne of God." Faith looks *out* instead of *in* and the whole life falls into line.

All this may seem too simple. But we have no apology to make. To those who would seek to climb into heaven after help or descend into hell, God says, "The word is nigh thee, even . . . the word of faith" (Romans 10:8).

The Word induces us to lift up our eyes unto the Lord and the blessed work of faith begins.

When we lift our inward eyes to gaze upon God we are sure to meet friendly eyes gazing back at us, for it is written that the eyes of the Lord run to and fro throughout all the earth. The sweet language of experience is "Thou God seest me" (Genesis 16:13). When the eyes of the soul looking out meet the eyes of God looking in, heaven has begun right here on this earth.

Nicholas of Cusa wrote four hundred years ago:

> When all my endeavor is turned toward Thee because all Thy endeavor is turned toward me; when I look unto Thee alone with all my attention, nor ever turn aside the eyes of my mind, because Thou dost enfold me with Thy constant regard; when I direct my love toward Thee alone because Thou, who art Love's self hast turned Thee toward me alone. And what, Lord, is my life, save that embrace wherein Thy delight-some sweetness doth so lovingly enfold me?[1]

I should like to say more about this old man of God. He is not much known today anywhere among Christian believers, and among current fundamentalists he is known not at all. I feel that we could gain much from a little acquaintance with men of his spiritual flavor and the school of Christian thought which they represent. Christian literature, to be accepted and approved by evangelical leaders of our times, must follow very closely the same train of thought, a kind of "party line" from which it is scarcely safe to depart. A half-century of this in America has made us smug and content. We imitate each other with slavish devotion. Our most strenuous efforts are put forth to try to say the same thing that everyone around us is saying—and yet to find an excuse for saying it, some little safe variation on the approved theme or, if no more, at least a new illustration.

Nicholas was a true follower of Christ, a lover of the Lord, radiant and shining in his devotion to the person of Jesus. His theology was orthodox but fragrant and sweet as everything about Jesus might properly be expected to be. His conception of eternal life, for instance, is beautiful in itself and, if I mistake not, is nearer in spirit to John 17:3 than that which is current among us today. Life eternal, says Nicholas, is

> nought other than that blessed regard wherewith Thou never ceasest to behold me, yes, even the secret places of my soul. With Thee, to behold is to give life; 'tis unceasingly to impart sweetest love of Thee; 'tis to inflame me to love of Thee by love's imparting, and to feed me by inflaming, and by feeding to kindle my yearning, and by kindling to make me drink of the dew of gladness, and by drinking to infuse in me a fountain of life, and by infusing to make it increase and endure.[2]

Now, if faith is the gaze of the heart at God, and if this gaze is but the raising of the inward eyes to meet the all-seeing eyes of God, then it follows that it is one of the easiest things possible to do. It would be like God to make the most vital thing easy and place it within the range of possibility for the weakest and poorest of us.

Several conclusions may fairly be drawn from all this. The simplicity of it, for instance. Since believing is looking, it can be done without special equipment or religious paraphernalia. God has seen to it that the one life-and-death essential can never be subject to the caprice of accident. Equipment can break down or get lost, water can leak away, records can be destroyed by fire, the minister can be delayed or the church can burn down. All these are external to the soul and are subject to accident or mechanical failure. But looking is of the heart and can be done successfully by any man standing up or kneeling down or lying in his last agony a thousand miles from any church.

Since believing is looking it can be done any time. No season is superior to another season for this sweetest of all acts. God never made salvation depend upon new moons or holy days or sabbaths. A man is not nearer to Christ on Easter Sunday than he is, say, on Saturday, August 3, or Monday, October 4. As long as Christ sits on the mediatorial throne, every day is a good day and all days are days of salvation.

Neither does place matter to this blessed work of believing God. Lift your heart and let it rest upon Jesus and you are instantly in a sanctuary though it be a Pullman berth or a factory or a kitchen. You can see God from anywhere if your mind is set to love and obey Him.

Now, someone may ask, "Is not this of which you speak for special persons such as monks or ministers who have, by the nature of their calling, more time to devote to quiet meditation? I am a busy worker and have little time to spend alone." I am happy to say that the life I describe is for every one of God's children regardless of calling. It is, in fact, happily practiced every day by many hardworking persons and is beyond the reach of none.

Many have found the secret of which I speak and, without giving much thought to what is going on within them, constantly practice this habit of inwardly gazing upon God. They know that something inside their hearts sees God. Even when they are compelled to withdraw their conscious attention in order to engage in earthly affairs, there is within them a secret communion always going on. Let their attention but be released for a moment from necessary business and it flies at once to God again. This has been the testimony of many Christians, so many that even as I state it thus I have a feeling that I am quoting, though from whom or from how many I cannot possibly know.

I do not want to leave the impression that the ordinary means of grace have no value. They most assuredly have. Private prayer should be practiced by every Christian. Long periods of Bible meditation will purify our gaze and direct it; church attendance will enlarge our outlook and increase our love for others. Service and work and activity—all are good and should be engaged in by every Christian. But at the bottom of all these things, giving meaning to them, will be the inward habit of beholding God. A new set of eyes (so to speak) will develop within us enabling us to be looking at God while our outward eyes are seeing the scenes of this passing world.

Someone may fear that we are magnifying private religion out of all proportion, that the "us" of the New Testament is being displaced by a selfish "I." Has it ever occurred to you that one hundred pianos all tuned to the same fork are automatically tuned to each other? They are of one accord by being tuned, not to each other, but to another standard to which one must individually bow. So one hundred worshipers meeting together, each one looking away to Christ, are in heart nearer to each other than they could possibly be were they to become "unity" conscious and turn their eyes away from God to strive for closer fellowship. Social religion is perfected when private religion is purified. The body becomes stronger as its members become healthier. The whole church of God gains when the members that compose it begin to seek a better and a higher life.

All the foregoing presupposes true repentance and a full committal of the life to God. It is hardly necessary to mention this, for only persons who have made such a committal will have read this far.

When the habit of inwardly gazing Godward becomes fixed within us, we shall be ushered onto a new level of spiritual life more in keeping with the promises of God and the mood of the New Testament. The Triune God will be our dwelling place even while our feet walk the low road of simple duty here among men. We will have found life's *summum bonum* indeed.

> There is the source of all delights that can be desired; not only can nought better be thought out by men and angels, but nought better can exist in any mode of being! For it is the absolute maximum of every rational desire, than which a greater cannot be.[3]

O Lord, I have heard a good word inviting me to look away to Thee and be satisfied.

My heart longs to respond, but sin has clouded my vision till I see Thee but dimly. Be pleased to cleanse me in Thine own precious blood, and make me inwardly pure, so that I may with unveiled eyes gaze upon Thee all the days of my earthly pilgrimage.

Then shall I be prepared to behold Thee in full splendor in the day when Thou shalt appear to be glorified in Thy saints and admired in all them that believe.

Amen.

NOTES

1. Nicholas of Cusa, *The Vision of God*, E.P. Dutton & Co., Inc., New York, 1928. This and the following used by kind permission of the publishers.
2. Ibid.
3. Ibid.

CHAPTER 8

Restoring the Creator-Creature Relation

Be thou exalted, O God, above the heavens;
let thy glory be above all the earth.

PSALM 57:5

It is true that order in nature depends upon right relationships; to achieve harmony each thing must be in its proper position relative to each other thing. In human life it is not otherwise. I have hinted before in these chapters that the cause of all our human miseries is a radical moral dislocation, an upset in our relation to God and to each other. For whatever else the fall may have been, it was certainly a sharp change in man's relation to his Creator. He adopted toward God an altered attitude, and by so doing destroyed the proper Creator-creature relation in which, unknown to him, his true happiness lay. Essentially, salvation is the restoration of a right relation between man and his Creator, a bringing back to normal of the Creator-creature relation.

A satisfactory spiritual life will begin with a complete change in relation between God and the sinner; not a judicial change merely, but a conscious and experienced change affecting the sinner's whole nature. The atonement in Jesus' blood makes such a change judicially possible and the working of the Holy Spirit makes it emotionally satisfying. The story of the prodigal son perfectly illustrates this latter phase. He had brought a world of trouble upon himself by forsaking the position which he had properly held as son of his father. At bottom of his restoration was nothing more than a reestablishing of the father-son relation which had existed from his birth and had been altered temporarily by his act of sinful rebellion. This story overlooks the legal aspects of redemption, but it makes beautifully clear the experiential aspects of salvation.

In determining relationships we must begin somewhere. There must be somewhere a fixed center against which everything else is measured, where the law of relativity does not enter and we can say "IS" and make no allowances. Such a center is God. When God would make His name known to mankind He could find no better word than "I AM." When He speaks in the first person He says, "I AM"; when we speak *of* Him we say, "He is"; when we speak *to* Him we say, "Thou art." Everyone and everything else measures from that fixed point. "I AM

THAT I AM," (Exodus 3:14) says God, "I change not" (Malachi 3:6).

As the sailor locates his position on the sea by "shooting" the sun, so we may get our moral bearings by looking at God. We must begin with God. We are right when, and only when, we stand in a right position relative to God, and we are wrong so far and so long as we stand in any other position.

Much of our difficulty as seeking Christians stems from our unwillingness to take God as He is and adjust our lives accordingly. We insist upon trying to modify Him and to bring Him nearer to our own image. The flesh whimpers against the rigor of God's inexorable sentence and begs like Agag for a little mercy, a little indulgence of its carnal ways. It is no use. We can get a right start only by accepting God as He is and learning to love Him for what He is. As we go on to know Him better we shall find it a source of unspeakable joy that God is just what He is. Some of the most rapturous moments we know will be those we spend in reverent admiration of the Godhead. In those holy moments the very thought of change in Him will be too painful to endure.

So let us begin with God. Back of all, above all, before all is God; first in sequential order, above in rank and station, exalted in dignity and honor. As the self-existent One He gave being to all things, and all things exist out of Him and for Him. "Thou art worthy, O Lord, to receive glory and honour and power: for thou hast created

all things, and for thy pleasure they are and were created"
(Revelation 4:11).

Every soul belongs to God and exists by His pleasure.
God being who and what He is, and we being who and
what we are, the only thinkable relation between us is
one of full lordship on His part and complete submission
on ours. We owe Him every honor that is in our power to
give Him. Our everlasting grief lies in giving Him anything less.

The pursuit of God will embrace the labor of bringing
our total personality into conformity to His. And this
not judicially, but actually. I do not here refer to the act
of justification by faith in Christ. I speak of a voluntary
exalting of God to His proper station over us and a willing surrender of our whole being to the place of worshipful submission which the Creator-creature circumstance
makes proper.

The moment we make up our minds that we are going
on with this determination to exalt God over all, we step
out of the world's parade. We shall find ourselves out of
adjustment to the ways of the world, and increasingly so
as we make progress in the holy way. We shall acquire a
new viewpoint; a new and different psychology will be
formed within us; a new power will begin to surprise us
by its upsurgings and its outgoings.

Our break with the world will be the direct outcome
of our changed relation to God. For the world of fallen
men does not honor God. Millions call themselves by

His name, it is true, and pay some token respect to Him, but a simple test will show how little He is really honored among them. Let the average man be put to the proof on the question of who or what is *above*, and his true position will be exposed. Let him be forced into making a choice between God and money, between God and men, between God and personal ambition, God and self, God and human love, and God will take second place every time. Those other things will be exalted above. However the man may protest, the proof is in the choices he makes day after day throughout his life.

"Be thou exalted" (Psalm 21:13) is the language of victorious spiritual experience. It is a little key to unlock the door to great treasures of grace. It is central in the life of God in the soul. Let the seeking man reach a place where life and lips join to say continually, "Be thou exalted," and a thousand minor problems will be solved at once. His Christian life ceases to be the complicated thing it had been before and becomes the very essence of simplicity. By the exercise of his will he has set his course, and on that course he will stay as if guided by an automatic pilot. If blown off course for a moment by some adverse wind, he will surely return again as by a secret bent of the soul. The hidden motions of the Spirit are working in his favor, and "the stars in their courses" (Judges 5:20) fight for him. He has met his life problem at its center, and everything else must follow along.

Let no one imagine that he will lose anything of human

dignity by this voluntary sell-out of his all to his God. He does not by this degrade himself as a man; rather he finds his right place of high honor as one made in the image of his Creator. His deep disgrace lay in his moral derangement, his unnatural usurpation of the place of God. His honor will be proved by restoring again that stolen throne. In exalting God over all he finds his own highest honor upheld.

Anyone who might feel reluctant to surrender his will to the will of another should remember Jesus' words, "Whosoever committeth sin is the servant of sin" (John 8:34). We must of necessity be servant to someone, either to God or to sin. The sinner prides himself on his independence, completely overlooking the fact that he is the weak slave of the sins that rule his members. The man who surrenders to Christ exchanges a cruel slave driver for a kind and gentle Master whose yoke is easy and whose burden is light.

Made as we were in the image of God, we scarcely find it strange to take again our God as our All. God was our original habitat and our hearts cannot but feel at home when they enter again that ancient and beautiful abode.

I hope it is clear that there is a logic behind God's claim to preeminence. That place is His by every right in earth or heaven. While we take to ourselves the place that is His, the whole course of our lives is out of joint. Nothing will or can restore order till our hearts make the great decision: God shall be exalted above.

"Them that honour me I will honour" (1 Samuel 2:30), said God once to a priest of Israel, and that ancient law of the kingdom stands today unchanged by the passing of time or the changes of dispensation. The whole Bible and every page of history proclaim the perpetuation of that law. "If any man serve me, him will my Father honour" (John 12:26), said our Lord Jesus, tying in the old with the new and revealing the essential unity of His ways with men.

Sometimes the best way to see a thing is to look at its opposite. Eli and his sons are placed in the priesthood with the stipulation that they honor God in their lives and ministrations. This they fail to do, and God sends Samuel to announce the consequences. Unknown to Eli this law of reciprocal honor has been all the while secretly working, and now the time has come for judgment to fall. Hophni and Phineas, the degenerate priests, fall in battle; the wife of Phineas dies in childbirth; Israel flees before her enemies; the ark of God is captured by the Philistines, and the old man Eli falls backward and dies of a broken neck. This stark, utter tragedy followed upon Eli's failure to honor God.

Now over against this set almost any Bible character who honestly tried to glorify God in his earthly walk. See how God winked at weakness and overlooked failures as He poured upon His servants grace and blessing untold. Let it be Abraham, Jacob, David, Daniel, Elijah or whom you will; honor followed honor as harvest the seed. The man of God set his heart to exalt God above all; God accepted his intention as fact and acted accordingly. Not perfection, but holy intention made the difference.

In our Lord Jesus Christ this law was seen in simple perfection. In His lowly manhood He humbled Himself and gladly gave all glory to His Father in heaven. He sought not His own honor, but the honor of God who sent Him. "If I honour myself," He said on one occasion, "my honour is nothing: it is my Father that honoureth me" (8:54). So far had the Pharisees departed from this law that they could not understand one who honored God at his own expense. "I honour my Father," said Jesus to them, "and ye do dishonour me" (8:49).

Another saying of Jesus, and a most disturbing one, was put in the form of a question. "How can ye believe, which receive honour one of another, and seek not the honour that cometh from God only?" (5:44). If I understand this correctly, Christ taught here the alarming doctrine that the desire for honor among men made belief impossible. Is this sin at the root of religious unbelief? Could it be that those "intellectual difficulties" which men blame for their inability to believe are but smoke screens to conceal the real cause that lies behind them? Was it this greedy desire for honor from man that made men into Pharisees and Pharisees into Deicides? Is this the secret back of religious self-righteousness and empty worship? I believe it may be. The whole course of the life is upset by failure to put God where He belongs. We exalt ourselves instead of God and the curse follows.

In our desire after God let us keep always in mind that God also has desire, and His desire is toward the sons of men, and more particularly toward those sons of men who will make the once-for-all decision to exalt Him over all. Such as these are precious to God above all treasures of earth or sea. In them God finds a theater where He can display His exceeding kindness toward us in Christ Jesus. With them God can walk unhindered; toward them He can act like the God He is.

In speaking thus I have one fear: that I may convince the mind before God can win the heart. For this God-above-all position is one not easy to take. The mind may approve it while not having the consent of the will to put it into effect. While the imagination races ahead to honor God, the will may lag behind and the man must make the decision before the heart can know any real satisfaction. God wants the whole person and He will not rest till He gets us in entirety. No part of the man will do.

Let us pray over this in detail, throwing ourselves at God's feet and meaning everything we say. No one who prays thus in sincerity need wait long for tokens of divine acceptance. God will unveil His glory before His servant's eyes, and He will place all His treasures at the disposal of such a one, for He knows that His honor is safe in such consecrated hands.

O God, be Thou exalted over my possessions. Nothing of earth's treasures shall seem dear unto me if only Thou art glorified in my life. Be Thou exalted over my friendships. I am determined that Thou shalt be above all, though I must stand deserted and alone in the midst of the earth. Be Thou exalted above my comforts. Though it mean the loss of bodily comforts and the carrying of heavy crosses, I shall keep my vow made this day before Thee. Be Thou exalted over my reputation. Make me ambitious to please Thee even if as a result I must sink into obscurity and my name be forgotten as a dream. Rise, O Lord, into Thy proper place of honor, above my ambitions, above my likes and dislikes, above my family, my health and even my life itself. Let me sink that Thou mayest rise above.

Ride forth upon me as Thou didst ride into Jerusalem mounted upon the humble little beast, a colt, the foal of an ass, and let me hear the children cry to Thee, "Hosanna in the highest."

Amen.

CHAPTER 9

Meekness and Rest

Blessed are the meek:
for they shall inherit the earth.

MATTHEW 5:5

A fairly accurate description of the human race might be furnished to one unacquainted with it by taking the Beatitudes, turning them wrong side out and saying, "Here is your human race." For the exact opposite of the virtues in the Beatitudes are the very qualities which distinguish human life and conduct.

In the world of men we find nothing approaching the virtues of which Jesus spoke in the opening words of the famous Sermon on the Mount. Instead of poverty of spirit we find the rankest kind of pride; instead of mourners we find pleasure seekers; instead of meekness, arrogance; instead of hunger after righteousness we hear men saying, "I am rich and increased with goods and have need of nothing"; instead of mercy we find cruelty;

315

instead of purity of heart, corrupt imaginings; instead of peacemakers we find men quarrelsome and resentful; instead of rejoicing in mistreatment we find them fighting back with every weapon at their command.

Of this kind of moral stuff civilized society is composed. The atmosphere is charged with it; we breathe it with every breath and drink it with our mother's milk. Culture and education refine these things slightly but leave them basically untouched. A whole world of literature has been created to justify this kind of life as the only normal one. And this is the more to be wondered at seeing that these are the evils which make life the bitter struggle it is for all of us. All our heartaches and a great many of our physical ills spring directly out of our sins. Pride, arrogance, resentfulness, evil imaginings, malice, greed are the sources of more human pain than all the diseases that ever afflicted mortal flesh.

Into a world like this the sound of Jesus' words comes wonderful and strange, a visitation from above. It is well that He spoke, for no one else could have done it as well; and it is good that we listen. His words are the essence of truth. He is not offering an opinion; Jesus never uttered opinions. He never guessed; He knew, and He knows. His words are not as Solomon's were, the sum of sound wisdom or the results of keen observation. He spoke out of the fullness of His Godhead, and His words are very Truth itself. He is the only one who could say "blessed" with complete authority, for He is the Blessed One come from the world above to confer blessedness upon mankind. And His words were supported by deeds mightier than any performed on this earth by any other man. It is wisdom for us to listen.

As was often so with Jesus, He used this word *meek* in a brief crisp sentence, and not till sometime later did He go on to explain it. In the same book of Matthew He tells us more about it and applies it to our lives. "Come unto me, all ye that labour and are heavy laden, and I will give you rest. Take my yoke upon you, and learn of me; for I am meek and lowly in heart: and ye shall find rest unto your souls. For my yoke is easy, and my burden is light" (11:28–30). Here we have two things standing in contrast to each other, a burden and a rest. The burden is not a local one, peculiar to those first hearers, but one which is borne by the whole human race. It consists not of political oppression or poverty or hard work. It is far deeper than that. It is felt by the rich as well as the poor, for it is something from which wealth and idleness can never deliver us.

The burden borne by mankind is a heavy and a crushing thing. The word Jesus used means "a load carried or toil borne to the point of exhaustion." Rest is simply release from that burden. It is not something we do; it is what comes to us when we cease to do. His own meekness, that is the rest.

Let us examine our burden. It is altogether an interior one. It attacks the heart and the mind and reaches the body only from within. First, there is the burden of *pride.* The labor of self-love is a heavy one indeed. Think for yourself whether much of your sorrow has not arisen from someone speaking slightingly of you. As long as you set yourself up as a little god to which you must be loyal there will be those who will delight to offer affront to your idol. How then can you hope to have inward peace? The heart's fierce effort to protect itself from every slight, to shield its touchy honor from the bad opinion of friend and enemy, will never let the mind have rest. Continue this fight through the years and the burden will become intolerable. Yet the sons of earth are carrying this burden continually, challenging every word spoken against them, cringing under every criticism, smarting under each fancied slight, tossing sleepless if another is preferred before them. Such a burden as this is not necessary to bear. Jesus calls us to His rest, and meekness is His method. The meek man cares not at all who is greater than he, for he has long ago decided that the esteem of the world is not worth the effort. He develops toward himself a kindly sense of humor and learns to say, "Oh, so you have been overlooked? They have placed someone else before you? They have whispered that you are pretty small stuff after all? And now you feel hurt because the world is saying about you the very things you have been saying about yourself? Only yesterday you were telling God that you were nothing, a mere worm of the dust. Where is your consistency? Come on, humble yourself and cease to care what men think."

The meek man is not a human mouse afflicted with a sense of his own inferiority. Rather, he may be in his moral life as bold as a lion and as strong as Samson; but he has stopped being fooled about himself. He has accepted God's estimate of his own life. He knows he is as weak and helpless as God has declared him to be, but paradoxically, he knows at the same time that he is, in the sight of God, more important than angels. In himself, nothing; in God, everything. That is his motto. He knows well that the world will never see him as God sees him and he has stopped caring. He rests perfectly content to allow God to place His own values. He will be patient to wait for the day when everything will get its own price tag and real worth will come into its own. Then the righteous shall shine forth in the kingdom of their Father. He is willing to wait for that day.

In the meantime, he will have attained a place of soul rest. As he walks on in meekness he will be happy to let God defend him. The old struggle to defend himself is over. He has found the peace which meekness brings.

Then also he will get deliverance from the burden of *pretense*. By this I mean not hypocrisy, but the common human desire to put the best foot forward and hide from the world our real inward poverty. For sin has played many evil tricks upon us, and one has been the infusing into us of a false sense of shame. There is hardly a man or woman who dares to be just what he or she is without doctoring up the impression. The fear of being found out gnaws like rodents within their hearts. The man of culture is haunted by the fear that he will someday come upon a man more cultured than himself. The learned man fears to meet a man more learned than he. The rich man sweats under the fear that his clothes or his car or his house will sometime be made to look cheap by comparison with those of another rich man. So-called "society" runs by a motivation not higher than this, and the poorer classes on their level are little better.

Let no one smile this off. These burdens are real, and little by little they kill the victims of this evil and unnatural way of life. And the psychology created by years of this kind of thing makes true meekness seem as unreal as a dream, as aloof as a star. To all the victims of the gnawing disease Jesus says, "Ye . . . [must] become as little children" (Matthew 18:3). For little children do not compare; they receive direct enjoyment from what they have without relating it to something else or someone else. Only as they get older and sin begins to stir within their hearts do jealousy and envy appear. Then they are unable to enjoy what they have if someone else has something larger or better. At that early age does the galling burden come down upon their tender souls, and it never leaves them till Jesus sets them free.

Another source of burden is *artificiality*. I am sure that most people live in secret fear that some day they will be careless and by chance an enemy or friend will be allowed to peep into their poor, empty souls. So they are never relaxed. Bright people are tense and alert in fear that they may be trapped into saying something common or stupid. Traveled people are afraid that they may meet some Marco Polo who is able to describe some remote place where they have never been.

This unnatural condition is part of our sad heritage of sin, but in our day it is aggravated by our whole way of life. Advertising is largely based upon this habit of pretense. "Courses" are offered in this or that field of human learning frankly appealing to the victim's desire to shine at a party. Books are sold, clothes and cosmetics are peddled by playing continually upon this desire to appear what we are not. Artificiality is one curse that will drop away the moment we kneel at Jesus' feet and surrender ourselves to His meekness. Then we will not care what people think of us so long as God is pleased. Then *what we are* will be everything; what we appear will take its place far down the scale of interest for us. Apart from sin we have nothing of which to be ashamed. Only an evil desire to shine makes us want to appear other than we are.

The heart of the world is breaking under this load of pride and pretense. There is no release from our burden apart from the meekness of Christ. Good, keen reasoning may help slightly, but so strong is the vice that if we push it down one place, it will come up somewhere else. To men and women everywhere Jesus says, "Come unto me, and I will give you rest." The rest He offers is the rest of meekness, the blessed relief which comes when we accept ourselves for what we are and cease to pretend. It will take some courage at first, but the needed grace will come as we learn that we are sharing this new and easy yoke with the strong Son of God Himself. He calls it "My yoke," and He walks at one end while we walk at the other.

Lord, make me childlike. Deliver me from the urge to compete with another for place or prestige or position. I would be simple and artless as a little child. Deliver me from pose and pretense. Forgive me for thinking of myself. Help me to forget myself and find my true peace in beholding Thee. That Thou may answer this prayer I humble myself before Thee.

Lay upon me Thy easy yoke of self-forgetfulness that through it I may find rest.

Amen.

CHAPTER 10

The Sacrament of Living

Whether therefore ye eat, or drink,
or whatsoever ye do, do all to the glory of God.

1 CORINTHIANS 10:31

O ne of the greatest hindrances to internal peace which the Christian encounters is the common habit of dividing our lives into two areas—the sacred and the secular. As these areas are conceived to exist apart from each other and to be morally and spiritually incompatible, and as we are compelled by the necessities of living to be always crossing back and forth from the one to the other, our inner lives tend to break up so that we live a divided instead of a unified life.

Our trouble springs from the fact that we who follow Christ inhabit at once two worlds—the spiritual and the natural. As children of Adam we live our lives on earth subject to the limitations of the flesh and the weaknesses and ills to which human nature is heir. Merely to live among men requires of us years of hard toil and much care and attention to the things of this world. In sharp contrast to this is our life in the Spirit. There we enjoy another and higher kind of life—we are children of God; we possess heavenly status and enjoy intimate fellowship with Christ.

This tends to divide our total life into two departments. We come unconsciously to recognize two sets of actions. The first are performed with a feeling of satisfaction and a firm assurance that they are pleasing to God. These are the sacred acts and they are usually thought to be prayer, Bible reading, hymn singing, church attendance, and such other acts as spring directly from faith. They may be known by the fact that they have no direct relation to this world, and would have no meaning whatever except as faith shows us another world, "an house not made with hands, eternal in the heavens" (2 Corinthians 5:1).

Over against these sacred acts are the secular ones. They include all of the ordinary activities of life which we share with the sons and daughters of Adam: eating, sleeping, working, looking after the needs of the body and performing our dull and prosaic duties here on earth. These we often do reluctantly and with many misgivings, often apologizing to God for what we consider a waste of time and strength. The upshot of this is that we are uneasy most of the time. We go about our common tasks with a feeling of deep frustration, telling ourselves pensively that there's a better day coming when we shall slough off this earthly shell and be bothered no more with the affairs of this world.

This is the old sacred-secular antithesis. Most Christians are caught in its trap. They cannot get a satisfactory adjustment between the claims of the two worlds. They try to walk the tightrope between two kingdoms and they find no peace in either. Their strength is reduced, their outlook confused and their joy taken from them.

I believe this state of affairs to be wholly unnecessary. We have gotten ourselves on the horns of a dilemma, true enough, but the dilemma is not real. It is a creature of misunderstanding. The sacred-secular antithesis has no foundation in the New Testament. Without doubt, a more perfect understanding of Christian truth will deliver us from it.

The Lord Jesus Christ Himself is our perfect example, and He knew no divided life. In the presence of His Father He lived on earth without strain from babyhood to His death on the cross. God accepted the offering of His total life, and made no distinction between act and act. "I do always those things that please him," was His brief summary of His own life as it related to the Father (John 8:29). As He moved among men He was poised and restful. What pressure and suffering He endured grew out of His position as the world's sin bearer; they were never the result of moral uncertainty or spiritual maladjustment.

Paul's exhortation to "do all to the glory of God" is more than pious idealism. It is an integral part of the sacred revelation and is to be accepted as the very Word of Truth. It opens before us the possibility of making every act of our lives contribute to the glory of God. Lest we should be too timid to include everything, Paul mentions specifically eating and drinking. This humble privilege we share with the beasts that perish. If these lowly animal acts can be so performed as to honor God, then it becomes difficult to conceive of one that cannot.

That monkish hatred of the body which figures so prominently in the works of certain early devotional writers is wholly without support in the Word of God. Common modesty is found in the sacred Scriptures, it is true, but never prudery or a false sense of shame. The New Testament accepts as a matter of course that in His incarnation our Lord took upon Him a real human body, and no effort is made to steer around the downright implications of such a fact. He lived in that body here among men and never once performed a non-sacred act. His presence in human flesh sweeps away forever the evil notion that there is about the human body something innately offensive to the Deity. God created our bodies, and we do not offend Him by placing the responsibility where it belongs. He is not ashamed of the work of His own hands.

Perversion, misuse and abuse of our human powers should give us cause enough to be ashamed. Bodily acts done in sin and contrary to nature can never honor God. Wherever the human will introduces moral evil we have no longer our innocent and harmless powers as God made them; we have instead an abused and twisted thing which can never bring glory to its Creator.

Let us, however, assume that perversion and abuse are not present. Let us think of a Christian believer in whose life the twin wonders of repentance and the new birth have been wrought. He is now living according to the will of God as he understands it from the written Word. Of such a one it may be said that every act of his life is or can be as truly sacred as prayer or baptism or the Lord's Supper. To say this is not to bring all acts down to one dead level; it is rather to lift every act up into a living kingdom and turn the whole life into a sacrament. If a sacrament is an external expression of an inward grace, then we need not hesitate to accept the above thesis. By one act of consecration of our total selves to God we can make every subsequent act express that consecration. We need no more be ashamed of our body—the fleshly servant that carries us through life— than Jesus was of the humble beast upon which He rode into Jerusalem. "The Lord hath need of [him]" (Matthew 21:3) may well apply to our mortal bodies. If Christ dwells in us, we may bear about the Lord of glory as the little beast did of old and give occasion to the multitudes to cry, "Hosanna in the highest."

That we *see* this truth is not enough. If we would escape from the toils of the sacred-secular dilemma, the truth must "run in our blood" and condition the complex of our thoughts. We must practice living to the glory of God, actually and determinedly. By meditation upon this truth, by talking it over with God often in our prayers, by recalling it to our minds frequently as we move about among men, a sense of its wondrous meaning will take hold of us. The old painful duality will go down before a restful unity of life. The knowledge that we are all God's, that He has received all and rejected nothing, will unify our inner lives and make everything sacred to us.

This is not quite all. Long-held habits do not die easily. It will take intelligent thought and a great deal of reverent prayer to escape completely from the sacred-secular psychology. For instance, it may be difficult for the average Christian to get hold of the idea that his daily labors can be performed as acts of worship acceptable to God by Jesus Christ. The old antithesis will crop up in the back of his head sometimes to disturb his peace of mind. Nor will that old serpent, the devil, take all this lying down. He will be there in the cab or at the desk or in the field to remind the Christian that he is giving the better part of his day to the things of this world and allotting to his religious duties only a trifling portion of his time. And unless great care is taken, this will create confusion and bring discouragement and heaviness of heart.

We can meet this successfully only by the exercise of an aggressive faith. We must offer all our acts to God and believe that He accepts them. Then hold firmly to that position and keep insisting that every act of every hour of the day and night be included in the transaction. Keep reminding God in our times of private prayer that we mean every act for His glory; then supplement those times by a thousand thought-prayers as we go about the job of living. Let us practice the fine art of making every work a priestly ministration. Let us believe that God is in all our simple deeds and learn to find Him there.

A concomitant of the error which we have been discussing is the sacred-secular antithesis as applied to places. It is little short of astonishing that we can read the New Testament and still believe in the inherent sacredness of some places. This error is so widespread that one feels all alone when he tries to combat it. It has acted as a kind of dye to color the thinking of religious persons and has colored the eyes as well so that it is all but impossible to detect its fallacy. In the face of every New Testament teaching to the contrary, it has been said and sung throughout the centuries and accepted as a part of the Christian message, that which it most surely is not. Only the Quakers, so far as my knowledge goes, have had the perception to see the error and the courage to expose it. Here are the facts as I see them. For four hundred years Israel had dwelt in Egypt, surrounded by the crassest idolatry. By the hand of Moses they were brought out at last and started toward the land of promise. The very idea of holiness had been lost to them. To correct this, God began at the bottom. He localized Himself in the cloud and fire, and later when the tabernacle had been built He dwelt in fiery manifestation in the Holy of Holies. By innumerable distinctions God taught Israel the difference between holy and unholy. There were holy days, holy vessels, holy garments. There were washings, sacrifices, offerings of many kinds. By these means, Israel learned that *God is holy*. It was this that He was teaching them, not the holiness of things or places. The holiness of Jehovah was the lesson they must learn.

Then came the great day when Christ appeared. Immediately He began to say, "Ye have heard that it was said by them of old time . . . but I say unto you" (Matthew 5:21–22). The Old Testament schooling was over. When Christ died on the cross, the veil of the temple was rent from top to bottom. The Holy of Holies was opened to everyone who would enter in faith. Christ's words were remembered, "The hour cometh, when ye shall neither in this mountain, nor yet at Jerusalem, worship the Father. . . . But the hour cometh, and now is, when the true worshippers shall worship the Father in spirit and in truth: for the Father seeketh such to worship him. God is a Spirit: and they that worship him must worship him in spirit and in truth" (John 4:21, 23–24).

Shortly after, Paul took up the cry of liberty and declared all meats clean, every day holy, all places sacred and every act acceptable to God. The sacredness of times and places, a half-light necessary to the education of the race, passed away before the full sun of spiritual worship.

The essential spirituality of worship remained the possession of the church until it was slowly lost with the passing of the years. Then the natural *legality* of the fallen hearts of men began to introduce the old distinctions. The church came to observe again days and seasons and times. Certain places were chosen and marked out as holy in a special sense. Differences were observed between one and another day or place or person. The "sacraments" were first two, then three, then four, until with the triumph of Romanism they were fixed at seven.

In all charity, and with no desire to reflect unkindly upon any Christian, however misled, I would point out that the Roman Catholic church represents today the sacred-secular heresy carried to its logical conclusion. Its deadliest effect is the complete cleavage it introduces between religion and life. Its teachers attempt to avoid this snare by many footnotes and multitudinous explanations, but the mind's instinct for logic is too strong. In practical living the cleavage is a fact.

From this bondage reformers and puritans and mystics have labored to free us. Today, the trend in conservative circles is back toward that bondage again. It is said that a horse, after it has been led out of a burning building, will sometimes, by a strange obstinacy, break loose from its rescuer and dash back into the building again to perish in the flame. By some such stubborn tendency toward error, fundamentalism in our day is moving back toward spiritual slavery. The observation of days and times is becoming more and more prominent among us. "Lent" and "holy week" and "good" Friday are words heard more and more frequently upon the lips of gospel Christians. We do not know when we are well off.

In order that I may be understood and not be misunderstood, I would throw into relief the practical implications of the teaching for which I have been arguing, i.e., the sacramental quality of everyday living. Over against its positive meanings, I should like to point out a few things it does not mean.

It does not mean, for instance, that everything we do is of equal importance with everything else we do or may do. One act of a good man's life may differ widely from another in importance. Paul's sewing of tents was not equal to his writing of an Epistle to the Romans, but both were accepted of God and both were true acts of worship. Certainly it is more important to lead a soul to Christ than to plant a garden, but the planting of the garden *can* be as holy an act as the winning of a soul.

Again, it does not mean that every man is as useful as every other man. Gifts differ in the body of Christ. A Billy Bray is not to be compared with a Luther or a Wesley for sheer usefulness to the church and to the world; but the service of the less gifted brother is as pure as that of the more gifted, and God accepts both with equal pleasure.

The "layman" need never think of his humbler task as being inferior to that of his minister. Let every man abide in the calling wherein he is called and his work will be as sacred as the work of the ministry. It is not what a man does that determines whether his work is sacred or secular, it is why he does it. The motive is everything. Let a man sanctify the Lord God in his heart and he can thereafter do no common act. All he does is good and acceptable to God through Jesus Christ. For such a man, living itself will be a priestly ministration. As he performs his never-so-simple task, he will hear the voice of the seraphim saying, "Holy, holy, holy, is the LORD of hosts: the whole earth is full of his glory" (Isaiah 6:3).

Lord, I would trust Thee completely; I would be altogether Thine; I would exalt Thee above all. I desire that I may feel no sense of possessing anything outside of Thee. I want constantly to be aware of Thy overshadowing presence and to hear Thy speaking voice. I long to live in restful sincerity of heart. I want to live so fully in the Spirit that all my thoughts may be as sweet incense ascending to Thee and every act of my life may be an act of worship.

Therefore I pray in the words of Thy great servant of old, "I beseech Thee so for to cleanse the intent of mine heart with the unspeakable gift of Thy grace, that I may perfectly love Thee and worthily praise Thee."

And all this I confidently believe Thou wilt grant me through the merits of Jesus Christ Thy Son.

Amen.

God's Pursuit
of Man

*To all those pilgrims of eternity
whose distrust with earth
has constrained them
to seek in God a more enduring substance,
this little work is offered
in humble dedication.*

FOREWORD

This book contains strong medicine, bitter to the taste but potent if taken in contrition and in belief. For a generation content in its own smugness, emotionally exhausted by the claptrap and bunkum of some well-meaning but misled leaders, glibly familiar with all the niceties of careful theological phrases, the medicine may be too bitter. Only the hopeless will benefit. May the slain of the Lord be many; may the hopeless be multiplied. Only then can we experience what some of us know by rote.

Some will point out where they disagree. Too much this or too much that will be the dodge. Don't be among them. What if something is said differently? What if the preacher holds another view of sovereignty, of holiness, of man (he may be right)? Don't miss the pith because you are engrossed in a study of the bark.

The author is a prophet, a man of God; his life as well as his sermons attest the fact. Here he speaks; no, he preaches; no, he thunders the message of God for those of us who are dreadfully poverty-stricken, though we think we are rich and have need of nothing. Don't be afraid of the thunderings of the language. Don't even fear the bold, jagged stroke of lightning of the speech. For all who will hear, for all who will obey, here is God's answer to our need—Himself.

WILLIAM CULBERTSON
Past President, Moody Bible Institute

PREFACE

It is, I suppose, quite impossible for anyone familiar with the Old Testament to sit down to the writing of a book without remembering with some uneasiness the words of the preacher, the son of David, king in Jerusalem, "And further, by these, my son, be admonished: of making many books there is no end; and much study is a weariness of the flesh" (Ecclesiastes 12:12).

I think we may safely conclude that the world has by that tired utterance been spared the ordeal of a vast number of worthless books which might otherwise have gotten themselves written. For this we may be indebted to the wise old king more deeply than we know. But if this remembrance of the many books already written has helped even a little to check the making of other poor ones, may it not also have worked to prevent the appearance of some which might indeed have held an authentic message for mankind? I do not think so.

The only book that should ever be written is one that flows up from the heart, forced out by the inward pressure. When such a work has gestated within a man it is almost certain that it will be written. The man who is thus charged with a message will not be turned back by any blasé consideration. His book will be to him not only imperative, it will be inevitable.

This little book of the spiritual way has not been "made" in any mechanical sense; it has been born out of inward necessity. At the risk of getting myself into doubtful company I might claim for myself the testimony of Elihu, the son of Barachel the Buzite, of the kindred of Ram, "For I am full of matter, the spirit within me constraineth me" (Job 32:18). And his fear that if he did not speak he must, as a new bottle, "burst asunder" is well understood by me. The sight of the languishing church around me and the operations of a new spiritual power within me have set up a pressure impossible to resist. Whether or not the book ever reaches a wide public, still it has to be written if for no other reason than to relieve an unbearable burden on my heart.

Along with this frank account of its spiritual genesis, let me further say (and waive the seeming contradiction) that I claim for the book neither originality nor any degree of inspiration beyond that which may be enjoyed by any of the servants of Christ. The "pressure" of which I speak may prove to be nothing more than the squeeze and stress which result from the effort to be good in a bad world and to honor God in the midst of a generation of Christians which seems bent upon giving glory to everyone else but Him.

As for originality, has not someone remarked that no one since Adam has been wholly original? "Every man," said Emerson, "is a quotation from his ancestors." All that I can hope is that this book may be a right emphasis coming at a right time. If the reader should discover here anything really new he is in conscience bound to reject it, for whatever in religion is new is by the same token false.

Without a doubt the reader will detect upon these pages traces of other hearts beside my own. I would be the first to point out that the influence of many minds is everywhere upon them. The masters of the inner life are here (however imperfectly represented), the saintly teachers at whose feet I have sat long and lovingly and from whose wells I have drawn water with reverence and gratitude. I lift thankful eyes to God for the men who have taught me to desire the better way: Nicholas Herman and that other Nicholas of Cusa and Meister Eckhart and Fenelon and Faber. These I name because they have helped me most, but there have been many others also. Among them is quaint old "John Smith, M.A.," whose name renders him almost anonymous. I know almost nothing about him except that his style is like that of Lord Francis Bacon and his spirit like the spirit of the fourth Gospel and that he once thoughtfully published a few of his sermons, one of which, in a happy moment, a veteran missionary kindly placed in my hands.

Toward anything like thorough scholarship I make no claim. I am not an authority on any man's teaching; I have never tried to be. I take my help where I find it and set my heart to graze where the pastures are greenest.

Only one stipulation do I make: my teacher must know God, as Carlyle said, "otherwise than by hearsay," and Christ must be all in all to him. If a man have only correct doctrine to offer me I am sure to slip out at the first intermission to seek the company of someone who has seen for himself how lovely is the face of Him who is the Rose of Sharon and the Lily of the Valley. Such a man can help me, and no one else can.

The argument of this book is the *essential interiority* of true religion. I expect to show that if we would know the power of the Christian message our nature must be invaded by an Object from beyond it; that That which is external must become internal; that the objective Reality which is God must cross the threshold of our personality and take residence within.

In arguing thus it could be said that I am wrong, but as Blake once wrote, "If I am wrong, I am wrong in good company." For is it not simply another way of saying, "It is the spirit that quickeneth; the flesh profiteth nothing" (John 6:63)? The essentiality of a right interior life was the burden of Christ's teaching and was without doubt one of the main causes of His rejection by those notorious externalists, the Pharisees. Paul also preached continually the doctrine of the indwelling Christ, and history will reveal that the church has gained or lost power exactly as she has moved toward or away from the inwardness of her faith.

Perhaps a word of warning would not be amiss here:

It is that we beware the common habit of putting confidence in books, as such. It takes a determined effort of the mind to break free from the error of making books and teachers ends in themselves.

The worst thing a book can do for a Christian is to leave him with the impression that he has received from it anything really good; the best it can do is to point the way to the Good he is seeking. The function of a good book is to stand like a signpost directing the reader toward the Truth and the Life. That book serves best which early makes itself unnecessary, just as a signpost serves best after it is forgotten, after the traveler has arrived safely at his desired haven. The work of a good book is to incite the reader to moral action, to turn his eyes toward God and urge him forward. Beyond that it cannot go.

Something should be said here also about the word *religion* as it occurs throughout these pages. I know how carelessly the word has been used by many and how many definitions it has received at the hands of philosophers and psychologists. In order that I may be as clear as possible let me state that the word *religion* as I use it here means the total of God's work in a man and the total of the man's response to that inner working. I mean the power of God at work in the soul as the individual knows and experiences it. But the word has other denotations as well. Sometimes it will mean doctrine, again it will mean the Christian faith or Christianity in its broadest sense. It is a good word and a scriptural one. I shall try to use it carefully, but I invoke the reader's charity to forgive the fault should he encounter it more frequently than he would wish.

It is impossible to travel south without turning one's back upon the north. One cannot plant until he has plowed nor move forward until he has removed the obstacles before him. It is quite to be expected therefore that a bit of gentle criticism should be found here occasionally. Whatever stands in the way of spiritual progress I have felt it my duty to oppose, and it is hardly possible to oppose without injuring the feelings of some. The dearer the error, the more dangerous and the more difficult to correct, always.

But I would bring everything to the test of the Word and the Spirit. Not the Word only, but the Word and the Spirit. "God is a Spirit," said our Lord, "and they that worship him must worship him in spirit and in truth" (John 4:24). While it is never possible to have the Spirit without at least some measure of truth, it is, unfortunately, possible to have the shell of truth without the Spirit. Our hope is that we may have both the Spirit and the truth in fullest measure.

CHAPTER 1

———————— • ————————

The Eternal Continuum

"As I was with Moses, so I will be with thee."

JOSHUA 1:5

The unconditioned priority of God in His universe is a truth celebrated both in the Old Testament and in the New. The prophet Habakkuk sang it in ecstatic language, "Art thou not from everlasting, O LORD my God, mine Holy One?" (1:12). The apostle John set it forth in careful words deep with meaning, "In the beginning was the Word, and the Word was with God, and the Word was God. The same was in the beginning with God. All things were made by him; and without him was not any thing made that was made" (1:1–3).

This truth is so necessary to right thoughts about God and ourselves that it can hardly be too strongly emphasized. It is a truth known to everyone, a kind of common property of all religious persons, but for the very reason that it is so common it now has but little meaning for any of us. It has suffered the fate of which Coleridge writes:

> Truths, of all others the most awful and interesting,
> are too often considered as *so* true that they lose
> all the power of truth and lie bed-ridden in the
> dormitory of the soul, side by side with the most
> despised and exploded errors.

The divine priority is one of those "bed-ridden" truths. I desire to do what I can to rescue it "from the neglect caused by the very circumstance of its universal admission." Neglected Christian truths can be revitalized only when by prayer and long meditation we isolate them from the mass of hazy ideas with which our minds are filled and hold them steadily and determinedly in the focus of the mind's attention.

For all things God is the great Antecedent. Because He is, we are and everything else is. He is that "dread, unbeginning One," self-caused, self-contained and self-sufficient. Faber saw this when he wrote his great hymn in celebration of God's eternity.

> Thou hast no youth, great God,
> An Unbeginning End Thou art;
> Thy glory in itself abode,
> And still abides in its own tranquil heart:
> No age can heap its outward years on Thee:
> Dear God! Thou art Thyself Thine own eternity.

Do not skip this as merely another poem. The difference between a great Christian life and any other kind lies in the quality of our religious concepts, and the ideas expressed in these six lines *can* be like rungs on Jacob's ladder leading upward to a sounder and more satisfying idea of God.

We cannot think rightly of God until we begin to think of Him as always being *there,* and *there first.* Joshua had this to learn. He had been so long the servant of God's servant Moses, and had with such assurance received God's word at his mouth, that Moses and the God of Moses had become blended in his thinking, so blended that he could hardly separate the two thoughts; by association they always appeared together in his mind. Now Moses is dead, and lest the young Joshua be struck down with despair God spoke to assure him, "As I was with Moses, so I will be with thee" (Joshua 1:5; 3:7). Nothing had changed and nothing had been lost. Nothing of God dies when a man of God dies.

"As I was—so I will be." Only God could say this. Only the Eternal One could stand in the timeless I AM and say, "I was" and "I will be."

Here we acknowledge (and there is fear and wonder in the thought) the essential unity of God's nature, the timeless persistence of His changeless being throughout eternity and time. Here we begin to see and feel the eternal continuum. Begin where we will, God is there first. He is Alpha and Omega, the beginning and the ending, which was, and which is and which is to come, the Almighty. If we grope back to the farthest limits of thought where imagination touches the pre-creation void, we shall find God there. In one unified present glance He comprehends all things from everlasting, and the flutter of a seraph's wing a thousand ages hence is seen by Him now without moving His eyes.

Once I should have considered such thoughts to be mere metaphysical bric-a-brac without practical meaning for anyone in a world such as this. Now I recognize them as sound and easy-to-grasp truths with unlimited potential for good. Failure to get a right viewpoint in the beginning of our Christian lives may result in weakness and sterility for the rest of our days. May not the inadequacy of much of our spiritual experience be traced back to our habit of skipping through the corridors of the kingdom like children through the marketplace, chattering about everything, but pausing to learn the true value of nothing?

In my creature impatience I am often caused to wish that there were some way to bring modern Christians into a deeper spiritual life painlessly by short, easy lessons; but such wishes are vain. No shortcut exists. God has not bowed to our nervous haste nor embraced the methods of our machine age. It is well that we accept the hard truth now: *The man who would know God must give time to Him.* He must count no time wasted which is spent in the cultivation of His acquaintance. He must give himself to meditation and prayer hours on end. So did the saints of old, the glorious company of the apostles, the goodly fellowship of the prophets and the believing members of the holy church in all generations. And so must we if we would follow in their train.

We would think of God, then, as maintaining the unity of His uncreated being throughout all His works and His years, as ever saying not only, "I did," and "I will do," but also "I do" and "I am doing."

A robust faith requires that we grasp this truth firmly, yet we know how seldom such a thought enters our minds. We habitually stand in our *now* and look back by faith to see the past filled with God. We look forward and see Him inhabiting our future; but our *now* is uninhabited except for ourselves. Thus we are guilty of a kind of temporary atheism which leaves us alone in the universe while, for the time, God is not. We talk of Him much and loudly, but we secretly think of Him as being absent, and we think of ourselves as inhabiting a parenthetic interval between the God who was and the God who will be. And we are lonely with an ancient and cosmic loneliness. We are each like a little child lost in a crowded market, who has strayed but a few feet from its mother, yet because she cannot be seen the child is inconsolable. So we try by every method devised by religion to relieve our fears and heal our hidden sadness; but with all our efforts we remain unhappy still, with the settled despair of men alone in a vast and deserted universe.

But for all our fears we are not alone. Our trouble is

that we *think* of ourselves as being alone. Let us correct the error by thinking of ourselves as standing by the bank of a full flowing river; then let us think of that river as being none else but God Himself. We glance to our left and see the river coming full out of our past; we look to the right and see it flowing on into our future. *But we see also that it is flowing through our present.* And in our today it is the same as it was in our yesterday, not less than, nor different from, but the very same river, one unbroken continuum, undiminished, active and strong as it moves sovereignly on into our tomorrow.

Wherever faith has been original, wherever it has proved itself to be real, it has invariably had upon it a sense of the *present God.* The holy Scriptures possess in marked degree this feeling of actual encounter with a real Person. The men and women of the Bible talked with God. They spoke to Him and heard Him speak in words they could understand. With Him they held person-to-person interaction, and a sense of shining reality is upon their words and deeds.

The world's own prophets, the unbelieving psychologists (those eyeless seekers who seek for a light which is not God's light) have been forced to recognize at the bottom of religious experience this sense of *something there.* But better far is the sense of *Someone there.* It was this that filled with abiding wonder the first members of the church of Christ. The solemn delight which those early disciples knew sprang straight from the conviction that there was One in the midst of them. They knew that the Majesty in the heavens was confronting them on earth: They were in the very Presence of God. And the power of that conviction to arrest attention and hold it for a lifetime, to elevate, to transform, to fill with uncontrollable moral happiness, to send men singing to prison and to death, has been one of the wonders of history and a marvel of the world.

Our fathers have told us and our own hearts confirm how wonderful is this sense of Someone there. It makes religion invulnerable to critical attack. It secures the mind against collapse under the battering of the enemy. They who worship the God who is present may ignore the objections of unbelieving men. Their experience is self-verifying and needs neither defense nor proof. What they see and hear overwhelms their doubts and confirms their assurance beyond the power of argument to destroy.

Some who desire to be teachers of the Word, but who understand neither what they say, nor whereof they affirm, insist upon "naked" faith as the only way to know spiritual things. By this they mean a conviction of the trustworthiness of the Word of God (a conviction, it may be noted, which the devils share with them).

But the man who has been taught even slightly by the Spirit of Truth will rebel at this perversion. His language will be, "I have heard Him and observed Him. What have I to do any more with idols?" For he cannot love a God who is no more than a deduction from a text.

He will crave to know God with a vital awareness that goes beyond words and to live in the intimacy of personal communion. To seek our divinity merely in books and writings is *to seek the living among the dead;* we do but in vain many times seek God in these, where His truth too often is not so much enshrined as entombed. He is best discerned by an intellectual touch of Him. We must see with our eyes, and hear with our ears, and our hands must handle of the Word of Life.

Nothing can take the place of the *touch* of God in the soul and the sense of Someone there. Real faith, indeed, brings such realization, for real faith is never the operation of reason upon texts. Where true faith is, the knowledge of God will be given as a fact of consciousness altogether apart from the conclusions of logic.

Were a man to awaken in the pitch dark at midnight and hear someone moving about in his room and know that the unseen presence was a loved member of his family who had every right to be there, his heart might be filled with a sense of quiet pleasure; but should he have reason to believe that an intruder had entered, perhaps to rob or to kill, he would lie in terror and stare at the darkness not knowing from which direction the expected blow might come. But *the difference between experience and no experience would be that acute sense of someone there.* Is it not true that for most of us who call ourselves Christians there is no real experience? We have substituted theological ideas for an arresting encounter; we are full of religious notions, but our great weakness is that for our hearts there is no one there.

Whatever else it embraces, true Christian experience must always include a genuine encounter with God. Without this, religion is but a shadow, a reflection of reality, a cheap copy of an original once enjoyed by someone else of whom we have heard. It cannot but be a major tragedy in the life of any man to live in a church from childhood to old age and know nothing more real than some synthetic god compounded of theology and logic, but having no eyes to see, no ears to hear and no heart to love.

The spiritual giants of old were men who at some time became acutely conscious of the real Presence of God and maintained that consciousness for the rest of their lives. The first encounter may have been one of terror, as when a "horror of great darkness" fell upon Abram, or as when Moses at the bush hid his face because he was afraid to look upon God. Usually this fear soon lost its content of terror and changed after a while to delightsome awe, to level off finally into a reverent sense of complete nearness to God. The essential point is, *they experienced God.* How otherwise can the saints and prophets be explained? How otherwise can we account for the amazing power for good they have exercised over countless generations? Is it not that they walked in conscious communion with the real Presence and addressed their prayers to God with the artless conviction that they were addressing Someone actually there?

Without doubt we have suffered the loss of many spiritual treasures because we have let slip the simple truth that the miracle of the perpetuation of life is in God. God did not create life and toss it from Him like some petulant artist disappointed with his work. All life is in Him and out of Him, flowing from Him and returning to Him again, a moving indivisible sea of which He is the Fountainhead. That eternal life which was with the Father is now the possession of believing men, and that life is not God's gift only, but His very self.

Redemption is not a strange work which God for a moment turned aside to do; rather it is His same work performed in a new field, the field of human catastrophe. The regeneration of a believing soul is but a recapitulation of all His work done from the moment of creation. It is hard to miss the parallel between generation as described in the Old Testament and regeneration as described in the New. How, for instance, could the condition of a lost soul better be described than by the words, "without form, and void" with darkness "upon the face of the deep" (Genesis 1:2)? And how could the strong yearnings of God's heart over that lost soul be more perfectly expressed than by saying that "the Spirit of God brooded upon the face of the waters" (see 1:2)? And from what source could light come to that sin-shrouded soul had God not said, "Let there be light" (1:3)? At His word the light breaks and the lost man arises to drink of eternal life and follow the Light of the World. As order and fruitfulness came next to that ancient creation, so moral order and spiritual fruit follow next in human experience. And we know that God is the same and His years fail not. He will always act like Himself wherever He is found at work and whatever work He is doing.

We need to seek deliverance from our vain and weakening wish to go back and recover the past. We should seek to be cleansed from the childish notion that to have lived in Abram's day, or in Paul's, would have been better than to live today. With God Abram's day and this day are the same. By one single impulse of life He created all days and all times, so that the life of the first day and the life of the remotest future day are united in Him. We may well sing again (and believe) the truth our fathers sang:

> *Eternity with all its years,*
> *Stands present in Thy view;*
> *To Thee there's nothing old appears;*
> *Great God, there's nothing new.*

In saving men God is but doing again (or rather continuing to do) the same creative work as at the beginning of the world. To Him each ransomed soul is a world wherein He performs again His pleasant work as of old.

We who experience God in this day may rejoice that we have in Him all that Abraham or David or Paul could have; indeed the very angels before the throne can have no more than we, for they can have no more God and can want nothing apart from Him. And all that He is and all that He has done is for us and for all who share the common salvation. With full consciousness of our own demerit we may yet take our place in the love of God, and the poorest and weakest of us may without offense claim for ourselves all the riches of the Godhead in mercy given. I have every right to claim all for myself, knowing that an infinite God can give all of Himself to each of His children. He does not distribute Himself that each may have a part, but to each one He gives all of Himself as fully as if there were no others.

What a difference it makes when we cease being general (a dodge, incidentally, for pseudo-humility and unbelief) and become pointed and personal in our approach to God. Then we shall not fear the personal pronoun but shall with the friends of God relate it to the One who gave it and claim each one for himself the Person and work of the Triune God. Then we shall see that all that God did was for each of us. Then we can sing:

For me Thou didst cover Thyself with light as with a garment and stretch out the heavens like a curtain and lay the foundations of the earth. For me Thou didst appoint the moon for seasons and the sun knoweth his going down. For me Thou didst make every beast of the earth after his kind and every herb bearing seed and every tree in which is the fruit of a tree. For me prophet wrote and psalmist sang. For me holy men spake as they were moved by the Holy Ghost.

For me Christ died, and the redemptive benefits of that death are by the miracle of His present life perpetuated forever, as efficacious now as on the day He bowed His head and gave up the ghost. And when He arose the third day it was for me; and when He poured out upon the disciples the promised Holy Spirit it was that He might continue *in me* the work He had been doing *for me* since the morning of the creation.

CHAPTER 2

In Word, or in Power

*For our gospel came not unto you in word only,
but also in power, and in the Holy Ghost.*

1 THESSALONIANS 1:5

If any man be in Christ, he is a new creature.

2 CORINTHIANS 5:17

*I know thy works, that thou hast
a name that thou livest, and art dead.*

REVELATION 3:1

To one who is a student merely, these verses might be interesting, but to a serious man intent upon gaining eternal life they might well prove more than a little disturbing. For they evidently teach that the message of the gospel may be received in either of two ways: in word only, without power, or in word with power. Yet it is the same message whether it comes in word or in power. And these verses teach also that when the message is received in power it effects a change so radical as to be called a new creation. But the message may be received without power, and apparently some have so received it, for they have a name to live and are dead. All this is present in these texts.

By observing the ways of men at play I have been able to understand better the ways of men at prayer. Most men, indeed, play at religion as they play at games, religion itself being of all games the one most universally played. The various sports have their rules and their balls and their players; the game excites interest, gives pleasure and consumes time, and when it is over the competing teams laugh and leave the field. It is common to see a player leave one team and join another and a few days later play against his old mates with as great zest as he formerly displayed when playing *for* them. The whole thing is arbitrary. It consists in solving artificial problems and attacking difficulties which have been deliberately created for the sake of the game. It has no moral roots and is not supposed to have. No one is the better for his self-imposed toil. It is all but a pleasant activity which changes nothing and settles nothing at last.

If the condition we describe were confined to the ballpark we might pass it over without further thought, but what are we to say when this same spirit enters the sanctuary and decides the attitude of men toward God and religion? For the church has also its fields and its rules and its equipment for playing the game of pious words. It has its devotees, both laymen and professionals, who support the game with their money and encourage it with their presence, but who are no different in life or character from many who take in religion no interest at all.

As an athlete uses a ball, so do many of us use words: words spoken and words sung, words written and words uttered in prayer. We throw them swiftly across the field; we learn to handle them with dexterity and grace; we build reputations upon our word skill and gain as our reward the applause of those who have enjoyed the game. But the emptiness of it is apparent from the fact that after the pleasant religious game *no one is basically any different from what he had been before.* The bases of life remain unchanged, the same old principles govern, the same old Adam rules.

I have not said that religion without power makes no changes in a man's life, only that it makes no fundamental difference. Water may change from liquid to vapor and still be fundamentally the same. So powerless religion may put a man through many surface changes and leave him exactly what he was before. Right there is where the snare lies. *The changes are in form only, they are not in kind.* Behind the activities of the non-religious man and the man who has received the gospel without power lie the very same motives. An unblessed ego lies at the bottom of both lives, the difference being that the religious man has learned better to disguise his vice. His sins are refined and less offensive than before he took up religion, but the man himself is not a better man in the sight of God. He may indeed be a worse one, for always God hates artificiality and pretense. Selfishness still throbs like an engine at the center of the man's life. True, he may learn to "redirect" his selfish impulses, but his woe is that self still lives unrebuked and even unsuspected within his deep heart. He is a victim of religion without power.

The man who has received the Word without power has trimmed his hedge, but it is a thorn hedge still and can never bring forth the fruits of the new life. Yet such a man may be a leader in the church and his influence and his vote may go far to determine what religion shall be in his generation.

The truth received in power shifts the bases of life from Adam to Christ and a new set of motives goes to work within the soul. A new and different Spirit enters the personality and makes the believing man new in every department of his being. His interests shift from things external to things internal, from things on earth to things in heaven. He loses faith in the soundness of external values, he sees clearly the deceptiveness of outward appearances and his love for and confidence in the unseen and eternal world become stronger as his experience widens.

With the ideas here expressed most Christians will agree, but the gulf between theory and practice is so great as to be terrifying. For the gospel is too often preached and accepted without power, and the radical shift which the truth demands is never made. There may be, it is true, a change of some kind; an intellectual and emotional bargain may be struck with the truth, but whatever happens is not enough, not deep enough, not radical enough. The "creature" is changed, but he is not "new." And right there is the tragedy of it. The gospel is concerned with a new life, with a birth upward onto a new level of being, and until it has effected such a rebirth it has not done a saving work within the soul.

Wherever the Word comes without power its essential content is missed. For there is in divine truth an imperious note, there is about the gospel an urgency, a finality which will not be heard or felt except by the enabling of the Spirit. We must constantly keep in mind that the gospel is not good news only, but a judgment as well upon everyone that hears it. The message of the cross is good news indeed for the penitent, but to those who "obey not the gospel" it carries an overtone of warning. The Spirit's ministry to the impenitent world is to tell of sin and righteousness and judgment. For sinners who want to cease being willful sinners and become obedient children of God the gospel message is one of unqualified peace, but it is by its very nature also an arbiter of the future destinies of men.

This secondary aspect is almost wholly overlooked in our day. The *gift* element in the gospel is held to be its exclusive content, and the *shift* element is accordingly ignored. Theological assent is all that is required to make Christians. This assent is called faith and is thought to be the only difference between the saved and the lost. Faith is thus conceived as a kind of religious magic, bringing to the Lord great delight and possessing mysterious power to open the kingdom of heaven.

I want to be fair to everyone and to find all the good I can in every man's religious beliefs, but the harmful effects of this faith-as-magic creed are greater than could be imagined by anyone who has not come face to face with them. Large assemblies today are being told fervently that the one essential qualification for heaven is to be an evil man, and the one sure bar to God's favor is to be a good one. The very word *righteousness* is spoken only in cold scorn, and the moral man is looked upon with pity. "A Christian," says these teachers, "is not morally better than a sinner, the only difference is that he has taken Jesus, and so he has a Savior." I trust it may not sound flippant to inquire, "A savior from what?" If not from sin and evil conduct and the old fallen life, then from what? And if the answer is, "From the consequences of past sins and from judgment to come," still we are not satisfied. Is justification from past offenses all that distinguishes a Christian from a sinner? Can a man become a believer in Christ and be no better than he was before? Does the gospel offer no more than a skillful advocate to get the guilty sinners off free at the day of judgment?

I think the truth of the matter is not too deep nor too difficult to discover. Self-righteousness is an effective bar to God's favor because it throws the sinner back upon his own merits and shuts him out from the imputed righteousness of Christ. And to be a sinner confessed and consciously lost is necessary to the act of receiving salvation through our Lord Jesus Christ. This we joyously admit and constantly assert, but here is the truth which has been overlooked in our day, *A sinner cannot enter the kingdom of God.* The Bible passages which declare this are too many and too familiar to need repeating here, but the skeptical might look at Galatians 5:19–21 and Revelation 21:8.

How then can a man be saved? The penitent sinner meets Christ and after that saving encounter he is a sinner no more. The power of the gospel changes him, shifts the basis of his life from self to Christ, faces him about in a new direction and makes him a new creation. The moral state of the penitent when he comes to Christ does not affect the result, for the work of Christ sweeps away both his good and evil and turns him into another man. The returning sinner is not saved by some judicial transaction apart from a corresponding moral change. Salvation must include a judicial change of status, but what is overlooked by most teachers is that *it also includes an actual change in the life of the individual.* And by this we mean more than a surface change—we mean a transformation as deep as the roots of his human life. If it does not go that deep it does not go deep enough.

If we had not first suffered a serious decline in our expectations we should not have accepted this same technical view of faith. The churches (even the gospel churches) are worldly in spirit, morally anemic, on the defensive, imitating instead of initiating and in a wretched state generally because for two full generations they have been told that justification is no more than a "not guilty" verdict pronounced by the heavenly Father upon a sinner who can present the magic coin *faith* with the wondrous "open-sesame" engraved upon it. If it is not stated as bluntly as that, at least the message is so presented as to create such an impression. The whole business is the result of hearing the Word preached without power and receiving it in the same way.

Now faith is indeed the "open-sesame" to eternal blessedness. Without faith it is impossible to please God; neither can any man be saved apart from faith in the risen Savior. But the true quality of faith is almost universally missed, namely, its moral quality. It is more than mere confidence in the veracity of a statement made in Holy Writ. It is a highly moral thing and of a spiritual essence. It invariably effects radical transformation in the life of the one who exercises it. It shifts the inward gaze from self to God. It introduces its possessor into the life of heaven upon earth.

It is not my desire to minimize the justifying effect of faith. No man who knows the depths of his own wickedness would dare to appear before the ineffable Presence with nothing to recommend him but his own character. Nor would any Christian, wise after the discipline of failures and imperfections, want his acceptance with God to depend upon any degree of holiness to which he might have attained through the operations of inward grace. All who know their own hearts and the provisions of the gospel will join in the prayer of the man of God:

> *When He shall come with trumpet sound,*
> *Oh, may I then in Him be found,*
> *Dressed in His righteousness alone,*
> *Faultless to stand before the throne!*

It is a distressing thing that a truth so beautiful should have been so perverted. But perversion is the price we pay for failure to emphasize the moral content of truth; it is the curse that follows rational orthodoxy when it has quenched or rejected the Spirit of Truth.

In asserting that faith in the gospel effects a change of life-motive from self to God I am but stating the sober facts. Every man with moral intelligence must be aware of the curse that afflicts him inwardly; he must be conscious of the thing we call *ego*, by the Bible called *flesh* or *self*, but by whatever name called, a cruel master and a deadly foe.

Pharaoh never ruled Israel as tyrannically as this hidden enemy rules the sons and daughters of men. The words of God to Moses concerning Israel in bondage may well describe us all: "I have surely seen the affliction of my people which are in Egypt, and have heard their cry by reason of their taskmasters; for I know their sorrows" (Exodus 3:7). The Nicene Creed so tenderly states that our Lord Jesus Christ for us men and for our salvation, came down from heaven, and was incarnate by the Holy Ghost of the Virgin Mary, and was made man; and was crucified also for us under Pontius Pilate. He suffered and was buried; and the third day He rose again according to the Scriptures, and ascended into heaven, and sitteth on the right hand of the Father.

What was it all for? That He might pronounce us technically free and leave us in our bondage? Never. God said to Moses:

> I am come down to deliver them out of the hand of the Egyptians, and to bring them up out of that land unto a good land and a large, unto a land flowing with milk and honey. . . . Go unto Pharaoh, and say unto him . . . Let my people go. (Exodus 3:8; 8:1)

For sin's human captives God never intends anything less than full deliverance. The Christian message rightly understood means this: The God who by the *word* of the gospel *proclaims* men free, by the *power* of the gospel *actually makes them free.* To accept less than this is to know the gospel in word only, without its power.

They to whom the Word comes in power know this deliverance, this inward migration of the soul from slavery to freedom, this release from moral position, a real crossing over, and they stand consciously on another soil under another sky and breathe another air. Their life motives are changed and their inward drives made new.

What are these old drives that once forced obedience at the end of a lash? What but little taskmasters, servants of the great taskmaster, *self,* who stand before him and do his will? To name them all would require a book in itself, but we would point out one as a type or sample of the rest. It is the desire for social approval.

This is not bad in itself and might be perfectly innocent if we were living in a sinless world, but since the race of men has fallen off from God and joined itself to His foes, to be a friend of the world is to be a collaborator with evil and an enemy of God. Still the desire to please men is back of all social acts from the highest civilizations to the lowest levels upon which human life is found. No one can escape it. The outlaw who flouts the rules of society and the philosopher who rises in thought above its common ways may *seem* to have escaped from the snare, but they have in reality merely narrowed the circle of those they desire to please. The outlaw has his pals before whom he seeks to shine; the philosopher his little coterie of superior thinkers whose approval is necessary to his happiness. For both, the motive-root remains uncut. Each draws his peace from the thought that he enjoys the esteem of his fellows, though each will interpret the whole business in his own way.

Every man looks to his fellow men because he has no one else to whom he can look. David could say, "Whom have I in heaven but thee? and there is none upon earth that I desire beside thee" (Psalm 73:25). But the sons of this world have not God; they have only each other, and they walk holding to each other and looking to one another for assurance like frightened children. But their hope will fail them, for they are like a group of men, none of whom has learned to fly a plane, who suddenly find themselves aloft without a pilot, each looking to the other to bring them safely down. Their desperate but mistaken trust cannot save them from the crash which must certainly follow.

With this desire to please men so deeply implanted within us how can we uproot it and shift our life-drive from pleasing men to pleasing God? Well, no one can do it alone, nor can he do it with the help of others, nor by education nor by training nor by any other method known under the sun. What is required is a reversal of nature (that it is a fallen nature does not make it any the less powerful) and this reversal must be a supernatural act. That act the Spirit performs through the power of the gospel when it is received in living faith. Then He displaces the old with the new. Then He invades the life as sunlight invades a landscape and drives out the old motives as light drives away darkness from the sky.

The way it works in experience is something like this: The believing man is overwhelmed suddenly by a powerful feeling that *only God matters;* soon this works itself out into his mental life and conditions all his judgments and all his values. Now he finds himself free from slavery to man's opinions. Soon he learns to love above all else the assurance that he is well pleasing to the Father in heaven.

It is this complete switch in their pleasure source that has made believing men invincible. So could saints and martyrs stand alone, deserted by every earthly friend, and die for Christ under the universal displeasure of mankind. When, to intimidate him, Athanasius' judges warned him that the whole world was against him, he dared to reply, "Then is Athanasius against the world!" That cry has come down the years and today may remind us that the gospel has power to deliver men from the tyranny of social approval and make them free to do the will of God.

I have singled out this one enemy for consideration, but it is only one, and there are many others. They seem to stand by themselves and have existence apart from each other, but it is only seeming. Actually they are but branches of the same poison vine, growing from the same evil root, and they die together when the root dies. That root is *self*, and the cross is its only effective destroyer.

The message of the gospel, then, is the message of a new creation in the midst of an old, the message of the invasion of our human nature by the eternal life of God and the displacing of the old by the new. The new life seizes upon the believing man's nature and sets about its benign conquest, a conquest which is not complete until the invading life has taken full possession and a new creation has emerged. And this is an act of God without human aid, for it is a moral miracle and a spiritual resurrection.

CHAPTER 3

The Mystery of the Call

Called to be an apostle . . . called to be saints.

1 CORINTHIANS 1:1–2

The little word *called* as used here by the apostle is like a door opening into another world, and when we enter we shall find ourselves in another world indeed. For the new world into which we pass is the world of God's sovereign will where the will of man cannot come, or if it comes, it is as a dependent and a servant, never as a lord.

Paul here explains his apostleship: It is by an effectual call, not by his own wish or will or determination, and this call is a divine thing, free, uninfluenced and altogether out of the hands of man. The *response* is from man, but the call, never. That is from God alone.

There are two worlds, set over against each other, dominated by two wills: the will of man and the will of God, respectively. The old world of fallen nature is the world of human will. There man is king and his will decides events. So far as he is able in his weakness he decides who and what and when and where. He fixes values: what is to be esteemed, what despised, what received and what rejected. His will runs through everything. "I determined," "I decided," "I decree," "Be it enacted." These words are heard continually springing from the lips of little men. And how they rejoice in their fancied "right of self-determination," and with what comic vanity do they boast of the "sovereign voter." They do not know, or refuse to consider, that they are but for a day, soon to pass away and be no more.

> *Time, like an ever rolling stream,*
> *Bears all its sons away;*
> *They fly forgotten as a dream*
> *Dies at the break of day.*
>
> *The busy tribes of flesh and blood*
> *With all their cares and fears,*
> *Are carried downward like a flood*
> *And lost in following years.*
> —Isaac Watts

Yet in their pride men assert their will and claim ownership of the earth. Well, for a time it is true that this is man's world. God is admitted only by man's sufferance. He is treated as visiting royalty in a democratic country.

Everyone takes His name upon his lips and (especially at certain seasons) He is feted and celebrated and hymned. But behind all this flattery men hold firmly to their right of self-determination. As long as man is allowed to play host he will honor God with his attention, but always He must remain a guest and never seek to be Lord. Man will have it understood that this is his world; he will make its laws and decide how it shall be run. God is permitted to decide nothing. Man bows to Him and as he bows, manages with difficulty to conceal the crown upon his own head.

When we enter the kingdom of God, however, we are in another kind of world. It is altogether other than the old world from which we came; always it is different from and mostly it is contrary to the old. Where the two appear to be alike it is only in appearance, "the first man is of the earth, earthy: the second man is the Lord from heaven" (1 Corinthians 15:47). "That which is born of the flesh is flesh; and that which is born of the Spirit is spirit" (John 3:6). The first will perish, the last abides forever.

Paul was made an apostle by the direct call of God. "No man taketh this honour unto himself" (Hebrews 5:4). Among men we see that noted artists sometimes appear before royalty and their appearance is called a "command performance." However gifted they may be and however famous, they dare not intrude into the king's presence except by royal call, a call that amounts to an order. That call leaves no place for refusal except at the risk of affront to majesty. And with Paul it was not otherwise. God's call was also his command. Had Paul been running for political office the voters would have determined the outcome. Had he been trying for a place in the literary world his own abilities would have decided that place for him. Had he been competing in the prize ring his own strength and skill would have won or lost for him. But his apostleship was not so determined.

How delightful are God's ways and the goings forth of His will! Not by might nor by power, neither by native ability nor by training are men made apostles, but by God's effectual calling. So it is with every office within the church. Men are permitted to recognize the call and make public acknowledgment before the congregation, but never are they permitted themselves to make the choice. But where divine ways and the ways of men mix and mingle there is confusion and failure continually. Good men who are yet not called of God may, and often do, take upon them the sacred work of the ministry. Worse still is it when men who belong yet to the old world and have not been renewed by the miracle of regeneration try to carry on God's holy work. How sad is the sight and how tragic the consequences, for the ways of man and the ways of God are forever contrary one to the other.

Is this one of the reasons behind our present state of spiritual weakness? How can the flesh serve the Spirit? How can men from another tribe than Levi's minister before the altar? How vain to try to serve the new after the ways of the old. From this stems the rank growth of evil methods which characterizes the churches of our day. The bold and self-assertive push forward and the weak ones follow without asking for a proof of their right to lead. The divine call is ignored, and sterility and confusion result.

It is time for us to seek again the leadership of the Holy Ghost. Man's lordship has cost us too much. Man's intrusive will has introduced such a multiplicity of unscriptural ways and unscriptural activities as positively to threaten the life of the church. These divert annually millions of dollars from the true work of God and waste Christian man-hours in such vast numbers as to be heartbreaking.

There is another and worse evil which springs from this basic failure to grasp the radical difference between the natures of two worlds. It is the habit of languidly "accepting" salvation as if it were a small matter and one wholly in our hands. Men are exhorted to think things over and "decide" for Christ, and in some places one day each year is set aside as "Decision Day," at which time people are expected to condescend to grant Christ the right to save them, a right which they have obviously refused Him up to that time. Christ is thus made to stand again before men's judgment seat; He is made to wait upon the pleasure of the individual, and after long and humble waiting is either turned away or patronizingly admitted. By a complete misunderstanding of the noble and true doctrine of the freedom of the human will, salvation is made to depend perilously upon the will of man instead of upon the will of God.

However deep the mystery, however many the paradoxes involved, it is still true that men become saints not at their own whim but by sovereign calling. Has not God by such words as these taken out of our hands the ultimate choice?

> It is the spirit that quickeneth; the flesh profiteth nothing. . . . No man can come to me, except the Father which hath sent me draw him. . . . No man can come unto me, except it were given unto him of my Father. . . . Thou hast given him power over all flesh, that he should give eternal life to as many as thou hast given him. . . . It pleased God, who separated me from my mother's womb, and called me by his grace, to reveal his Son in me. (John 6:63, 44, 65; 17:2; Galatians 1:15–16)

God has made us in His likeness, and one mark of that likeness is our free will. We hear God say, "Whosoever will, let him come." We know by bitter experience the woe of an unsurrendered will and the blessedness or terror which may hang upon our human choice. But back of all this and preceding it is the sovereign right of God to call saints and determine human destinies. The master choice is His, the secondary choice is ours. Salvation is from our side a choice, from the divine side it is a seizing upon, an apprehending, a conquest of the Most High God. *Our "accepting" and "willing" are reactions rather than actions.* The right of determination must always remain with God.

God has indeed lent to every man the power to lock his heart and stalk away darkly into his self-chosen night, as He has lent to every man the ability to respond to His overtures of grace, but while the "no" choice may be ours, the "yes" choice is always God's. He is the Author of our faith as He must be its Finisher. Only by grace can we continue to believe; we can persist in willing God's will only as we are seized upon by a benign power that will overcome our natural bent to unbelief.

So keenly do we men enjoy dominion that we like to think that we hold in our own hands the power of life and death. We love to think that hell will be easier to bear from the fact of our having gone there in defiance of some power that sought to rule us. He knew this well who put into the mouth of Satan that speech of proud defiance:

> *What though the field be lost?*
> *All is not lost; the unconquerable will,*
> *The study of revenge, immortal hate,*
> *And courage never to submit or yield,*
> *And what is else not to be overcome;*
> *That glory never shall His wrath or might*
> *Extort from us.*

While few would dare thus to voice their secret feelings, there are millions who have imbibed the notion that they hold in their hands the keys of heaven and hell. The whole content of modern evangelistic preaching contributes to this attitude. Man is made large and God small; Christ is placed in a position to excite pity rather than respect as He stands meekly, lantern in hand, outside a vine-covered door.

How deeply do men err who conceive of God to our human will or as standing respectfully to wait upon our human pleasure. Though He in condescending love may seem to place Himself at our disposal, yet never for the least division of a moment does He abdicate His throne or void His right as Lord of man and nature. He is that Majesty on high. To Him all angels cry aloud, the heavens and all power therein: to Him cherubim and seraphim continually do cry, "Holy, Holy, Holy, Lord God of Sabaoth, heaven and earth are full of the majesty of thy glory." He is the Fear of Isaac and the Dread of Jacob, and before Him prophet and patriarch and saint have knelt in breathless awe and adoration.

The gradual disappearance of the idea and feeling of majesty from the church is a sign and a portent. The revolt of the modern mind has had a heavy price, how heavy is becoming more apparent as the years go by. Our God has now become our servant to wait on our will. "The Lord is my *shepherd*," we say, instead of "*The Lord* is my shepherd," and the difference is as wide as the world.

We need to have restored again the lost idea of sovereignty, not as a doctrine only but as the source of a solemn religious emotion. We need to have taken from our dying hand the shadow scepter with which we fancy we rule the world. We need to feel and know that we are but dust and ashes and that God is the disposer of the destinies of men. How ashamed we Christians should be that a pagan king should teach us to fear the Majesty on high. For it was the chastened Nebuchadnezzar who said:

> I . . . lifted up mine eyes unto heaven, and mine understanding returned unto me, and I blessed the most High, and I praised and honored him that liveth for ever, whose dominion is an everlasting dominion, and his kingdom is from generation to generation: and all the inhabitants of the earth are reputed as nothing: and he doeth according to his will in the army of heaven, and among the inhabitants of the earth: and none can stay his hand, or say unto him, What doest thou? (Daniel 4:34–35)

"At the same time," added the humbled king, "my reason returned unto me" (4:36). This whole passage is apt to be overlooked, occurring as it does in one of the less popular books of the Bible, but is it not of great significance that *humility* and *reason* returned together? "Now I Nebuchadnezzar praise and extol and honour the King of heaven, all whose works are truth, and his ways judgment: and those that walk in pride he is able to abase" (4:37). The king's pride was to him a kind of insanity which drove him at last into the fields to dwell with the beasts. While he saw himself large and God small he was insane; sanity returned only as he began to see God as all and himself as nothing.

Such moral madness as Nebuchadnezzar suffered is now upon the nations. Men of reputed learning have long been chanting with Swinburne,* "Glory to man in the highest," and the masses have picked up the chant. A strange amentia has resulted, marked by acute self-importance and delusions of moral grandeur. Men who refuse to worship the true God now worship themselves with tender devotion. A return to spiritual sanity waits for repentance and true humility. God grant that we may soon know again how small and how sinful we are.

*English poet (1837–1909) known for his libertarian themes

—————•—————

CHAPTER 4

Victory through Defeat

*And he said, Thy name shall be called no more
Jacob, but Israel: for as a prince hast thou
power with God and with men, and hast prevailed.*

GENESIS 32:28

*But God forbid that I should glory, save in the cross
of our Lord Jesus Christ, by whom the world
is crucified unto me, and I unto the world.*

GALATIANS 6:14

The experiences of men who walked with God in olden times agree to teach that the Lord cannot fully bless a man until He has first conquered him. The degree of blessing enjoyed by any man will correspond exactly with the completeness of God's victory over him. This is a badly neglected tenet of the Christian's creed, not understood by many in this self-assured age, but it is nevertheless of living importance to us all. This spiritual principle is well illustrated in the book of Genesis.

Jacob was the wily old heel-catcher whose very strength was to him a near-fatal weakness. For two-thirds of his total life he had carried in his nature something hard and unconquered. Not his glorious vision in the wilderness nor his long bitter discipline in Haran had broken his harmful strength. He stood at the ford of Jabbok at the time of the going down of the sun, a shrewd, intelligent old master of applied psychology learned the hard way. The picture he presented was not a pretty one. He was a vessel marred in the making. His hope lay in his own defeat. This he did not know at the setting of the day, but had learned before the rising of the sun. All night he resisted God until in kindness God touched the hollow of his thigh and won the victory over him. It was only after he had gone down to humiliating defeat that he began to feel the joy of release from his own evil strength, the delight of God's conquest over him. Then he cried aloud for the blessing and refused to let go till it came. It had been a long fight, but for God (and for reasons known only to Him) Jacob had been worth the effort. Now he became another man, the stubborn and self-willed rebel was turned into a meek and dignified friend of God. He had prevailed indeed, but through weakness, not through strength.

Only the conquered can know true blessedness. This is sound philosophy, based upon life, and necessary by the constitution of things. We need not accept this truth blindly; the reasons are discoverable, among them being these: We are created beings, and as such are derived, not self-existent. Not to us has it been given to have life in ourselves. For life we are wholly and continually dependent upon God, the Source and Fountain of life. Only by full dependence upon Him are the hidden potentialities of our natures realized. Apart from this we are but half-men, malformed and unbeautiful members of a noble race once made to wear the image of its Creator.

Once in olden times the Lord declared that the end of all flesh had come before Him, and the years have brought no mitigation of that sentence. "They that are in the flesh cannot please God. . . . The carnal mind is enmity against God; for it is not subject to the law of God, neither indeed can be. . . . To be carnally minded is death" (Romans 8:8, 7, 6). By such words as these has God perpetuated the ancient sentence of condemnation. Whether we admit it or not the stroke of death is upon us, and it will be saving wisdom for us to learn to trust not in ourselves but in Him that raiseth the dead. For how dare we put confidence in anything so fugitive, so fleeting, as human life?

> *The wise man, I affirm, can find no rest*
> *In that which perishes: nor will he lend*
> *His heart to aught which doth on time depend.*

From the sixteenth century these words have come to us, and in our moments of quiet wisdom we feel and know them to be true. Why then do we put our trust in things that perish and so become the dupes of time and the fools of change? Who has poisoned our cup and turned us into rebels? That old serpent, the devil, he it was who first beguiled us into that rash declaration of independence, a declaration which, in view of the circumstances, is both deeply comic and profoundly tragic. For our enemy must laugh at the incredible vanity that would lead us to match strength with the Almighty. That is the cynical comedy of it all; the tragedy drops with every tear and sorrows beside every grave.

A little acquaintance with our own hearts will force us to acknowledge that there is no hope within us, and the briefest glance around should show us that we need expect no help from without. Nature itself will teach us that (apart from God) we are but orphans of the creation, waifs of the wide spaces, caught helpless amid the whirl of forces too great to comprehend. Onward through this world roars an immense and sightless power leaving in its wake generations, cities, civilizations. The earth, our brief home, offers us at last only a grave. For us there is nothing safe, nothing kind. In the Lord there is mercy, but in the world there is none, for nature and life move on as if unaware of good or evil, of human sorrow or human pain.

It was to save Jacob from deceptive hope that God confronted him that night on the bank of the river. To save him from self-trust it was necessary for God to conquer him, to wrest control away from him, to take His great power and rule with a rod of love. Charles Wesley, the sweet singer of England, with a spiritual penetration rare even among advanced Christians, wrote from the mouth of Jacob what he conceived to be his prayer as he wrestled with God at the ford of Jabbok:

> *My strength is gone, my nature dies;*
> *I sink beneath Thy weighty hand;*
> *Faint to revive, and fall to rise:*
> *I fall, and yet by faith I stand.*
> *I stand, and will not let Thee go,*
> *Till I Thy Name, Thy Nature know.*
>
> *Lame as I am, I take the prey;*
> *Hell, earth, and sin, with ease o'ercome;*
> *I leap for joy, pursue my way,*
> *And as a bounding hart fly home,*
> *Through all eternity to prove,*
> *Thy Nature and Thy Name is love.*

We might well pray for God to invade and conquer us, for until He does, we remain in peril from a thousand foes. We bear within us the seeds of our own disintegration. Our moral imprudence puts us always in danger of accidental or reckless self-destruction. The strength of our flesh is an ever present danger to our souls. Deliverance can come to us only by the defeat of our old life. Safety and peace come only after we have been forced to our knees. God rescues us by breaking us, by shattering our strength and wiping out our resistance. Then He invades our natures with that ancient and eternal life which is from the beginning. So He conquers us and by that benign conquest saves us for Himself.

With this open secret awaiting easy discovery, why do we in almost all our busy activities work in another direction from this? Why do we build our churches upon human flesh? Why do we set such store by that which the Lord has long ago repudiated and despise those things which God holds in such high esteem? For we teach men not to die with Christ but to live in the strength of their dying manhood. We boast not in our weakness but in our strength. Values which Christ has declared to be false are brought back into evangelical favor and promoted as the very life and substance of the Christian way. How eagerly do we seek the approval of this or that man of worldly reputation. How shamefully do we exploit the converted celebrity. Anyone will do to take away the reproach of obscurity from our publicity-hungry leaders: famous athletes, congressmen, world travelers, rich industrialists; before such we bow with obsequious smiles and honor them in our public meetings and in the religious press. Thus we glorify men to enhance the standing of the church of God, and the glory of the Prince of Life is made to hang upon the transient fame of a man who shall die.

It is amazing that we can claim to be followers of Christ and yet take so lightly the words of His servants.

We could not act as we do if we took seriously the admonition of James the servant of God:

> My brethren, have not the faith of our Lord Jesus Christ, the Lord of glory, with respect of persons. For if there come unto your assembly a man with a gold ring, in goodly apparel, and there come in also a poor man in vile raiment; and ye have respect to him that weareth the gay clothing, and say unto him, Sit thou here in a good place; and say to the poor, Stand thou there, or sit here under my footstool: Are ye not then partial in yourselves, and are become judges of evil thoughts? Hearken, my beloved brethren, hath not God chosen the poor of this world rich in faith, and heirs of the kingdom which he hath promised to them that love him? (James 2:1–5)

Paul saw these things in another light than did those of whom James makes his complaint. "By the cross," he said, "I am crucified unto the world" (see Galatians 6:14). The cross where Jesus died became also the cross where His apostle died. The loss, the rejection, the shame, belong both to Christ and to all who in very truth are His. The cross that saves them also slays them, and anything short of this is a pseudo-faith and not true faith at all. But what are we to say when the great majority of our evangelical leaders walk not as crucified men but as those who accept the world at its own value—rejecting only its grosser elements? How can we face Him who was crucified and slain when we see His followers accepted and praised? Yet they preach the cross and protest loudly that they are true believers. Are there then two crosses? And did Paul mean one thing and they another? I fear that it is so, that there are two crosses, the old cross and the new.

Remembering my own deep imperfections I would think and speak with charity of all who take upon them the worthy Name by which we Christians are called. But if I see aright, the cross of popular evangelicalism is not the cross of the New Testament. It is, rather, a new bright ornament upon the bosom of self-assured and carnal Christianity whose hands are indeed the hands of Abel, but whose voice is the voice of Cain. The old cross slew men; the new cross entertains them. The old cross condemned; the new cross amuses. The old cross destroyed confidence in the flesh; the new cross encourages it. The old cross brought tears and blood; the new cross brings laughter. The flesh, smiling and confident, preaches and sings about the cross; before the cross it bows and toward the cross it points with carefully staged histrionics—but upon that cross it will not die, and the reproach of that cross it stubbornly refuses to bear.

I well know how many smooth arguments can be marshalled in support of the new cross. Does not the new cross win converts and make many followers and so carry the advantage of numerical success? Should we not adjust ourselves to the changing times? Have we not heard the new slogan "New days, new ways"? And who but someone very old and very conservative would insist upon death as the appointed way to life? And who today is interested in a gloomy mysticism that would sentence its flesh to a cross and recommend self-effacing humility as a virtue actually to be practiced by modern Christians? These are the arguments, along with many more flippant still, which are brought forward to give an appearance of wisdom to the hollow and meaningless cross of popular Christianity.

Doubtless there are many whose eyes are open to the tragedy of our times, but why are they so silent when their testimony is so sorely needed? In the name of Christ men have made void the cross of Christ. "The noise of them that sing do I hear" (Exodus 32:18). Men have fashioned a golden cross with a graving tool, and before it they sit down to eat and drink and rise up to play. In their blindness they have substituted the work of their own hands for the working of God's power. Perhaps our greatest present need may be the coming of a prophet to dash the stones at the foot of the mountain and call the church out to repentance or to judgment.

Before all who wish to follow Christ the way lies clear. It is the way of death unto life. Always life stands just beyond death and beckons the man who is sick of himself to come and know the life more abundant. But to reach the new life he must pass through the valley of the shadow of death, and I know that at the sound of those words many will turn back and follow Christ no more. But "to whom shall we go? thou hast the words of eternal life" (John 6:68).

It may be that there are some well-disposed followers who draw back because they cannot accept the morbidity which the idea of the cross seems to connote. They are lovers of the sun and find it too hard to think of living always in the shadows. They do not wish to dwell with death nor to live forever in an atmosphere of dying. And their instinct is sound. The church has made altogether too much of deathbed scenes and churchyards and funerals. The musty smell of churches, the slow and solemn step of the minister, the subdued quiet of the worshipers and the fact that many enter a church only to pay their last respects to the dead all add up to the notion that religion is something to be dreaded and, like a major operation, suffered only because we are caught in a crisis. All this is not the religion of the cross; it is rather a gross parody on it. Churchyard Christianity, though not ever remotely related to the doctrine of the cross, may yet be partly to blame for the appearance of the new and jolly cross of today. Men crave life, but when they are told that life comes by the cross they cannot understand how it can be, for they have learned to associate with the cross such typical images as memorial plaques, dim-lit aisles and ivy. So they reject the true message of the cross and with that message they reject the only hope of life known to the sons of man.

The truth is that God has never planned that His children should live forever stretched upon a cross. Christ Himself endured His cross for only six hours. When the cross had done its work life entered and took over. "Wherefore God also hath highly exalted him, and given him a name which is above every name" (Philippians 2:9).

His joyful resurrection followed hard upon His joyless crucifixion. But the first had to come before the second. The life that halts short of the cross is but a fugitive and condemned thing, doomed at last to be lost beyond recovery. That life which goes to the cross and loses itself there to rise again with Christ is a divine and deathless treasure. Over it death hath no more dominion. Whoever refuses to bring his old life to the cross is but trying to cheat death, and no matter how hard we may struggle against it, he is nevertheless fated to lose his life at last. The man who takes his cross and follows Christ will soon find that his direction is *away* from the sepulcher. Death is behind him and a joyous and increasing life before. His days will be marked henceforth not by ecclesiastical gloom, the churchyard, the hollow tone, the black robe (which are all but the cerements of a dead church), but by "joy unspeakable and full of glory" (1 Peter 1:8).

Real faith must always mean more than passive acceptance. It dare mean nothing less than surrender of our doomed Adam-life to a merciful end upon the cross. That is, we won God's just sentence against our evil flesh and admit His right to end its unlovely career. We reckon ourselves to have been crucified with Christ and to have risen again to newness of life. Where such faith is, God will always work in line with our reckoning. Then begins the divine conquest of our lives. This God accomplishes by an effective seizing upon, a sharp but love-impelled invasion of our natures. When He has overpowered our resistance He binds us with the cords of love and draws us to Himself. There, "faint with His loveliness" we lie conquered and thank God again and again for the blessed conquest. There, with moral sanity restored, we lift up our eyes and bless the Most High God. Then we go forth in faith to apprehend that for which we were first apprehended of God.

I thank thee, O Father, Lord of heaven and earth, that thou hast hid these things from the wise and prudent, and hast revealed them unto babes: even so, Father; for so it seemed good in thy sight. (Luke 10:21)

CHAPTER 5

The Forgotten One

The Comforter, which is the Holy Ghost.

JOHN 14:26

Neglecting or denying the deity of Christ, the liberals have committed a tragic blunder, for it leaves them nothing but an imperfect Christ whose death was a mere martyrdom and whose resurrection is a myth. They who follow a merely human savior follow no savior at all, but an ideal only, and one furthermore that can do no more than mock their weaknesses and sins. If Mary's Son was not the Son of God in a sense no other man is, then there can be no more hope for the human race. If He who called Himself the Light of the World was only a flickering torch, then the darkness that enshrouds the earth is here to stay. So-called Christian leaders shrug this off, but their responsibility toward the souls of their flocks cannot be dismissed with a shrug. God will yet bring them to account for the injury they have done to the plain people who trusted them as spiritual guides.

But however culpable the act of the liberal in denying the Godhood of Christ, we who pride ourselves on our orthodoxy must not allow our indignation to blind us to our own shortcomings. Certainly this is no time for self-congratulations, for we too have in recent years committed a costly blunder in religion, a blunder paralleling closely that of the liberal. Our blunder (or shall we frankly say our sin?) has been to neglect the doctrine of the Spirit to a point where we virtually deny Him His place in the Godhead. This denial has not been by open doctrinal statement, for we have clung closely enough to the biblical position wherever our credal pronouncements are concerned. Our formal creed is sound; *the breakdown is in our working creed.*

This is not a trifling distinction. A doctrine has practical value only as far as it is prominent in our thoughts and makes a difference in our lives. By this test the doctrine of the Holy Spirit as held by evangelical Christians today has almost no practical value at all. In most Christian churches the Spirit is quite entirely overlooked. Whether He is present or absent makes no real difference to anyone. Brief reference is made to Him in the doxology and the benediction. Further than that He might as well not exist. So completely do we ignore Him that it is only by courtesy that we can be called Trinitarian. The Christian doctrine of the Trinity boldly declares the equality of the Three Persons and the right of the Holy Spirit to be worshiped and glorified. Anything less than this is something less than Trinitarianism.

Our neglect of the doctrine of the blessed Third Person has had and is having serious consequences. For doctrine is dynamite. It must have emphasis sufficiently sharp to detonate it before its power is released. Failing this it may lie quiescent in the back of our minds for the whole of our lives without effect. The doctrine of the Spirit is buried dynamite. Its power awaits discovery and use by the church. The power of the Spirit will not be given to any mincing asset to pneumatological truth. The Holy Spirit cares not at all whether we write Him into our creeds in the back of our hymnals; He awaits our *emphasis.* When He gets into the thinking of the teachers He will get into the expectation of the hearers. When the Holy Spirit ceases to be incidental and again becomes fundamental, the power of the Spirit will be asserted once more among the people called Christians.

The idea of the Spirit held by the average church member is so vague as to be nearly non-existent. When he thinks of the matter at all he is likely to try to imagine a nebulous substance like a wisp of invisible smoke which is said to be present in churches and to hover over good people when they are dying. Frankly he does not believe in any such thing, but he wants to believe something, and not feeling up to the task of examining the whole truth in the light of Scripture he compromises by holding belief in the Spirit as far out from the center of his life as possible, letting it make no difference in anything that touches him practically. This describes a surprisingly large number of earnest persons who are sincerely trying to be Christians.

Now, how should we think of the Spirit? A full answer might well run to a dozen volumes. We can at best only point to the "gracious unction from above" and hope that the reader's own desire may provide the necessary stimulus to urge him on to know the blessed Third Person for himself.

If I read aright the record of Christian experience through the years, those who most enjoyed the power of the Spirit have had the least to say about Him by way of attempted definition. The Bible saints who walked in the Spirit never tried to explain Him. In post-biblical times many who were filled and possessed by the Spirit were by the limitations of their literary gifts prevented from telling us much about Him. They had no gifts for self-analysis but lived from within in uncritical simplicity. To them the Spirit was One to be loved and fellowshiped the same as the Lord Jesus Himself. They would have been lost completely in any metaphysical discussion of the nature of the Spirit, but they had no trouble in claiming the power of the Spirit for holy living and fruitful service.

This is as it should be. Personal experience must always be first in real life. The most important thing is that we experience reality by the shortest and most direct method. A child may eat nutritious food without knowing anything about the chemistry or dietetics. A country boy may know the delights of pure love while never having heard of Sigmund Freud or Havelock Ellis.* Knowledge by acquaintance is always better than mere knowledge by description, and the first does not presuppose the second nor require it.

In religion more than in any other field of human experience a sharp distinction must always be made between *knowing about* and *knowing*. The distinction is the same as between knowing about food and actually eating it. A man can die of starvation knowing all about bread, and a man can remain spiritually dead while knowing all the historic facts of Christianity. "This is life eternal, that they might know thee the only true God, and Jesus Christ, whom thou hast sent" (John 17:3). We have but to introduce one extra word into this verse to see how vast is the difference between knowing about and knowing. "This is life eternal, that they might know *about* thee the only true God, and Jesus Christ, whom thou hast sent." That one word makes all the difference between life and death, for it goes to the very root of the verse and changes its theology radically and vitally.

For all this we would not underestimate the importance of mere knowing about. Its value lies in its ability to rouse us to desire to know in actual experience. Thus knowledge by description may lead on to knowledge by

*English physician (1859–1939) who wrote the seven-volume *Studies in the Psychology of Sex*.

acquaintance. *May* lead on, I say, but does not necessarily do so. Thus we dare not conclude that because we learn about the Spirit we for that reason actually know Him. Knowing Him comes only by a personal encounter with the Holy Spirit Himself.

How shall we think of the Spirit? A great deal can be learned about the Holy Spirit from the word *spirit* itself. Spirit means existence on a level above and beyond matter; it means life subsisting in another mode. Spirit is substance that has no weight, no dimension, no size nor extension in space. These qualities belong to matter and can have no application to spirit. Yet spirit has true being and is objectively real. If this is hard to visualize, just pass it up, for it is at best but a clumsy attempt of the mind to grasp that which is above the mind's powers. And no harm is done if in our thinking about the Spirit we are forced by the limitations of our intellects to clothe Him in the familiar habiliments of material form.

How shall we think of the Spirit? The Bible and Christian theology agree to teach that He is a Person, endowed with every quality of personality, such as emotion, intellect and will. He knows, He wills, He loves; He feels affection, antipathy and compassion. He thinks, sees, hears and speaks and performs any act of which personality is capable.

One quality belonging to the Holy Spirit, of great interest and importance to every seeking heart, is penetrability. He can penetrate mind; He can penetrate another spirit, such as the human spirit. He can achieve complete penetration of and actual intermingling with the human spirit. He can invade the human heart and make room for Himself without expelling anything essentially human. The integrity of the human personality remains unimpaired. Only moral evil is forced to withdraw.

The metaphysical problem involved here can no more be avoided than it can be solved. How can one personality enter another? The candid reply would be simply that we do not know, but a near approach to an understanding may be made by a simple analogy borrowed from the old devotional writers of several hundred years ago. We place a piece of iron in a fire and blow up the coals. At first we have two distinct substances, iron and fire. When we insert the iron in the fire we achieve the penetration of the iron and we have not only the iron in the fire but the fire in the iron as well. They are two distinct substances, but they have co-mingled and interpenetrated to a point where the two have become one.

In some such manner does the Holy Spirit penetrate our spirits. In the whole experience we remain our very selves. There is no destruction of substance. Each remains a separate being as before; the difference is that now the Spirit penetrates and fills our personalities and we are *experientially one with God*.

How shall we think of the Holy Spirit? The Bible declares that He is God. Every quality belonging to Almighty God is freely attributed to Him. All that God is, the Spirit is declared to be. The Spirit of God is one with and equal to God just as the spirit of a man is equal to and one with the man. This is so fully taught in the Scriptures that we may without loss to the argument omit the formality of proof texts. The most casual reader will have discovered it for himself.

The historic church when she formulated her "rule of faith" boldly wrote into her confession her belief in the Godhood of the Holy Ghost. The Apostles' Creed witnesses to faith in the Father and in the Son and in the Holy Ghost and makes no difference between the three. The fathers who composed the Nicene Creed testified in a passage of great beauty to their faith in the deity of the Spirit:

> And I believe in the Holy Ghost, the Lord and Giver
> of life, who proceedeth from the Father and the
> Son; who with the Father and the Son together is
> worshiped and glorified.

The Arian controversy of the fourth century compelled the fathers to state their beliefs with greater clarity than before. Among the important writings which appeared at the time is the Athanasian Creed. Who composed it matters little to us now. It was written as an attempt to state in as few words as possible what the Bible teaches about the nature of God; and this it has done with a comprehensiveness and precision hardly matched anywhere in the literature of the world. Here are a few quotations bearing on the deity of the Holy Ghost:

> There is one Person of the Father, another of the Son:
> and another of the Holy Ghost.
> But the Godhead of the Father, of the Son, and
> of the Holy Ghost, is all one: the Glory equal, the
> Majesty co-eternal.
> And in this Trinity none is afore, or after other:
> none is greater, or less than another;
> But the whole three Persons are co-eternal
> together: and co-equal.
> So that in all things, as is aforesaid: the Unity in
> Trinity, and Trinity in Unity is to be worshiped.

In her sacred hymnody the church has freely acknowledged the Godhead of the Spirit and in her inspired song she has worshiped Him with joyous abandon. Some of our hymns to the Spirit have become so familiar that we tend to miss their true meaning by the very circumstances of their familiarity. Such a hymn is the wondrous "Holy Ghost, with Light Divine"; another is the more recent "Breathe on Me, Breath of God"; and there are many others. They have been sung so often by persons who have had no experiential knowledge of their content that for the most of us they have become almost meaningless.

In the poetical works of Frederick Faber I have found a hymn to the Holy Spirit which I would rank among the finest ever written, but so far as I know it has not been set to music, or if it has, it is not sung today in any church with which I am acquainted. Could the reason be that it embodies a personal experience of the Holy Spirit so deep, so intimate, so fiery hot that it corresponds to nothing in the hearts of the worshipers in present-day evangelicalism? I quote three stanzas:

> *Fountain of Love!*
> *Thyself true God!*
> *Who through eternal days*
> *From Father and from Son*
> *hast flowed in uncreated ways!*
>
> *I dread Thee, Unbegotten Love!*
> *True God! sole Fount of Grace!*
> *And now before Thy blessed throne*
> *My sinful self abase.*
>
> *O Light! O Love! O very God*
> *I dare no longer gaze*
> *Upon Thy wondrous attributes*
> *And their mysterious ways.*

These lines have everything to make a great hymn—sound theology, smooth structure, lyric beauty, high compression of profound ideas and a full charge of lofty religious feeling. Yet they are in complete neglect. I believe that a mighty resurgence of the Spirit's power among us will open again wells of hymnody long forgotten. For song can never bring the Holy Spirit, but the Holy Spirit does invariably bring song.

What we have in the Christian doctrine of the Holy Spirit is Deity present among us. He is not God's messenger only; *He is God.* He is God in contact with His creatures, doing in them and among them a saving and renewing work.

The Persons of the Godhead never work separately. We dare not think of them in such a way as to "divide the substance." Every act of God is done by all three Persons. God is never anywhere present in one Person without the other two. He cannot divide Himself. Where the Spirit is, there also is the Father and the Son. "We will come unto him, and make our abode with him" (John 14:23). For the accomplishment of some specific work one Person may for the time be more prominent than the others are, but never is He alone. God is altogether present wherever He is present at all.

To the reverent question, "What is God like?" a proper answer will always be, "He is like Christ." For Christ is God, and the Man who walked among men in Palestine was God acting like Himself in the familiar situation where His incarnation placed Him. To the question, "What is the Spirit like?" the answer must always be, "He is like Christ." For the Spirit is the essence of the Father and the Son. As they are, so is He. As we feel toward Christ and toward our Father who art in heaven, so should we feel toward the Spirit of the Father and the Son.

The Holy Spirit is the Spirit of life and light and love. In His uncreated nature He is a boundless sea of fire, flowing, moving ever, performing as He moves the eternal purposes of God. Toward nature He performs one sort of work, toward the world another and toward the church still another. And every act of His accords with the will of the Triune God. Never does He act on impulse nor move after a quick or arbitrary decision. Since He is the Spirit of the Father He feels toward His people exactly as the Father feels, so there need be on our part no sense of strangeness in His presence. He will always act like Jesus, toward sinners in compassion, toward saints in warm affection, toward human suffering in tenderest pity and love.

It is time for us to repent, for our transgressions against the blessed Third Person have been many and much aggravated. We have bitterly mistreated Him in the house of His friends. We have crucified Him in His own temple as they crucified the Eternal Son on the hill above Jerusalem. And the nails we used were not of iron, but of finer and more precious stuff of which human life is made. Out of our hearts we took the refined metals of will and feeling and thought, and from them we fashioned the nails of suspicion and rebellion and neglect. By unworthy thoughts about Him and unfriendly attitudes toward Him we grieved and quenched Him days without end.

The truest and most acceptable repentance is to reverse

the acts and attitudes of which we repent. A thousand years of remorse over a wrong act would not please God as much as a change of conduct and a reformed life. "Let the wicked forsake his way, and the unrighteous man his thoughts: and let him return unto the LORD, and he will have mercy upon him; and to our God, for he will abundantly pardon" (Isaiah 55:7).

We can best repent our neglect by neglecting Him no more. Let us begin to think of Him as One to be worshiped and obeyed. Let us throw open every door and invite Him in. Let us surrender to Him every room in the temple of our hearts and insist that He enter and occupy as Lord and Master within His own dwelling. And let us remember that He is drawn to the sweet name of Jesus as bees are drawn to the fragrance of clover. Where Christ is honored the Spirit is sure to feel welcome; where Christ is glorified He will move about freely, pleased and at home.

CHAPTER 6

The Illumination
of the Spirit

John answered and said,
A man can receive nothing,
except it be given him from heaven.

JOHN 3:27

Here in a brief sentence is the hope and despair of mankind. "A man can receive nothing." From the context we know that John is speaking of spiritual truth. He is telling us that there is a kind of truth which can never be grasped by the intellect, for the intellect exists for the apprehension of ideas, and this truth consists not in ideas but in life. Divine truth is of the nature of spirit and for that reason can be received only by spiritual revelation. "Except it be given him from heaven."

This was no new doctrine which John here set forth, but an advance rather upon truth already taught in the

Old Testament. The prophet Isaiah, for instance, has this passage.

> My thoughts are not your thoughts, neither are your
> ways my ways, saith the LORD. For as the heavens are
> higher than the earth, so are my ways higher than
> your ways, and my thoughts than your thoughts.
> (Isaiah 55:8–9)

Perhaps this had meant to its readers no more than that God's thoughts, while similar to ours, were loftier, and His ways as high above ours as would befit the ways of One whose wisdom is infinite and whose power is without bounds. Now John says plainly enough that God's thoughts are not only greater than ours quantitatively by qualitatively wholly different from ours. God's thoughts belong to the world of spirit, man's to the world of intellect, and while spirit can embrace intellect, the human intellect can never comprehend spirit. Man's thoughts cannot cross over into God's. "How unsearchable are his judgments, and his ways past finding out!" (Romans 11:33).

God made man in His own image and placed within him an organ by means of which he could know spiritual things. When man sinned that organ died. "Dead in sin" is a description not of the body nor yet of the intellect, but of the organ of God-knowledge within the human soul. Now men are forced to depend upon another and inferior organ and one furthermore which is wholly in-adequate to the purpose. I mean, of course, the mind as the seat of his powers of reason and understanding.

Man by reason cannot know God; he can only *know about* God. Through the light of reason certain important facts about God may be discovered.

> Because that which may be known of God is manifest in them; for God hath showed it unto them. For the invisible things of him from the creation of the world are clearly seen, being understood by the things that are made, even his eternal power and Godhead; so that they are without excuse. (Romans 1:19–20)

Through the light of nature man's moral reason may be enlightened, but the deeper mysteries of God remain hidden to him until he has received illumination from above.

> But the natural man receiveth not the things of the Spirit of God: for they are foolishness unto him: neither can he know them, because they are spiritually discerned. (1 Corinthians 2:14)

When the Spirit illuminates the heart, then a part of the man sees which never saw before; a part of him knows which never knew before, and that with a kind of know-ing which the most acute thinker cannot imitate. He knows now in a deep and authoritative way, and what he knows needs no reasoned proof. His experience of knowing is above reason, immediate, perfectly convincing and inwardly satisfying.

"A man can receive nothing." That is the burden of the Bible. Whatever men may think of human reason God takes a low view of it. "Where is the wise? where is the scribe? where is the disputer of this world? hath not God made foolish the wisdom of this world?" (1 Corinthians 1:20). Man's reason is a fine instrument and useful within its field. It is a gift of God and God does not hesitate to appeal to it, as when He cries to Israel, "Come now, and let us reason together" (Isaiah 1:18). The inability of human reason as an organ of divine knowledge arises not from its own weakness but from its unfittedness for the task by its own nature. It was not given as an organ by which to know God.

The doctrine of the inability of the human mind and the need for divine illumination is so fully developed in the New Testament that it is nothing short of astonishing that we should have gone so far astray from the whole thing. Fundamentalism has stood aloof from the liberal in self-conscious superiority and has on its own part fallen into error, the error of textualism, which is simply orthodoxy without the Holy Ghost. Everywhere among conservatives we find persons who are Bible-taught but not Spirit-taught. They conceive truth to be something which they can grasp with the mind. If a man holds to the fundamentals of the Christian faith he is thought to possess divine truth. But it does not follow. There is no truth apart from the Spirit. The most brilliant intellect may be imbecilic when confronted with the mysteries of God. For a man to understand revealed truth requires an act of God equal to the original act which inspired the text.

"Except it be given him from heaven." Here is the other side of the truth; here is hope for all, for these words do certainly mean that there is such a thing as a gift of knowing, a gift that comes from heaven. Christ taught His disciples to expect the coming of the Spirit of Truth who would teach them all things. He explained Peter's knowledge of His Saviorhood as being a direct revelation from the Father in heaven. And in one of His prayers He said:

I thank thee, O Father, Lord of heaven and earth, because thou hast hid these things from the wise and prudent, and hast revealed them unto babes. (Matthew 11:25)

By "wise and prudent" our Lord meant not Greek philosophers but Jewish Bible students and teachers of the Law.

This basic idea, the inability of human reason as an instrument of God-knowledge, was fully developed in the epistles of Paul. The apostle frankly rules out every natural faculty as instruments for discovering divine truth and throws us back helpless upon the inworking Spirit.

Eye hath not seen, nor ear heard, neither hath entered into the heart of man, the things which God hath prepared for them that love him. But God hath revealed them unto us by his Spirit: for the Spirit searcheth all things, yea, the deep things of God. For what man knoweth the things of a man, save the spirit of man which is in him? even so the things of God knoweth no man, but the Spirit of God. Now we have received, not the spirit of the world, but the spirit which is of God; that we might know the things that are freely given to us of God.
(1 Corinthians 2:9–12)

The passage just quoted is taken from Paul's first epistle to the Corinthians and is not lifted out of context nor placed in a setting which would tend to distort its meaning. Indeed it expresses the very essence of Paul's spiritual philosophy and fully accords with the rest of the epistle, and I might add, with the rest of Paul's writings as we have them preserved in the New Testament. That type of theological rationalism which is so popular today would have been wholly foreign to the mind of the great apostle. He had no faith in man's ability to comprehend truth apart from the direct illumination of the Holy Ghost.

I have just now used the word *rationalism* and I must either retract it or justify its use in association with orthodoxy. The latter I think I shall have no trouble doing. For the textualism of our times is based upon the same premise as the old-line rationalism, that is, the belief that the human mind is the supreme authority in the judgment of truth. Or otherwise stated, it is *confidence in the ability of the human mind to do that which the Bible declares it was never created to do and consequently is wholly incapable of doing.* Philosophical rationalism is honest enough to reject the Bible flatly. Theological rationalism rejects it while pretending to accept it and in so doing puts out its own eyes.

The inward kernel of truth has the same configuration as the outward shell. The mind can grasp the shell but only the Spirit of God can lay hold of the internal essence. Our great error has been that we have trusted to the shell and have believed we were sound in faith because we were able to explain the external shape of truth as found in the letter of the Word.

From this mortal error fundamentalism is slowly dying. We have forgotten that the essence of spiritual truth cannot come to the one who knows the external shell of truth unless there is first a miraculous operation of the Spirit within the heart. Those overtones of religious delight which accompany truth when the Spirit illuminates it are all but missing from the church today. Those transporting glimpses of the celestial country are few and dim; the fragrance of "Sharon's dewy Rose" is hardly discernible. Consequently we have been forced to look elsewhere for our delights and we have found them in the dubious artistry of converted opera singers or the tinkling melodies of odd and curious musical arrangements. We have tried to secure spiritual pleasures by working upon fleshly emotions and whipping up synthetic feeling by means wholly carnal. And the total effect has been evil.

In a remarkable sermon on "The True Way of Attaining Divine Knowledge," John Smith states the truth I am attempting to set forth here.

> Were I indeed to define divinity I should rather call it a divine *life* than a divine science; it is something rather to be understood by a spiritual sensation, than by any *verbal description*. . . . Divinity is indeed a true *efflux* from the eternal Light, which like the sunbeams, does not only enlighten, but *heat* and *enliven*. . . . We must not think that we have attained to the right knowledge of truth, when we have broken through the outward shell of words and phrases that house it up. . . . There is a knowing of Truth as it is in Jesus, as it is in a Christlike nature, as it is in that sweet, mild, humble and loving Spirit of Jesus, which spreads itself like a morning sun upon the souls of good men, full of life and light. It profits little to know Christ Himself after the flesh; but He gives His Spirit to good men that search the deep things of God. There is an inward beauty, life and loveliness in divine Truth, which can be known only when it is digested into life and practice.

This old divine held that a pure life was absolutely necessary to any real understanding of spiritual truth.

> There is an inward sweetness and deliciousness in divine truth, which no sensual mind can taste or relish: this is that "natural" man that savors not the things of God. . . . Divinity is not so much perceived by a subtle wit as by a purified sense.

Twelve hundred years before these words were uttered Athanasius had written a profound treatise called, "The Incarnation of the Word of God." In this treatise he boldly attacked the difficult problems inherent in the doctrine of the incarnation. The whole thing is a remarkable demonstration of pure reason engaged with divine revelation. He makes a great case for the deity of Christ and, for all who believe the Bible, settles the matter for all time. Yet so little does he trust the human mind to comprehend divine mysteries that he closed his great work with a strong warning against a mere intellectual understanding of spiritual truth. His words should be printed in large type and tacked on the desk of every pastor and theological student in the world:

> But for the searching of the Scriptures and true knowledge of them, an honorable life is needed, and a pure soul, and that virtue which is according to Christ; so that the intellect guiding its path by it may

be able to attain what it desires, and to comprehend it, in so far as it is accessible to human nature to learn concerning the Word of God. For without a pure mind and a modeling of the life after the saints, a man could not possibly comprehend the words of the saints. . . . He that would comprehend the mind of those who speak of God needs begin by washing and cleansing his soul.

The old Jewish believers of pre-Christian times who gave us the (to modern Protestants little-known) books, the Wisdom of Solomon and Ecclesiasticus, believed that it is impossible for an impure heart to know divine truth.

For into a malicious soul wisdom will not enter; nor dwell in the body that is subject unto sin. For the holy spirit of discipline will flee deceit, and remove from thoughts that are without understanding, and will not abide when unrighteousness cometh in.

These books, along with our familiar Book of Proverbs, teach that true spiritual knowledge is the result of a visitation of heavenly wisdom, a kind of baptism of the Spirit of Truth which comes to God-fearing men. This wisdom is always associated with righteousness and humility and is never found apart from godliness and true holiness of life.

Conservative Christians in this day are stumbling over this truth. We need to re-examine the whole thing. We need to learn that truth consists not in correct doctrine, but in correct doctrine *plus the inward enlightenment of the Holy Spirit.* We must declare again the mystery of wisdom from above. A re-preachment of this vital truth could result in a fresh breath from God upon a stale and suffocating orthodoxy.

CHAPTER 7

The Spirit as Power

But ye shall receive power,
after that the Holy Ghost is come upon you.

ACTS 1:8

S ome good christians have misread this text and have assumed that Christ told His disciples that they were to receive the Holy Spirit *and* power, the power to come after the coming of the Spirit. A superficial reading of the King James text might conceivably lead to the conclusion, but the truth is that Christ taught not the coming of the Holy Spirit *as* power; the power and the Spirit are the same.

Our mother tongue is a beautiful and facile instrument, but it can also be a tricky and misleading one, and for this reason it must be used with care if we would avoid giving and receiving wrong impressions by its means. Especially is this true when we are speaking of God, for God being wholly unlike anything or anybody in His universe, our very thoughts of Him as well as our words are in constant danger of going astray. One example is found in the words, "The power of God." The danger is that we think of "power" as something belonging to God as muscular energy belongs to a man, as something which He *has* and which might be separated from Him and still have existence in itself. We must remember that the "attributes" of God are not component parts of the blessed Godhead nor elements out of which He is composed. A god who could be *composed* would not be God at all but the work of something or someone greater than he, great enough to compose him. We would then have a synthetic god made out of the pieces we call attributes, and the true God would be another being altogether, One indeed who is above all thought and all conceiving.

The Bible and Christian theology teach that God is an indivisible unity, being what He is in undivided oneness, from whom nothing can be taken and to whom nothing can be added. Mercy, for instance, immutability, eternity these are but names which we have given to something which God has declared to be true of Himself. All the "of God" expressions in the Bible must be understood to mean not what God has but *what God is* in His undivided and indivisible unity. Even the word "nature" when applied to God should be understood as an accommodation to our human way of looking at things and not as an accurate description of anything true of the mysterious Godhead. God has said, "I AM THAT I AM" (Exodus 3:14), and we can only repeat in reverence, "O God, Thou art."

Our Lord before His ascension said to His disciples, "Tarry ye in the city of Jerusalem, until ye be endued with power from on high" (Luke 24:49). That word *until* is a time-word; it indicates a point in relation to which everything is either before or after. So the experience of those disciples could be stated like this: Up to that point they *had not* received the power; at that point they *did* receive the power; after that point they *had* received the power. Such is the plain historic fact. Power came upon the church, such power as had never been released into human nature before (with the lone exception of that mighty anointing which came upon Christ at the waters of Jordan). That power, still active in the church, has enabled her to exist for nearly twenty centuries, even though for all of that time she has remained a highly unpopular minority group among the nations of mankind and has always been surrounded by enemies who would gladly have ended her existence if they could have done so.

"Ye shall receive power." By those words our Lord raised the expectation of His disciples and taught them to look forward to the coming of a supernatural potency into their natures from a source outside of themselves. It was to be something previously unknown to them, but suddenly to come upon them from another world. It was to be nothing less than God Himself entering into them with the purpose of ultimately reproducing His own likeness within them.

Here is the dividing line that separates Christianity from all occultism and from every kind of oriental cult, ancient or modern. These all are built around the same ideas, varying only in minor details, each with its own peculiar set of phrases and apparently vying with each other in vagueness and obscurity. They each advise, "Get in tune with the infinite," or "Wake the giant within you," or "Tune in to your hidden potential" or "Learn to think creatively." All this may have some fleeting value as a psychological shot in the arm, but its results are not permanent because at its best it builds its hopes upon the fallen nature of man and knows no invasion from above. And whatever may be said in its favor, *it most certainly is not Christianity.*

Christianity takes for granted the absence of any self-help and offers a power which is nothing less than the power of God. This power is to come upon powerless men as a gentle but resistless invasion from another world, bringing a moral potency infinitely beyond anything that might be stirred up from within. This power is sufficient; no additional help is needed, no auxiliary source of spiritual energy, for it is the Holy Spirit of God come where the weakness lay to supply power and grace to meet the moral need.

Set over against such a mighty provision as this ethical Christianity (if I may be allowed the term) is seen to be no Christianity at all. An infantile copying of Christ's "ideals," a pitiable effort to carry out the teachings of the

Sermon on the Mount! All this is but religious child's play and is not the faith of Christ and the New Testament.

"Ye shall receive power." This was and is a unique afflatus, an enduement of supernatural energy affecting every department of the believer's life and remaining with him forever. It is not physical power nor even mental power though it may touch everything both mental and physical in its benign outworking. It is, too, another kind of power than that seen in nature, in the lunar attraction that creates the tides or the angry flash that splits the great oak during a storm. This power from God operates on another level and affects another department of His wide creation. It is spiritual power. It is the kind of power that God is. It is the ability to achieve spiritual and moral ends. Its long-range result is to produce Godlike character in men and women who were once wholly evil by nature and by choice.

Now how does this power operate? At its purest it is an unmediated force directly applied by the Spirit of God to the spirit of man. The wrestler achieves his ends by the pressure of his physical body upon the body of his opponent; the teacher by the pressure of ideas upon the mind of the student; the moralist by the pressure of duty upon the conscience of the disciple. So the Holy Spirit performs His blessed work by direct contact with the human spirit.

It would be less than accurate to say that the power of God is always experienced in a direct and unmediated form, for when He so wills the Spirit may use other means as Christ used spittle to heal a blind man. But always the power is above and beyond the means. While the Spirit may use appropriate means to bless a believing man, He never need do so, for they are at best but temporary concessions made to our ignorance and unbelief. Where adequate power is present almost any means will suffice, but where the power is absent not all the means in the world can secure the desired end. The Spirit of God may use a song, a sermon, a good deed, a text or the mystery and majesty of nature, but always the final work will be done by the pressure of the inliving Spirit upon the human heart.

In the light of this it will be seen how empty and meaningless is the average church service today. All the means are in evidence; the one ominous weakness is the absence of the Spirit's power. The form of godliness is there, and often the form is perfected till it is an aesthetic triumph. Music and poetry, art and oratory, symbolic vesture and solemn tones combine to charm the mind of the worshiper, but too often the supernatural afflatus is not there. The power from on high is neither known nor desired by pastor or people. This is nothing less than tragic, and all the more so because it falls within the field of religion where the eternal destinies of men are involved.

To the absence of the Spirit may be traced that vague sense of unreality which almost everywhere invests religion in our times. In the average church service the most real thing is the shadowy unreality of everything. The worshiper sits in a state of suspended thought; a kind of dreamy numbness creeps upon him; he hears words but they do not register; he cannot relate them to anything on his own life-level. He is conscious of having entered a kind of halfworld; his mind surrenders itself to a more or less pleasant mood which passes with the benediction, leaving no trace behind. It does not affect anything in his everyday life. He is aware of no power, no presence, no spiritual reality. There is simply nothing in his experience corresponding to the things which he heard from the pulpit or sang in the hymns.

One meaning of the word "power" is "ability to do." There precisely is the wonder of the Spirit's work in the church and in the hearts of Christians, His sure ability to make spiritual things real to the soul. This power can go straight to its object with piercing directness; it can diffuse itself through the mind like an infinitely fine volatile essence securing ends above and beyond the limits of the intellect. Reality is its subject matter, reality in heaven and upon earth. It does not create objects which are not there but reveals objects already present and hidden from the soul. In actual human experience this is likely to be first felt in a heightened sense of the presence of Christ. He is felt to be a real Person and to be intimately, ravishingly near. Then all other spiritual objects begin to stand out clearly before the mind. Grace, forgiveness, cleansing take on a form of almost bodily clearness. Prayer loses its unmeaning quality and becomes a sweet conversation with Someone actually there. Love for God and for the children of God takes possession of the soul. We feel ourselves near to heaven and it is now the earth and the world that begin to seem unreal. We know them now for what they are, realities indeed, but like stage scenery here for one brief hour and soon to pass away. The world to come takes on a hard outline before our minds and begins to invite our interest and our devotion. Then the whole life changes to suit the new reality and the change is permanent. Slight fluctuations there may be like the rise and dip of the line on a graph, but the established direction is upward and the ground taken is held.

This is not all, but it will give a fair idea of what is meant when the New Testament speaks of *power,* and perhaps by contrast we may learn how little of the power we enjoy.

I think there can be no doubt that the need above all other needs in the church of God at this moment is the power of the Holy Spirit. More education, better organization, finer equipment, more advanced methods—all are unavailing. It is like bringing a better respirator after the patient is dead. Good as these are they can never give life. "It is the spirit that quickeneth" (John 6:63). Good as they are they can never bring power. "Power belongeth unto God" (Psalm 62:11). Protestantism is on the wrong road when it tries to win merely by means of a "united front." It is not organizational unity we need most; the great need is power. The headstones in the cemetery present a united front, but they stand mute and helpless while the world passes by.

I suppose my suggestion will not receive much serious attention, but I should like to suggest that we Bible-believing Christians announce a moratorium on religious activity and set our house in order preparatory to the coming of an afflatus from above. So carnal is the body of Christians which composes the conservative wing of the church, so shockingly irreverent are our public services in some quarters, so degraded are our religious tastes in still others that the need for power could scarcely have been greater at any time in history. I believe we should profit immensely were we to declare a period of silence and self-examination during which each one of us searched his own heart and sought to meet every condition for a real baptism of power from on high.

We may be sure of one thing, that for our deep trouble there is no cure apart from a visitation, yes, an *invasion* of power from above. Only the Spirit Himself can show us what is wrong with us and only the Spirit can prescribe the cure. Only the Spirit can save us from the numbing unreality of Spiritless Christianity. Only the Spirit can show us the Father and the Son. Only the inworking of the Spirit's power can discover to us the solemn majesty and the heart ravishing mystery of the Triune God.

———————•———————

CHAPTER 8

The Holy Spirit as Fire

*And there appeared unto them cloven tongues
like as of fire, and it sat upon each of them.*

ACTS 2:3

Christian theology teaches that God in His essential nature is both inscrutable and ineffable. This by simple definition means that He is incapable of being searched into or understood and that He cannot tell forth or utter what He is. This inability lies not in God but in the limitations of our creaturehood. "Why asketh thou thus after my name, seeing it is secret?" (Judges 13:18). Only God knows God in any final meaning of the word "know." "Even so the things of God knoweth no man, but the Spirit of God" (1 Corinthians 2:11).

To the average Christian today this may sound strange, if not downright confusing, for the temper of religious thinking in our times is definitely not theological. We may live out a full lifetime and die without once

431

having our minds challenged by the sweet mystery of the Godhead if we depend upon the churches to do the challenging. They are altogether too busy playing with shadows and getting "adjusted" to one thing and another to spend much time thinking about God. It might be well, therefore, to consider for a moment longer the divine inscrutability.

God in His essential being is unique in the only sense that word will bear. That is, there is nothing conceived by the mind because He is "altogether other" than anything with which we have had experience before. The mind has no material with which to start. No man has ever entertained a thought which can be said to describe God in any but the vaguest and most imperfect sense. Where God is known at all it must be otherwise than by our creature-reason.

Novatian, in a famous treatise on the Trinity written sometime about the middle of the third century, says:

> In all our meditations upon the qualities of the attributes and content of God, we pass beyond our powers of fit conception, nor can human eloquence put forth a power commensurate with His greatness. At the contemplation and utterance of His majesty, all eloquence is rightly dumb, all mental effort is feeble. For God is greater than mind itself. His greatness cannot be conceived. Nay, if we could conceive of His greatness, He would be less than the

human mind which could form the conception. He is greater than all language, and no statement can express Him. Indeed, if any statement could express Him, He would be less than human speech, which could by such statement comprehend and gather up all that He is. Up to a certain point, of course, we can have experience of Him, without language, but no man can express in words all that He is in Himself. Suppose, for instance, one speaks of Him as light; this is an account of part of His creation, not of Himself. It does not express what He is. Or suppose one speaks of Him as power. This too sets forth in words His attribute of might, rather than His being. Or suppose one speaks of Him as majesty. Once again, we have a declaration of the honor which is His own, rather than of Him in Himself . . . . To sum up the matter in a single sentence, every possible statement that can be made about God expresses some possession or virtue of God, rather than God Himself. What words or thoughts are worthy Him, who is above all language and all thought? The conception of God as He is can only be grasped in one way, and even that is impossible for us, beyond our grasp and understanding; by thinking of Him as a Being whose attributes and greatness are beyond our powers of understanding, or even of thought.

Just because God cannot tell us *what He is* He very often tells us *what He is like.* By these "like" figures He leads our faltering minds as close as they can come to that "light which no man can approach unto" (1 Timothy 6:16). Through the more cumbersome medium of the intellect the soul is prepared for the moment when it can, through the operation of the Holy Spirit, know God as He is in Himself. God has used a number of these similitudes to hint at His incomprehensible being, and judging from the Scriptures one would gather that *His favorite similitude is fire.* In one place the Spirit speaks expressly, "For our God is a consuming fire" (Hebrews 12:29). This accords with His revelation of Himself as recorded throughout the Bible. As a fire He spoke to Moses from the burning bush; in the fire He dwelt above the camp of Israel through all the wilderness journey; as fire He dwelt between the wings of the cherubim in the Holy of Holies; to Ezekiel He revealed Himself as a strange brightness of "a fire infolding itself" (Ezekiel 1:4).

> I saw as it were the appearance of fire, and it had brightness round about. As the appearance of the bow that is in the cloud in the day of rain, so was the appearance of the brightness round about. This was the appearance of the likeness of the glory of the LORD. And when I saw it, I fell on my face, and I heard a voice of one that spake. (1:27–28)

With the coming of the Holy Spirit at Pentecost the same imagery was continued. "And there appeared unto them cloven tongues like as of fire, and it sat upon each of them" (Acts 2:3). That which came upon the disciples in that upper room was nothing less than God Himself. To their mortal eyes He appeared as fire, and may we not safely conclude that those Scripture-taught believers knew at once what it meant? The God who had appeared to them as fire throughout all their long history was now dwelling in them as fire. He had moved from without to the interior of their lives. The Shekinah that had once blazed over the mercy seat now blazed on their foreheads as an external emblem of the fire that had invaded their natures. This was Deity giving Himself to ransomed men. The flame was the seal of a new union. They were now men and women of the Fire.

Here is the whole final message of the New Testament: Through the atonement in Jesus' blood sinful men may now become one with God. Deity indwelling men! That is Christianity in its fullest effectuation, and even those greater glories of the world to come will be in essence but a greater and more perfect experience of the soul's union with God.

Deity indwelling men! That, I say, is Christianity, and no man has experienced rightly the power of Christian belief until he has known this for himself as a living reality. Everything else is preliminary to this. Incarnation, atonement, justification, regeneration—what are these but acts of God preparatory to the work of invading and the act of indwelling the redeemed human soul? Man, who moved out of the heart of God by sin, now moves back into the heart of God by redemption. God, who moved out of the heart of man because of sin, now enters again His ancient dwelling to drive out His enemies and once more make the place of His feet glorious.

That visible fire on the day of Pentecost had for the church a deep and tender significance, for it told to all ages that they upon whose heads it sat were men and women apart; they were "creatures out of the fire" (see Ezekiel 1:13) as surely as were they whom Ezekiel in his vision saw by the river Chebar. The mark of the fire was the sign of divinity; they who received it were forever a peculiar people, sons and daughters of the Flame.

One of the most telling blows which the enemy ever struck at the life of the church was to create in her a fear of the Holy Spirit. No one who mingles with Christians in these times will deny that such a fear exists. Few there are who without restraint will open their whole heart to the blessed Comforter. He has been and is so widely misunderstood that the very mention of His name in some circles is enough to frighten many people into resistance. The source of this unreasoning fear may easily by traced, but it would be fruitless labor to do it here. Sufficient to say that the fear is groundless. Perhaps we may help to destroy its power over us if we examine that fire which is the symbol of the Spirit's Person and presence.

The Holy Spirit is first of all a *moral flame.* It is not an accident of language that He is called the *Holy* Spirit, for whatever else the word *holy* may mean it does undoubtedly carry with it the idea of moral purity. And the Spirit, being God, must be absolutely and infinitely pure. With Him there are not (as with men) grades and degrees of holiness. He is holiness itself, the sum and essence of all that is unspeakably pure.

No one whose senses have been exercised to know good and evil but must grieve over the sight of zealous souls seeking to be filled with the Holy Spirit while they are yet living in a state of moral carelessness or borderline sin. Such a thing is a moral contradiction. Whoever would be filled and indwelt by the Spirit should first judge his life for any hidden iniquities; he should courageously expel from his heart everything which is out of accord with the character of God as revealed by the Holy Scriptures.

At the base of all true Christian experience must lie a sound and sane morality. No joys are valid, no delights legitimate where sin is allowed to live in life or conduct. No transgression of pure righteousness dare excuse itself on the ground of superior religious experience. To seek high emotional states while living in sin is to throw our whole life open to self-deception and the judgment of God. "Be ye holy" is not a mere motto to be framed and hung on the wall. It is a serious commandment from the Lord of the whole earth.

Cleanse your hands, ye sinners; and purify your
hearts, ye double minded. Be afflicted, and mourn,
and weep: let your laughter be turned to mourning,
and your joy to heaviness. (James 4:8–9)

The true Christian ideal is not to be happy but to be
holy. The holy heart alone can be the habitation of the
Holy Ghost.

The Holy Spirit is also a *spiritual flame.* He alone can
raise our worship to true spiritual levels. For we might as
well know once for all that morality and ethics, however
lofty, are still not Christianity. The faith of Christ under-
takes to raise the soul to actual communion with God, to
introduce into our religious experiences a suprarational
element as far above mere goodness as the heavens are
above the earth. The coming of the Spirit brought to the
book of Acts this very quality of supramundaneness, this
mysterious elevation of tone not found in as high intensity even in the Gospels. The key of the book of Acts is
definitely the major. There is in it no trace of creature-
sadness, no lingering disappointment, no quaver of uncertainty. The mood is heavenly. A victorious spirit is
found there, a spirit which could never be the result of
mere religious belief. The joy of the first Christians was
not the joy of logic working on facts. They did not reason, "Christ is risen from the dead; therefore we ought
to be glad." Their gladness was as great a miracle as the
resurrection itself; indeed these were and are organically

related. The moral happiness of the Creator had taken residence in the breasts of redeemed creatures and they could not but be glad.

The flame of the Spirit is also *intellectual*. Reason, say the theologians, is one of the divine attributes. There need be no incompatibility between the deepest experiences of the Spirit and the highest attainments of the human intellect. *It is only required that the Christian intellect be fully surrendered to God and there need be no limit to its activities* beyond those imposed upon it by its own strength and size. How cold and deadly is the unblessed intellect. A superior brain without the saving essence of godliness may turn against the human race and drench the world with blood, or worse, it may loose ideas into the earth which will continue to curse mankind for centuries after it has turned to dust again. But a Spirit-filled mind is a joy to God and a delight to all men of good will. What would the world have missed if it had been deprived of the love-filled mind of a David or a John or an Isaac Watts?

We naturally shy away from superlatives and from comparisons which praise one virtue at the expense of another, yet I wonder whether there is on earth anything as exquisitely lovely as a brilliant mind aglow with the love of God. Such a mind sheds a mild and healing ray which can actually be *felt* by those who come near it. Virtue goes forth from it and blesses those who merely touch the hem of its garment. One has, for instance, but to read

The Celestial Country by Bernard of Cluny to understand what I mean. There a sensitive and shining intellect warm with the fire of the inliving Spirit writes with a vast and tender sympathy of those longings for immortality which have dwelt deep in the human breast since the first man knelt down upon the earth out of whose bosom he came and into whose bosom he must soon return again. For loftiness of concept, for sheer triumph of the Christian spirit over mortality, for ability to rest the soul and raise the mind to rapturous worship its equal is hardly found anywhere in uninspired literature. I submit it as my respectful opinion that this single hymn may have ministered more healing virtue to distressed spirits than all the writings of secular poets and philosophers since the art of writing was invented. No unblessed intellect, however sure its genius, would be remotely capable of producing such a work. One closes the book after reading it with the feeling, yes, the solemn conviction, that he has heard the voice of the cherubim and the sound of harpers strumming beside the sea of God.

This same feeling of near-inspiration is experienced also in the letters of Samuel Rutherford, in the *Te Deum,* in many of the hymns of Watts and Wesley and occasionally in a work of some lesser-known saint whose limited gifts may have been for one joyous moment made incandescent by the fire of the indwelling Spirit.

The blight of the Pharisee's heart in olden times was doctrine without love. With the teachings of the Pharisees

Christ had little quarrel, but with the pharisaic spirit He carried on unceasing warfare to the end. It was religion that put Christ on the cross, religion without the indwelling Spirit. It is no use to deny that Christ was crucified by persons who would today be called fundamentalists. This should prove most disquieting if not downright distressing to us who pride ourselves on our orthodoxy. An unblessed soul filled with the letter of truth may actually be worse off than a pagan kneeling before a fetish. We are safe only when the love of God is shed abroad in our hearts by the Holy Ghost, only when our intellects are indwelt by the loving Fire that came at Pentecost. For the Holy Spirit is not a luxury, not something added now and again to produce a deluxe type of Christian once in a generation. No, He is for every child of God a vital necessity, and that He fill and indwell His people is more than a languid hope. It is rather an inescapable imperative.

The Spirit is also a *volitional flame.* Here as elsewhere the imagery is inadequate to express all the truth, and unless care is taken we may easily gain a wrong impression from its use. For fire as we see and know it every day is a *thing,* not a person, and for that reason it has no will of its own. But the Holy Spirit is a Person, having those attributes of personality of which volition is one. He does not, upon entering the human soul, void any of His attributes, nor does He surrender them in part or in full to the soul into which He enters. Remember, the Holy Spirit is Lord. "Now the Lord is that Spirit,"

441

said Paul to the Corinthians (2 Corinthians 3:17). The Nicene Creed says, "And I believe in the Holy Ghost, the Lord and Giver of life," and the Athanasian Creed declares, "So likewise the Father is Lord, the Son Lord, and the Holy Ghost Lord. And yet not three Lords: but one Lord." Whatever problems this may pose for the understanding, our faith must accept it and make it a part of our total belief about God and the Spirit. Now it hardly need be said that the Sovereign Lord will never abandon the prerogatives of His Godhood. Wherever He is He must continue to act like Himself. When He enters the human heart He will be there what He has always been, Lord in His own right.

The deep disease of the human heart is a will broken loose from its center, like a planet which has left its central sun and started to revolve around some strange body from outer space which may have moved in close enough to draw it away. When Satan said, "I will," he broke loose from his normal center, and the disease with which he has infected the human race is the disease of disobedience and revolt. Any adequate scheme of redemption must take into account this revolt and must undertake to restore again the human will to its proper place in the will of God. In accord with this underlying need for the healing of the will, the Holy Spirit, when He effects His gracious invasion of the believing heart, must win that heart to glad and voluntary obedience to the whole will of God. The cure must be wrought from within; no outward conformity will do. Until the will is sanctified the man is still a rebel just as an outlaw is still an outlaw at heart even though he may be yielding grudging obedience to the sheriff who is taking him to prison.

The Holy Spirit achieves this inward cure by merging the will of the redeemed man with His own. This is not accomplished at one stroke. There must be, it is true, some kind of overall surrender of the will to Christ before any work of grace can be done, but the full mergence of every part of life with the life of God in the Spirit is likely to be a longer process than we in our creature impatience would wish. The most advanced soul may be shocked and chagrined to discover some private area within his life where he had been, unknown to himself, acting as lord and proprietor of that which he thought he had given to God. It is the work of the in-living Spirit to point out these moral discrepancies and correct them. He does not, as is sometimes said, "break" the human will, but He does invade it and bring it gently to a joyous union with the will of God.

To will the will of God is to do more than give unprotesting consent to it; it is rather to choose God's will with positive determination. As the work of God advances, the Christian finds himself free to choose whatever he will, and he gladly chooses the will of God as his highest conceivable good. Such a man has found life's highest goal. He has been placed beyond the little disappointments that plague the rest of men. Whatever happens to him is the will of God for him and that is just what he most ardently desires. But it is only fair to state that this condition is one not reached by many of the busy Christians of our busy times. Until it is reached, however, the Christian's peace cannot be complete. There must be still a certain inward controversy, a sense of spiritual disquiet which poisons our joy and greatly reduces our power.

Another quality of the indwelling Fire is *emotion*. This must be understood in light of what has been said before about the divine inscrutability. What God is in His unique essence cannot be discovered by the mind nor uttered by the lips, but those qualities in God which may be termed rational, and so received by the intellect, have been freely set forth in the sacred Scriptures. They do not tell us what God is, but they do tell us what God is like, and the sum of them constitute a mental picture of the Divine Being seen, as it were, afar off and through a glass darkly.

Now the Bible teaches that there is something in God which is like emotion. He experiences something which is like our love, something that is like our grief, that is like our joy. And we need not fear to go along with this conception of what God is like. Faith would easily draw the inference that since we were made in His image, He would have qualities like our own. But such an inference, while satisfying to the mind, is not the ground of our belief. *God has said certain things about Himself, and these furnish all the grounds we require.*

The LORD thy God in the midst of thee is mighty;
he will save, he will rejoice over thee with joy; he will
rest in his love, he will joy over thee with singing.
(Zephaniah 3:17)

This is but one verse among thousands which serve to form our rational picture of what God is like, and they tell us plainly that God feels something like our love, like our joy, and what He feels makes Him act very much as we would in a similar situation; He rejoices over His loved ones with joy and singing.

Here is emotion on as high a plane as it can ever be seen, emotion flowing out of the heart of God Himself. Feeling, then, is not the degenerate son of unbelief that is often painted by some of our Bible teachers. Our ability to feel is one of the marks of our divine origin. We need not be ashamed of either tears or laughter. The Christian stoic who has crushed his feelings is only two-thirds of a man; an important third part has been repudiated.

Holy feeling had an important place in the life of our Lord. "For the joy that was set before him" (Hebrews 12:2) He endured the cross and despised its shame. He pictured Himself crying, "Rejoice with me; for I have found my sheep which was lost" (Luke 15:6). On the night of His agony He "sang a hymn" before going out to the Mount of Olives. After His resurrection He sang among His brethren in the great congregation (see Psalm 22:22). And if the Song of Solomon refers to Christ (as most Christians believe it does) then how are we to miss the sound of His rejoicing as He brings His Bride home after the night has ended and the shadows have fled away?

One of the very greatest calamities which sin has brought upon us is the debasement of our normal emotions. We laugh at things which are not funny; we find pleasure in acts which are beneath our human dignity; and we rejoice in objects which should have no place in our affections. The objection to "sinful pleasures," which has always been characteristic of the true saint, is at bottom simply a protest against the degradation of our human emotions. That gambling, for instance, should be allowed to engross the interests of men made in the image of God has seemed like a horrid perversion of noble powers; that alcohol should be necessary to stimulate the feeling of pleasure has seemed like a kind of prostitution; that men should turn to the man-made theater for enjoyment has seemed an affront to the God who placed us in the midst of a universe charged with high dramatic action. The world's artificial pleasures are all but evidence that the human race has to a large extent lost its power to enjoy the true pleasures of life and is forced to substitute for them false and degrading thrills.

The work of the Holy Spirit is, among other things, to rescue the redeemed man's emotions, to restring his harp and open again the wells of sacred joy which have been stopped by sin. That He does this is the unanimous testimony of the saints. And it is not inconsistent with the whole way of God in His creation. Pure pleasure is part of life, such an important part that it is difficult to see how human life could be justified if it were to consist of endless existence devoid of pleasurable feeling.

The Holy Spirit would set an aeolian harp in the window of our souls so that the winds of heaven may play sweet melody for a musical accompaniment to the humblest task we may be called to perform. The spiritual love of Christ will make constant music within our hearts and enable us to rejoice even in our sorrows.

———— • ————

CHAPTER 9

Why the World Cannot Receive

The Spirit of truth;
whom the world cannot receive.

JOHN 14:17

The christian faith, based upon the New Testament,
teaches the complete antithesis between the church
and the world. I have noted this briefly in a previous
chapter, but the matter is so important to the seeking
soul that I feel that I must here go into the whole thing
a little further.

It is no more than a religious platitude to say that the
trouble with us today is that we have tried to bridge the
gulf between two opposites, the world and the church,
and have performed an illicit marriage for which there is
no biblical authority. Actually no real union between the
world and the church is possible. When the church joins

up with the world it is the true church no longer but only a pitiful hybrid thing, an object of smiling contempt to the world and an abomination to the Lord.

The twilight in which many (or should we say *most?*) believers walk today is not caused by any vagueness on the part of the Bible. Nothing could be clearer than the pronouncements of the Scriptures on the Christian's relation to the world. The confusion which gathers around this matter results from the unwillingness of professing Christians to take the Word of the Lord seriously. Christianity is so entangled with the world that millions never guess how radically they have missed the New Testament pattern. Compromise is everywhere. The world is whitewashed just enough to pass inspection by blind men posing as believers, and those same believers are everlastingly seeking to gain acceptance with the world. By mutual concessions men who call themselves Christians manage to get on with men who have for the things of God nothing but quiet contempt.

This whole thing is spiritual in its essence. A Christian is what he is not by ecclesiastical manipulation but by the new birth. He is a Christian because of a Spirit which dwells in him. Only that which is born of the Spirit is spirit. The flesh can never be converted into spirit, no matter how many church dignitaries work on it. Confirmation, baptism, holy communion, confession of faith— none of these nor all of them together can turn flesh into spirit nor make a son of Adam a son of God. "Because

ye are sons," wrote Paul to the Galatians, "God hath sent
forth the Spirit of his Son into your hearts, crying, Abba,
Father" (Galatians 4:6). And to the Corinthians he wrote:

> Examine yourselves, whether ye be in the faith; prove
> your own selves. Know ye not your own selves, how
> that Jesus Christ is in you, except ye be reprobates?
> (2 Corinthians 13:5)

And to the Romans:

> But ye are not in the flesh, but in the Spirit, if so
> be that the Spirit of God dwell in you. Now if any
> man have not the Spirit of Christ, he is none of his.
> (Romans 8:9)

That terrible zone of confusion so evident in the whole
life of the Christian community could be cleared up in
one day if the followers of Christ would begin to follow
Christ instead of each other. For our Lord was very plain
in His teaching about the believer and the world.

On one occasion, after receiving unsolicited and carnal advice from sincere but unenlightened brethren, our
Lord replied:

> My time is not yet come: but your time is alway
> ready. The world cannot hate you; but me it hateth,

because I testify of it, that the works thereof are evil.
(John 7:6–7)

He identified His fleshly brethren with the world and said that they and He were of two different spirits. The world hated Him but could not hate them because it could not hate itself. A house divided against itself cannot stand. Adam's house must remain loyal to itself or it will tear itself apart. Though the sons of the flesh may quarrel among themselves they are at bottom one with each other. It is when the Spirit of God comes in that an alien element has entered. The Lord said to His disciples:

If the world hate you, ye know that it hated me
before it hated you. If ye were of the world, the
world would love his own: but because ye are not of
the world, but I have chosen you out of the world,
therefore the world hateth you. (John 15:18–19)

Paul explained to the Galatians the difference between the bond child and the free: "But as then he that was born after the flesh persecuted him that was born after the Spirit, even so it is now" (Galatians 4:29).

So throughout the entire New Testament a sharp line is drawn between the church and the world. There is no middle ground. The Lord recognizes no good-natured "agreeing to disagree" so that the followers of the Lamb may adopt the world's ways and travel along the world's path. The gulf between the true Christian and the world is as great as that which separated the rich man and Lazarus. And furthermore it is the same gulf, that is, it is the gulf that divides the world of ransomed from the world of fallen men.

I well know and feel deeply, how offensive such teaching as this must be to the great flock of worldlings which mills around the traditional sheepfold. I cannot hope to escape the charge of bigotry and intolerance which will undoubtedly be brought against me by the confused religionists who seek to make themselves sheep by association. But we may as well face the hard truth that men do not become Christians by associating with church people, nor by religious contact, nor by religious education; they become Christians only by invasion of their nature by the Spirit of God in the new birth. And when they do thus become Christians they are immediately members of a new race,

> a chosen generation, a royal priesthood, an holy nation, a peculiar people . . . which in time past were not a people, but are now the people of God: which had not obtained mercy, but now have obtained mercy. (1 Peter 2:9–10)

In the verses quoted there has been no wish to quote out of context nor to focus attention upon one side of truth to draw it away from another. The teaching of these passages is altogether one with all New Testament truth. It is as if we dipped a cup of water from the sea. What we took out would not be all the water in the ocean, but it would be a true sample and would perfectly agree with the rest.

The difficulty we modern Christians face is not misunderstanding the Bible, but persuading our untamed hearts to accept its plain instructions. Our problem is to get the consent of our world—loving minds to make Jesus Lord in fact as well as in word. For it is one thing to say, "Lord, Lord," and quite another thing to obey the Lord's commandments. We may sing, "Crown Him Lord of All," and rejoice in the tones of the loud-sounding organ and the deep melody of harmonious voices, but still we have done nothing until we have left the world and set our faces toward the city of God in hard practical reality. When faith becomes obedience then it is true faith indeed.

The world's spirit is strong, and it clings to us as close as the smell of smoke to our garments. It can change its face to suit any circumstance and so deceive many a simple Christian whose senses are not exercised to discern good and evil. It can play at religion with every appearance of sincerity. It can have fits of conscience (particularly during Lent) and even confess its evil ways in the public press. It will praise religion and fawn on the church for its ends. It will contribute to charitable causes and promote campaigns to furnish clothing for the poor. *Only let Christ keep His distance and never assert His lordship over it.* This it will positively not endure. And toward the true Spirit of Christ it will show only antagonism. The world's press (which is always its real mouthpiece) will seldom give a child of God a fair deal. If the facts compel a favorable report, the tone is apt to be condescending and ironic. The note of contempt sounds through.

Both the sons of this world and the sons of God have been baptized into a spirit, but the spirit of the world and the Spirit which dwells in the hearts of twice-born men are as far apart as heaven and hell. Not only are they the complete opposite of each other but they are sharply antagonistic to each other as well. To a son of earth the things of the Spirit are either ridiculous, in which case he is amused, or they are meaningless, in which case he is bored.

> But the natural man receiveth not the things of
> the Spirit of God: for they are foolishness unto
> him: neither can he know them, because they are
> spiritually discerned. (1 Corinthians 2:14)

In the first epistle of John two words are used over and over, the words *they* and *ye,* and they designate two wholly different worlds. *They* refers to the men and women of Adam's fallen world; *ye* refers to the chosen ones who have left all to follow Christ. The apostle does not genuflect to the little god Tolerance (the worship of which has become in America a kind of secondary surface religion); he is bluntly intolerant. He knows that tolerance may be merely another name for indifference. It takes a vigorous faith to accept the teaching of the man John. It is so much easier to blur the lines of separation and so offend no one. Pious generalities and the use of *we* to mean both Christians and unbelievers is much safer. The fatherhood of God can be stretched to include everyone from Jack the Ripper to Daniel the Prophet. Thus no one is offended and everyone feels quite snug and ready for heaven. But the man who laid his ear on Jesus' breast was not so easily deceived. He drew a line to divide the race of men into two camps, to separate the saved from the lost, those who shall rise to eternal reward from them that shall sink to final despair. On one side are *they* that know not God; on the other *ye* (or with a change of person, *we),* and between the two is a moral gulf too wide for any man to cross.

Here is the way John states it:

Ye are of God, little children, and have overcome them: because greater is he that is in you, than he that is in the world. They are of the world: therefore speak they of the world, and the world heareth them. We are of God: he that knoweth God heareth us; he that is not of God heareth not us. Hereby know we the spirit of truth, and the spirit of error. (1 John 4:4–6)

Such language as this is too plain to confuse anyone who honestly wants to know the truth. Our problem is not one of understanding, I repeat, but of faith and obedience. The question is not a theological one, What does this teach? It is a moral one, Am I willing to accept this and abide by its consequences? Can I endure the cold stare? Have I the courage to stand up to the slashing attack of the "liberal"? Dare I invite the hate of men who will be affronted by my attitude? Have I independence of mind sufficient to challenge the opinions of popular religion and go along with an apostle? Or briefly, can I bring myself to take up the cross with its blood and its reproach?

The Christian is called to separation from the world, but we must be sure we know what we mean (or more important, what God means) by the *world*. We are likely to make it mean something external only and thus miss its real meaning. The theater, cards, liquor, gambling—these are not the world; they are merely an external manifestation of the world. Our warfare is not against merely an external manifestation of the world. Our warfare is not against mere worldly ways, but against the *spirit* of the world. For man, whether he is saved or lost, is essentially spirit. The world, in the New Testament meaning of the word, is simply unregenerate human nature wherever it is found, whether in a tavern or in a church. Whatever springs out of, is built upon or receives support from fallen human nature is the world, whether it is morally base or morally respectable.

The ancient Pharisees, in spite of their zealous devotion to religion, were of the very essence of the world. The spiritual principles upon which they built their system were drawn not from above but from below. They employed against Jesus the tactics of men. They bribed men to tell lies in defense of truth. To defend God they acted like devils. To support the Bible they defied the teachings of the Bible. They scuttled religion to save religion. They gave rein to blind hate in the name of the religion of love. There we see the world in all of its grim defiance of God. So fierce was this spirit that it never rested till it had put to death the Son of God Himself. The spirit of the Pharisees was actively and maliciously hostile to the Spirit of Jesus as each was a kind of distillation of the two worlds from whence they came.

Those present-day teachers who place the Sermon on the Mount in some other dispensation than this and so release the church from its teachings little realize the evil they do. For the Sermon on the Mount gives in brief the characteristics of the kingdom of renewed men. The blessed poor who mourn for their sins and thirst after righteousness are true sons of the kingdom. In meekness they show mercy to their enemies; with guileless candor they gaze upon God; surrounded by persecutors they bless and curse not. In modesty they hide their good deeds. They go out of their way to agree with their adversaries and forgive those who sin against them. They serve God in secret in the depth of their hearts and wait with patience for His open reward. They freely surrender their earthly goods rather than use violence to protect them. They lay up treasures in heaven. They avoid praise and wait for the day of final reckoning to learn who is greatest in the kingdom of heaven.

If this is a fairly accurate view of things, what can we say then when Christian men vie with one another for place and position? What can we answer when we see them hungrily seeking for praise and honor? How can we excuse the passion for publicity which is so glaringly evident among Christian leaders? What about political ambition in church circles? What about the fevered palm that is stretched out for more and bigger "love offerings"? What about the shameless egotism among Christians? How can we explain the gross man-worship that habitually blows up one and another popular leader to the size of colossus? What about the obsequious hand-kissing of moneyed men by those purporting to be sound preachers of the gospel?

There is only one answer to these questions; it is simply that in these manifestations we see the world and nothing but the world. No passionate profession of love for "souls" can change evil into good. These are the very sins that crucified Jesus.

It is true also that the grosser manifestations of fallen human nature are part of the kingdom of this world. Organized amusements with their emphasis upon shallow pleasure, the great empires built upon vicious and unnatural habits, unrestrained abuse of normal appetites, the artificial world called "high society"—these are all of the world. They are all part of that which is flesh, which builds upon flesh and must perish with the flesh. And from these things the Christian must flee. All these he must put behind him and in them he must have no part. Against them he must stand quietly but firmly without compromise and without fear.

So whether the world presents itself in its uglier aspects or in its subtler and more refined forms, we must recognize it for what it is and repudiate it bluntly. We *must* do this if we would walk with God in our generation as Enoch did in his. A clean break with the world is imperative.

> Ye adulterers and adulteresses, know ye not that
> the friendship of the world is enmity with God?
> whosoever therefore will be a friend of the world is
> the enemy of God. (James 4:4)

> Love not the world, neither the things that are in
> the world. If any man love the world, the love of the
> Father is not in him. For all that is in the world, the
> lust of the flesh, and the lust of the eyes, and the pride
> of life, is not of the Father, but is of the world.
> (1 John 2:15–16)

These words of God are not before us for our consideration; they are there for our obedience and we have no right to claim the title of Christian unless we follow them.

For myself, I fear any kind of religious stir among Christians that does not lead to repentance and result in a sharp separation of the believer from the world. I am suspicious of any organized revival effort that is forced to play down the hard terms of the kingdom. No matter how attractive the movement may appear, if it is not founded in righteousness and nurtured in humility it is not of God. If it exploits the flesh it is a religious fraud and should not have the support of any God-fearing Christian. Only that is of God which honors the Spirit and prospers at the expense of the human ego. "That, according as it is written, He that glorieth, let him glory in the Lord" (1 Corinthians 1:31).

CHAPTER 10

The Spirit-filled Life

Be filled with the Spirit.

EPHESIANS 5:18

That every Christian can be and should be filled with the Holy Spirit would hardly seem to be a matter for debate among Christians. Yet some will argue that the Holy Spirit is not for plain Christians but for ministers and missionaries only. Others hold that the measure of the Spirit received at regeneration is identical with that received by the disciples at Pentecost and any hope of additional fullness after conversion simply rests upon error. A few will express a languid hope that someday they may be filled, and still others will avoid the subject as one about which they know very little and which can only cause embarrassment.

I want here boldly to assert that it is my happy belief that every Christian can have a copious outpouring of the Holy Spirit in a measure far beyond that received at conversion, and I might also say, far beyond that enjoyed by the rank and file of orthodox believers today. It is important that we get this straight, for until doubts are removed faith is impossible. God will not surprise a doubting heart with an effusion of the Holy Spirit, nor will He fill anyone who has doctrinal questions about the possibility of being filled.

To remove doubts and create a confident expectation I recommend a reverent study of the Word of God itself. I am willing to rest my case upon the teachings of the New Testament. If a careful and humble examination of the words of Christ and His apostles does not lead to a belief that we may be filled with the Holy Spirit now, then I see no reason to look elsewhere. For it matters little what this or that religious teacher has said for or against the proposition. If the doctrine is not taught in the Scriptures then it cannot be supported by any argument, and all exhortations to be filled are valueless.

I shall not here present a case for the affirmative. Let the inquirer examine the evidence for himself, and if he decides that there is no warrant in the New Testament for believing that he can be filled with the Spirit, let him shut this book and save himself the trouble of reading further. What I say from here on is addressed to men and women who have gotten over their questions and are confident that when they meet the conditions they may indeed be filled with the Holy Spirit.

Before a man can be filled with the Spirit *he must be*

sure he wants to be. And let this be taken seriously. Many Christians want to be filled, but their desire is a vague romantic kind of thing hardly worthy to be called desire. They have almost no knowledge of what it will cost them to realize it.

Let us imagine that we are talking to an inquirer, some eager young Christian, let us say, who has sought us out to learn about the Spirit-filled life. As gently as possible, considering the pointed nature of the questions, we would probe his soul somewhat as follows: "Are you sure you want to be filled with a Spirit who, though He is like Jesus in His gentleness and love, will nevertheless demand to be Lord of your life? Are you willing to let your personality to be taken over by another, even if that other be the Spirit of God Himself? If the Spirit takes charge of your life He will expect unquestioning obedience in everything. He will not tolerate in you the self-sins even though they are permitted and excused by most Christians. By the self-sins I mean self-love, self-pity, self-seeking, self-confidence, self-righteousness, self-aggrandizement, self-defense. You will find the Spirit to be in sharp opposition to the easy ways of the world and of the mixed multitude within the precincts of religion. He will be jealous over you for good. He will take the direction of your life away from you. He will reserve the right to test you, to discipline you, to chasten you for your soul's sake. He may strip you of those borderline pleasures which other Christians enjoy but which are to you a source of refined evil. Through it all He will enfold you in a love so vast, so mighty, so all-embracing, so wondrous that your very losses will seem like gains and your small pains like pleasures. Yet the flesh will whimper under His yoke and cry out against it as a burden too great to bear. And you will be permitted to enjoy the solemn privilege of suffering to 'fill up that which is behind of the afflictions of Christ' in your flesh for His body's sake, which is the church (Colossians 1:24). Now, with the conditions before you, do you still want to be filled with Holy Spirit?"

If this appears severe, let us remember that the way of the cross is never easy. The shine and glamour accompanying popular religious movements is as false as the sheen on the wings of the angel of darkness when he for a moment transforms himself into an angel of light. The spiritual timidity that fears to show the cross in its true character is not on any grounds to be excused. It can result only in disappointment and tragedy at last.

Before we can be filled with the Spirit *the desire to be filled must be all-consuming.* It must be for the time the biggest thing in life, so acute, so intrusive as to crowd out everything else. The degree of fullness in any life accords perfectly with the intensity of true desire. We have as much of God as we actually want. One great hindrance to the Spirit-filled life is the theology of complacency so widely accepted among gospel Christians today. According to this view acute desire is an evidence of unbelief and proof of lack of knowledge of the Scriptures. A sufficient refutation of this position is afforded by the Word of God itself and by the fact that it always fails to produce real saintliness among those who hold it.

Then I doubt whether anyone ever received that divine afflatus with which we are here concerned who did not first *experience a period of deep anxiety and inward agitation.* Religious contentment is the enemy of the spiritual life always. The biographies of the saints teach that the way to spiritual greatness has always been through much suffering and inward pain. The phrase, "the way of the cross," though it has come in certain circles to denote something very beautiful, even enjoyable, still means to the real Christian what it has always meant, the way of rejection and loss. No one ever enjoyed a cross, just as no one ever enjoyed a gallows.

The Christian who is seeking better things and who has to his consternation found himself in a state of complete self-despair need not be discouraged. Despair with self, where it is accompanied by faith, is a good friend, for it destroys one of the heart's most potent enemies and prepares the soul for the ministration of the Comforter. A sense of utter emptiness, of disappointment and darkness can (if we are alert and wise to what is going on) be the shadow in the valley of shadows that leads on to those fruitful fields that lie further in. If we misunderstand it and resist this visitation of God we may miss entirely every benefit a kind heavenly Father has in mind for us. If we cooperate with God He will take away the natural comforts which have served us as mother and nurse for so long and put us where we can receive no help except from the Comforter Himself. He will tear away that false thing the Chinese call "face" and show us how painfully small we really are. When he is finished with us we will know what our Lord meant when He said, "Blessed are the poor in spirit" (Matthew 5:3).

Be sure, however, that in these painful chastenings we shall not be deserted by our God. He will never leave us nor forsake us, nor will He be wroth with us nor rebuke us. He will not break His covenant nor alter that which has gone out of His mouth. He will keep us as the apple of His eye and watch over us as a mother watches over her child. His love will not fail even while He is taking us through this experience of self-crucifixion so real, so terrible, that we can express it only by crying, "My God, my God, why hast thou forsaken me?" (Psalm 22:1; Matthew 27:46; Mark 15:34).

Now let us keep our theology straight about all this. There is not in this painful stripping one remote thought of human merit. The "dark night of the soul" knows not one dim ray of the treacherous light of self-righteousness. We do not by suffering earn the anointing for which we yearn, nor does this devastation of soul make us dear to God nor give us additional favor in His eyes. The value of the stripping experience lies in its power to detach us from life's passing interests and to throw us back upon eternity. It serves to empty our earthly vessels and prepare us for the inpouring of the Holy Spirit.

The filling with the Spirit, then, requires that we give up our all, that we undergo an inward death, that we rid our hearts of that centuries-old accumulation of Adamic trash and open all rooms to the heavenly Guest.

The Holy Spirit is a living Person and should be treated as a person. We must never think of Him as a blind energy nor as an impersonal force. He hears and sees and feels as any person does. He speaks and hears us speak. We can please Him or grieve Him or silence Him as we can any other person. He will respond to our timid effort to know Him and will ever meet us over half the way.

However wonderful the crisis experience of being filled with the Spirit, we should remember that it is only a means toward something greater: that greater thing is the lifelong walk in the Spirit, indwelt, directed, taught and empowered by His mighty Person. And to continue thus to walk in the Spirit requires that we meet certain conditions. These are laid down for us in the sacred Scriptures and are there for all to see.

The Spirit-filled walk demands, for instance, that we live in the Word of God as a fish lives in the sea. By this I do not mean that we study the Bible merely, nor that we take a "course" in Bible doctrine. I mean that we should "meditate day and night" (Psalm 1:2) in the sacred Word, that we should love it and feast upon it and digest it every hour of the day and night. When the business of life compels our attention we may yet, by kind of blessed mental reflex, keep the Word of Truth ever before our minds.

Then if we would please the indwelling Spirit we must be all taken up with Christ. The Spirit's present work is to honor Him, and everything He does has this for its ultimate purpose. And we must make our thoughts a clean sanctuary for His holy habitation. He dwells in our thoughts, and soiled thoughts are as repugnant to Him as soiled linen to a king. Above all we must have a cheerful faith that will keep on believing however radical the fluctuation in our emotional states may be.

The Spirit indwelt life is not a special deluxe edition of Christianity to be enjoyed by a certain rare and privileged few who happen to be made of finer and more sensitive stuff than the rest. Rather, it is the normal state for every redeemed man and woman the world over. It is

> the mystery which hath been hid from ages and from generations, but now is made manifest to his saints: to whom God would make known what is the riches of the glory of this mystery among the Gentiles; which is Christ in you, the hope of glory. (Colossians 1:26–27)

Faber, in one of his sweet and reverent hymns, addressed this good word to the Holy Spirit:

Ocean, wide flowing Ocean, Thou
Of uncreated Love;
I tremble as within my soul
I feel Thy waters move.

Thou art a sea without a shore;
Awful, immense Thou art;
A sea which can contract itself
Within my narrow heart.